JN429389

East Asian Gender in Transition

Projected by the Keimyung Institute for Women's Studies
Edited by CHO Joo-hyun

Keimyung University Press

East Asian Gender in Transition

Edited by CHO Joo-hyun.
Printed in 2013. 02. 07.
Published in 2013. 02. 15.

Copyright ©2013 by SYNN Ilhi, the President of Keimyung University
All rights reserved

This book is a publication of Keimyung University Press
(704-701) 1095 Dalgubeoldaero, Dalseo-Gu , Daegu, Korea
TEL (053) 580-6233 FAX (053) 580-6235
www.kmupress.com
Registration 1970. 9. 1. (#347-1998-1)

ISBN 978-89-7585-611-2 93300
Price: ₩14,000

No part of this book may be reproduced, stored in a retrieval systems or transmitted in any form or by any means, electronic or mechanical, including photocopying, recording or any information storage and retrieval systems, without permission in writing from the copyright owner(s).

East Asian Gender in Transition

Projected by the Keimyung Institute for Women's Studies
Edited by CHO Joo-hyun

Contents

Contributors

Saskia SASSEN

Saskia SASSEN is the Robert S. Lynd Professor of Sociology and Co-Chair, The Committee on Global Thought, Columbia University (www.saskiasassen.com). Her recent books are *Territory, Authority, Rights: From Medieval to Global Assemblages* (Princeton University Press 2008), *A Sociology of Globalization* (W.W.Norton 2007), and the 4th fully updated edition of *Cities in a World Economy* (Sage 2012). Among older books is *The Global City* (Princeton University Press, 1991/2001). Her books are translated into over 20 languages. The 1st edition of *Cities in a World Economy*(Pine Forge Press, 1994) has been translated into Korean in 1998 by the Purungil Publisher (translated by NAM Gibeom, YOO Hwan-jong, and HONG In-ock) with the title of *Geongje-ui Saegyehwawa Doshi-ui Weegi*. She is the recipient of diverse awards and mentions, ranging from multiple doctor honoris causa to named lectures and being selected as one of the 100 Top Global Thinkers of 2011 by Foreign Policy Magazine. http://www.foreignpolicy.com/articles/2011/11/28/the_fp_top_100_global_thinkers?page=0,33 E-mail: sjs2@columbia.edu

WEI Guoying

WEI Guoying is professor and Executive Vice Director of the Women's Studies Center of Peking University. Her study covers the basic theory of the gender studies and contemporary women's issues. She has compiled and edited books on women's studies and published more than 40 papers and articles on women's studies. Her major works include: 1) *Introduction to Women's Studies* (Peking University Press 2000), editor-in-chief, which later was reprinted 6th time in 2012. The book was awarded the first session of the Chinese Women's Research Outstanding Achievement in 2004 and the fourth session of the National Award for Outstanding Women's Readings in 2006; 2) *Concise Reader of the Basic State Policies on Gender Equality* (Peking University Press 2008), as the first author; 3) *Some Issues of the Basic Theory of the Gender Studies* (Peking University Journal, vol. 1, 2003); 4) *Development by Leaps and Bounds and Domestic Experience: A Review of One Decade Development of Gender Studies as a Discipline Construction* (<Women's Studies Series> 2006, vol.6); and 5) *Gender Comparison of Employment and Career Development in China* (<Asian Women—Research Institute of Asian Women>, Spring 2011, Vol. 27, No.1, pp. 95-113). E-mail: weigy@pku.edu.cn

CHO Joo-hyun

CHO Joo-hyun is Professor of Women's Studies and Director of the Institute for Women's Studies at Keimyung University in Korea. She received her Ph.D. in Sociology from University of Illinois at Urbana-Champaign in 1988. She is the author of *Yeoseong Jeongcheseong-ui Jeongchihak* (Women's Identity Politics) (Seoul: Ttohana-ui Munhwa, 2000) and *Beolgeobeoseun Saengmyeong: Sinjayujuui Sidae-ui Saengmyeongjeongchi-wa peminijeum* (Bare Life: Feminism and Bio-politics in the Age of Neoliberalism) (Seoul: Ttohana-ui Munhwa, 2009). She also translated several books to Korean, including *Whose Science? Whose Knowledge? Thinking from Women's Lives* by Sandra Harding (Cornell University Press, 1991) published as *Nugu-ui Gwahak-imyeo Nugu-ui Jisik-inga?* (Paju: Nanam, 2009) and published many articles, including "Neoliberal Governmentality at Work: Post-IMF Korean Society and the Construction of Neoliberal Women" (*Korea Journal*, 2009). She is currently at work on a manuscript on neoliberal globalization and sexual violence. E-mail: juhyun@kmu.ac.kr

Emiko OCHIAI

Emiko Ochiai is Professor of Sociology and the Director of the Research Center for the Intimate and Public Spheres at Graduate School of Letters, Kyoto

University. She is a family sociologist and family historian who is also active in the field of gender studies. Her recent research projects combine family studies, welfare state studies, and migration studies to develop a new framework to understand the on-going transformations in private lives and public institutions intermingled with each other, especially focusing on Asian societies. Her English publications include *Asia's New Mothers: Crafting Gender Roles and Childcare Networks in East and Southeast Asian Societies* (co-editorship with Barbara Molony, Folkestone, Kent: Global Oriental, 2008), *The Stem Family in EurAsian Perspective* (co-editorship with Antoinette Fauve-Chamoux, Bern: Peter Lang, 2009) and *The Japanese Family System in Transition: A Sociological Analysis of Family Change in Postwar Japan* (LTCB International Library Foundation, 1997). Her books have been translated and published in English, Korean, Chinese and Thai. The Korean version of the last book is *21 Segi Gajokege: Ilbon wi Gajok goa Sahoe*, Seoul: Yangseowon. The Korean translation of another book of hers is *Geundae Gajok, Gilmotungi-reul Doraseoda*. E-mail: emikoo2@aol.com

WONG Wai Ching Angela

WONG Wai Ching Angela received her Ph.D. in religious studies from the University of Chicago Divinity School. She is an Associate Professor of the Department of Cultural and Religious Studies, Programme Director of MA in Intercultural Studies, and a concurrent Professor of the Chung Chi College Divinity School at the Chinese University of Hong Kong. She is the Co-Director of Gender Research Centre and had served as the Head of the Graduate Division of Gender Studies for many years. Her research interests include: religion and sexuality, gender, religion and nationalism, feminist hermeneutics and religious classics, and postcolonialism and Hong Kong Christianity. Her works have been published in many professional journals both in Chinese and English. Some representative publications include: "*The Poor Woman*": *A Critical Analysis of Asian Theology and Contemporary Chinese Fiction by Women* (Peter Lang, 2002), "Negotiating Gender: Postcolonialism and Hong Kong Christian Women," in *Gender and Society in Hong Kong* (UBC Press, 2003), "Our Bodies Our Stories:

Narrating Female Sexuality in Hong Kong," in *Mainstreaming Gender in Hong Kong* (CU Press, 2009), and co-ed. with CHOI Poking, *Chinese Women and Hong Kong Christianity: An Oral History* (In Chinese) (Oxford University Press, 2010). E-mail: waiching@cuhk.edu.hk

TAM Siumi Maria

TAM Siumi Maria is Associate Professor of anthropology, and Co-director of the Gender Studies Programme, at the Chinese University of Hong Kong. Her research interests include the family in transnational and cross-border mobility, gender and domesticity, and ethnic relations and equity in Hong Kong society. She is currently working on projects that examine the construction of South Asian identities through transplantation of traditions, especially foodways and religion, and how these shape and are shaped by individual subjectivity, and gender role and status. She is author of Dealing with Double Marginalization: Three Generations of Nepalese Women in Hong Kong (*Asian Journal of Women's Studies* 2010: 16(2)), and co-editor of several volumes, including *Hong Kong: The Anthropology of a Chinese Metropolis* (Curzon, 1997) and *Tung Chung before and after the New Airport: an ethnographic and historical study of a community in Hong Kong* (AMO, HKSAR, 2005). E-mail: siumitam@gamil.com

LEE Shin-Young

LEE Shin-Young is Associate Professor of department of social welfare at Keimyung University in Korea. She received her Ph.D. in social welfare from the State University of New York at Albany in 2001. She is the author of *Introduction to Social Welfare* (Seoul: Chong Mok, 2011) and *Skills and Techniques for Social Work Practice* (Paju: Yangseowon, 2012). She published many articles, including "The Social Support Patterns and Depression among the Elderly Living Alone and Their Friends and Neighbors" (*Journal of Welfare for the Aged*, 2012). She is currently at work on a manuscript on Social Welfare for the Elderly. E-mail: sylee@kmu.ac.kr

Acknowledgments

This volume brings together the engaging scholarship presented at "Women and Family-in-Transition in the Age of Globalization: The Cases of China and South Korea," an international conference held in May 2012 by the Institute for Women's Studies at Keimyung University, and sponsored jointly with the Women's Studies Center at Peking University and the Gender Research Centre and Gender Studies Program at the Chinese University of Hong Kong. Seven works were selected from the contributions and included in this volume after further revisions. This volume is the culmination of a concerted effort involving many friends and colleagues during the last two years, from the conception of the conference to its publication. I would like to place on record my heartfelt thanks to all.

The Institute for Women's Studies at Keimyung University signed MOUs with the Women's Studies Center at Peking University and the Gender Research Centre and Gender Studies Program at the Chinese University of Hong Kong, in 2005 and 2007 respectively, and held five joint international conferences since. As the host of the 2012 conference, the Institute for Women's Studies at Keimyung University decided to expand the conference by including keynote sessions and publishing the scholarship from the conference in separate volumes in English and Korean. From its inception to completion, Dr. SYNN Ilhi, the President of Keimyung University, gave full support and encouragement essential for the success of this project. The preparation committee (Professors

KANG Seyoung, PARK Sun-Young, YOU Ok Hee, LEE Shin-Young, CHUNG Moonyoung, and CHO Joo-hyun), formed in January 2011, started to work out a detailed schedule and began the selection process of keynote speakers.

At the conference, there were twelve presentations. Saskia SASSEN (Robert S. Lynd Professor of Sociology and Co-Chair, The Committee on Global Thought, Columbia University)[1] and Emiko OCHIAI (Professor of Sociology, Kyoto University) participated as keynote speakers. Professors WEI Guoying, MA Fengzhi, and WU Lijuan from Peking University, Professors WONG Wai Ching Angela, TAM Siumi Maria, and WANG Danning from the Chinese University of Hong Kong, and Professors YANG Jung-Hye, LEE Shing-Young, CHO Joo-hyun, and HONG Sung-Hee from Keimyung University gave their presentations at the conference.

Many friends and colleagues from Keimyung University and other institutions helped to make the conference a success. Professors KIM Shin-Hye, PARK Sun-Young, SHIN Ji Suk, YOU Ok Hee, YOO Ka Hyo, CHOI Yunkyeung, and HUH Koung-Mi served as moderators. Professors KIM Sung Sook, KIM Eun-Shil, KIM Hyun-Mee, BAE Eun-Kyung, AHN Sook-Young, YOO Ka Hyo, YI Lo Ri, LEE Jin-Ee, CHO Sungsook, and CHOI Jongryul served as discussants. Professors KIM Shin-Hye, SOHN Gyeom Seo, and Wiebke B. Omnus served as English/Korean translators. Professors CHOI Eun-Jeong and LI Chunji served as Chinese/Korean translators. Professors LEE Sun-Ho and RHEE Esther directed the cultural project. Three Doctoral Candidates at the Department of Women's Studies of Keimyung University,

1 Professor Saskia SASSEN could not participate in the conference due to inevitable personal reasons and instead sent her manuscript and the video file prepared for her lecture.

KIM Hyang Suk, LEE Won-Sim, and LIM Hyun Hee, and Master's Candidate KIM Kuna, researchers for the conference, prepared the conference and field trip programs superbly.

For the publication of volumes in English and Korean, the translation and editing processes formed one of essential parts of the whole project. Professor SOHN Gyeom Seo translated the Korean manuscript by Professor LEE Shin-Young into English. Professional copyeditor KIM Joo Ok meticulously copyedited all of the English manuscripts . After copyediting, each manuscript was sent to its author for a final review. The English manuscripts by Professors Saskia SASSEN, WEI Guoying, Emiko OCHIAI, and WONG Wai Ching Angela were translated into Korean by Doctoral Candidates at the Department of Women's Studies of Keimyung University: LIM Hyun Hee, OH Aeri, SHIN Young-Hee, and JEONG-PARK Eunja, respectively, and copyedited by Professors CHO Joo-hyun, PARK Sun-Young, SOHN Gyeom Seo, and CHUNG Moonyoung respectively. The Chinese manuscript by TAM Siumi Maria was translated into Korean by Doctoral Candidate at Ewha Womans University LI Haiying. The cover of this volume was designed by Professor RHEEM Hun Woo of Keimyung University. Mr. CHOI Sang-Geun of Keimyung University Press guided the publication process. Researcher LIM Hyun Hee, as an assistant, coordinated collecting manuscripts and communications, edited the style, terminology, footnotes, and references, and defined the final shape of the volume. Researcher KWON Myung Jin at the Institute for Women's Studies took over the responsibility of accounting and mailing.

In addition to those acknowledged explicitly above, many other friends helped me during the conference and throughout the publication process. Though I do not mention them here, I am always thankful for their help and support. In retrospect, there have been many happy memories as well as difficult times. Whenever I was stranded in difficulty, a great idea or proposal from my colleagues helped me regain my courage, and my colleague researchers lent me a hand and revived our team through cooperation and collaboration. As this volume leaves our hands, we hope it will help our readers to reinterpret shifting social realities and open new venues in their theoretical analyses and social policy designs.

CHO Joo-hyun
Director
Institute for Women's Studies at Keimyung University
January 2013

Introduction

CHO Joo-hyun

This volume presents contributions that developed from a conference aiming to understand the transformations of women's lives and family lives in East Asia in the context of neoliberal globalization. The contributors to this volume try to explicate the characteristics of transformations that East Asian women and families have experienced during the last few decades in relation to globalization. When we can explicate the universalities and particularities of these transformations, we can make concrete theoretical and policy models appropriate for the unique characteristics of East Asian countries.

Though neoliberal globalization presents a common problem confronting both Western and East Asian societies, each society presents specific cultural and economic conditions, and presents significant differences in their responses to those conditions. Especially in the cases of Asian countries, the historical and cultural background, the process of modernization, including the experiences of colonial occupation, and the present status of economic development of each country influence its response strategies against the effects of globalization. Transformations occurring in the lives of women and families occur in the contexts of market changes caused by globalization and the characteristic modes of response by each country. However, these transformations are not solely determined by market mechanisms and national policies. They are also the results of the survival strategies of East Asian women and families confronting neoliberal crises. Therefore, it is critical to pay careful attention to the agency of the women and families, and to the consequent gender realignments as well as the roles of market mechanisms and national policies affected by globalization.

This volume consists of two parts. Part 1 introduces theoretical models of and perspectives on neoliberal globalization, and presents the specific cases of China and South Korea. The contributions by Saskia Sassen, Wei Guoying, and Cho Joo-hyun are included here. Part 2 discusses the present conditions of transformations occurring in the lives of East Asian women and families along the axis of modernization, and presents the cases of migration and multiculturalism in China and the transformation of the filial piety culture in South Korea. The contributions by Emiko Ochiai, Wong Wai Ching Angela, Tam Siumi Maria, and Lee Shin-Young are inluded in this part.

In Chapter 1, "Strategic Instantiations of Gendering in the Global Economy: The Feminizing of Survival," Saskia SASSEN claims that though the global economic system is constituted at the key sites of global cities, alternative global circuits are also formed along with this process, which she characterizes as the 'feminizing circuit of global survival.' Globalization and immigration contribute to the loosening of the tenacious territory-citizen-state bond. According to Sassen, the strategic sites for this loosening are global cities, which are currently undergoing the process of realignment according to race and gender arrangements. In a global city, where the global economic system integrates finance, production, trade, and communication, there coexists alternative global circuits for survival, incorporating the organized immigration of women, trafficking, and remittance. Women emerge as key actors in both global cities and global circuits for survival.

Instead of following the literal itineraries of women, Sassen's theoretical model analyzing the kinds of changes brought on women by globalization opts to detect the strategic areas for gender dynamics related to the immigration of women and focuses on these strategic areas. As Sassen points out, "[t]his is an important and difficult analytical task." Sassen notes that as key actors in these strategic areas, the immigrant women themselves, their families dependent for survival on the immigration of women, business entrepreneurs and organized crime members profiting from these migrations, as well as governments of the home countries of immigrant women, became an important source of revenues. According to Sassen, women, family members, entrepreneurs, and governments are the key actors constituting alternative global circuits for survival, and each of these actors utilizes gendering as a strategic component of their economic processes. Last, by revealing the relationship of these circuits for survival with some core programs of economic globalization, Sassen shows that the processes of gendering, which might initially appear unrelated, is closely implicated in global economic systems and forms a strategic component of the circuits for survival.

Chapter 2, by WEI Guoying, is entitled "Analysis of Progress and Issues of Gender Equality in China." In recent years, China achieved remarkable progress in gender equality. For example, the employment rates for women and men who have received elementary education or beyond are gradually becoming equal. However, China also faces new problems, including the decreasing proportion of women among employed college and university graduates, deepening the gendered division of labor in the choices of professions, duties and posts, and decreasing women's chances for promotion. In light of the new types of gender difference unfolding in China, Wei emphasizes the necessity of initiating sincere discussions about "gender equality." Toward this goal, Wei examines issues such as equal opportunity and the equality of results, the equality of quantity and virtual equality, the equality of fair competition and the equality of social support, and the demand for identical equality and differentiated equality. Wei Guoying also emphasizes the role of the state and the government as the principal agents to resolve these problems, and urges the government to recognize gender difference and take effective measures to deal with new gender issues.

In Chapter 3, "Neoliberal Globalization and the Transformation of Women's Subjectivity: From the Perspective of Practice Theory," CHO Joo-hyun explores the transformation of women's subjectivity in late modern Korean society. According to Cho, neoliberal governmentality intent on applying economic logic to the whole socio-political area could have spread with little resistance because of the obvious effectiveness of increasing individual freedom in promoting creativity, efficiency, and independence coveted by almost every member of society. Cho situates the visibility of neoliberal governmentality in contrast to its less apparent consequences of increasing the uncertainty and inefficacy of individual action in achieving its intended goal and the difficulty of securing public goods. Moreover, Cho shows that in late modernity, rather than relying on laws and other formal institutions, power shares its principal channels of operation with self-empowering efforts to increase individual freedom, thus becoming all the more challenging to understand its constitutive nature.

When power in late modernity operates in this loose and mundane manner, Cho claims, we can no longer understand power as relatively invariant but instead as the effect of social practices that regulates each agent's performances and are in turn maintained or transformed by each agent's decisions during deontic scorekeeping, hence always involving possibility of changes . Therefore, when the constituted nature and the agency of women's subjectivity are so intertwined that it is no longer an easy matter to decide whether women's increased freedom of choices is a constitutive effect of neoliberal governmentality or simply a reflection of women's agency, we need a more sophisticated approach that incorporates this interconnectedness. Cho recommends a microscopic approach based on social practice theory that carefully traces the decision processes of each individual in everyday social contexts along with the introduction of Brandom's concept of 'expressive positive freedom' to replace the naïve neoliberal concept of freedom. Cho also claims that this approach naturally leads to the adoption of agonistic politics as its political implementation for successful transformations of social practices.

Though East Asian societies are known as traditionally dominated by the patriarchal family system and Confucian values, their women and family structures are undergoing rapid transformations under the influence of neoliberal globalization. However, as each transformation is influenced by internal conditions specific to each society as well as external factors, each society will surely reveal its distinct characteristics.

In Chapter 4, "The Logics of Family and Gender Changes in Early 21-st East Asia," Emiko OCHIAI shows that the changes in East Asian women and families have their own characteristic features distinct from those of the West, and searches for the causes of such changes in the combinations of effects from Confucian cultures, compressed modernity, and state welfare policies. According to Ochiai, one of the distinctive demographic characteristics of East Asian women and families is that there are no significant changes related to marriage despite plummeting fertility levels in this region. For example, the ratios of births out of wedlock remain within the range of 1%-4% in Japan, South Korea, Taiwan, and Singapore, in stark contrast to the cases in Europe, where about one third to more than half of births are out of wedlock. Moreover, whereas in Western countries the housewifization of women proceeded along with the modern gender division of labor during the first demographic transition (1880s-1920s) and de-housewifization, implying the labor force participation of women, has occurred during the second demographic transition since the 1970s, in East Asia both the housewifization and the de-housewifization phenomena are occurring simultaneously, and even showing a reverse transition from de-housewifization to housewifization, preventing easy generalizations.

Ochiai discusses three hypotheses (the influence of Confucianism, paths to modernity, and policy decisions) for the causes of changes in women's lives and families' lives. In the first case of Confucian influences, Ochiai claims that Confucianism has limited impacts for the women and family changes in East Asia, instead simply influencing the "traditionalization of modernity" in early modernity. For example, the concept of the 'wise wife and good mother' in China, the 'good wife and wise mother' in Japan, and the 'wise mother and good wife' in Korea believed to be an ancient precept deriving mainly from Confucianism should be more properly considered as concepts imported from Europe reflecting the influences of modern gender division of labor in the 19th and 20th centuries, recast as a concept reflecting an 'Asian tradition' after World War One. Ochiai explains this phenomenon as a result of identity politics based on "self-Orientalism" in Asia. Second, East Asian countries with the exception of Japan followed the paths of compressed modernity, and thus could not secure enough time to establish social welfare systems. This led East Asians to rely on the family structure as the only social resource. The paradoxical phenomena of East Asian women and families maintaining the family system despite plummeting fertility rates, increasing ages at first marriage, and rising divorce rates reflect the tendency to minimize family-related risks and hold on to the family system as a last resort for social safety, and are thus not related to individualism, as commonly believed. Third, welfare policies in East Asian countries share the common characteristics of a "familialist welfare regime" despite some differences originating from policy decisions at the state level. Ochiai concludes that these three causes in various combinations determined the present realities of East Asian women and families.

In Chapter 5, "Negotiating Between Cultures: Chinese Women Making Muslim Families in Hong Kong," WONG Wai Ching Angela explains how "minority Chinese Muslim women negotiated their religious enthusiasm with the modern role and place of women in a highly westernized society of Hong Kong." In in-depth interviews conducted with five Chinese Muslim women, Wong skillfully utilizes their roles as a window to the multicultural practices and lives of people. One interviewee confided that because of the traditional Chinese extended family network, she received substantial help when her family members had fallen ill, and that she could rely on her Muslim faith to regain meaning in her life when her life became unbearable. Thus, Wong suggests that multiculturalism in the Muslim community in Hong Kong is practiced in the everyday lives of men and women, and it is thus no longer meaningful to ask whether the Chinese tradition or the Islamic tradition is more oppressive to women. Significantly, these women did not remain helpless in their given social circumstances, and they successfully combined their religious devotion through practicing salah, eating halal food, and veiling with modern values for women including balancing work and family, flexible parenting, exercising women's right to divorce, and negotiating gender equality, all within the context of the Chinese tradition including filial piety, caring for sibling relationships, and a strong sense of male responsibility. In conclusion, Wong claims that the hybrid history of Hong Kong has managed to devise additional venues for women to negotiate in their lives by disallowing through the mixture of cultures the possibility of a single tradition to have the final say.

In Chapter 6, "Being Minority and Being Female: Gender and Social Capital among the Nepalese in Postcolonial Hong Kong," TAM Siumi Maria conducted in-depth interviews with twenty-six Nepalese migrant women aged between nineteen and seventy-two years old across three generations to explore their identities constructed from the intersectionality of gender, class, and race. They all have common family and working class backgrounds in that their husbands or fathers served in the British Army stationed in Hong Kong. The first generation of women married Nepalese Gurkha soldiers through arranged marriages by parents. After spending two years in British Army compounds, they returned to Nepal with their children and lived in Nepal until their husbands retired after fourteen to sixteen years. Their daughters, the second generation of Nepalese women, returned to Hong Kong after their marriages with yet another generation of Nepalese men. The second generation of women stayed in the Nepalese community formed in the outskirts of Hong Kong, separated from Hong Kong's mainstream community, subjected to the patriarchal influences of Nepalese families, and relying on marginal jobs, usually care work jobs. The third generation of females,without their working moms at home to take care of them, were sent to Nepal to be raised there. Even while in Hong Kong, they attended the schools for minorities taught in English, and were not incorporated into the Chinese cultural community. They remain marginalized, belonging to neither Nepalese culture nor Chinese culture. Tam emphasizes that while it is true that they were forced into arranged marriages and marriage immigration, we must recognize their agency in that the women exercise their decisions in their given social conditions. By carefully tracing the networks the women create in their social environments as well as the structures of gender, class, and race they negotiate, Tam asserts that we can gain better understandings of their agency at work.

In Chapter 7, "Intergenerational Exchange Patterns between Elderly Korean Women and Their Adult Children," LEE Shin-Young explores the problem of elderly women in Korea, which has already become a rapidly aging society and is expected to become an aged society. In 2011, the number of Korean women aged 65 and over was 3.167 million, with their average life expectancy at birth as 86.7 and their economic activity rate at 21.7%. In this work, based on the "2008 National Data on the Elderly," Lee evaluates the social support networks with non-cohabitant children for elderly women living separately from their adult children. According to her analysis, in the case of single-elderly women, though the exchange of emotional support such as phone contact or visits between mothers and their adult children was most frequent (67.3%), in cases of the exchange of instrumental support such as cleaning, meal preparation, or laundry, or physical support such as nursing, caring, or hospital accompaniment between mothers and their adult children, the numbers of elderly women with no such exchanges were highest (48.3% and 43.6% respectively) and the cases of unilateral support from adult children were the next frequent numbers (37.0% and 29.5% respectively). Lee diagnoses that the evaluation of filial piety as an ethical norm has started to change, and as the burden of taking care of elderly parents grew greater than ever as a consequence of an increasing number of women joining the workforce, related domestic conflicts are deepening. Lee urges the government to recognize that the welfare policies for the elderly are not only for the elderly in trouble, but should be actively directed to the entire elderly population as active and productive members of society.

East Asian societies belong to a region that experienced the most dynamic and intense political and social changes during modernization and neoliberal globalization. Responses to these changes, currently occurring in this region, portend an equally dramatic upheaval in the lives of women and families. An understanding of their lives should start from the careful analysis of influences from the previous and current political and social changes. Each contributor to this volume approaches this difficult and important task by presenting an analysis and/or a theoretical model of immigrant women and family lives in diverse global cities, state policies for gender equality and elderly women, demographic changes in family and gender, or the problem of women's subjection and agency in this region. We hope our work serves as an important starting point for future work on these important topics.

East Asian Gender in Transition

PART I

Globalization and Gender in East Asia

I GLOBALIZATION AND GENDER IN EAST ASIA

STRATEGIC INSTANTIATIONS OF GENDERING IN THE GLOBAL ECONOMY : THE FEMINIZING OF SURVIVAL[1]

Saskia SASSEN

Economic globalization has multiple localizations, many which typically fail to get recognized. In this paper I focus on a particular set of global circuits that form one such localization. These are cross-border circuits in which the role of women, and especially the condition of being a foreign-born woman, is crucial to the formation of those circuits. These circuits include the illegal trafficking

1 This is based on the author's larger multi-year project on "Governance and Accountability in the Global Economy" (published as *Territory, Authority, Rights*, Princeton University Press 2008, new ed.) and *A Sociology of Globalization* (Norton 2007, especially chapters 7 and 8). See also "A Savage Sorting of Winners and Losers: Contemporary Versions of Primitive Accumulation" in *Globalizations*, March–June 2010, Vol. 7, Nos. 1–2, pp. 23–50.
She is the Robert S. Lynd Professor of Sociology and Co-Chair of The Committee on Global Thought at Columbia University (www.saskiasassen).

of women and children for the sex industry; the mostly illegal trafficking of migrant workers, which is a growing source of profit for both legal and illegal contractors; and, more generally, emigration which has become an important source of hard currency for governments in home countries. The employment and/or use of foreign-born women covers an increasingly broad range of economic sectors, ranging from prostitution, which is illegal in many countries, to highly regulated occupations such as nursing. The key actors giving shape to these processes are the individuals themselves in search of work and, increasingly so, illegal traffickers and contractors as well as governments of home countries.

In the first section I conceptualize these alternative circuits so as to situate them in the global economic system. This will help explicate the analytic shift from detecting the presence of women to understanding the gender dynamics that I suggest are operating in the global economy. The second section seeks to ground these theorized circuits in the empirical conditions in developing countries that are associated with economic globalization, such as growing unemployment, the closures of a large number of typically small and medium-sized enterprises oriented to national rather than export markets, and large, often increasing government debt. The purpose is to establish the existence of systemic links between these conditions and the growth of these alternative circuits for survival, for profit-making, and for securing government revenue.

While these economies are frequently labeled as "developing," they are in some cases struggling or stagnant, and even shrinking. For the sake of briefness I will use "developing" as shorthand for this variety of situations. In fact, the poorest countries are not likely to have even the minimal resources necessary for setting up the alternative circuits examined in this paper. The third section interprets this combination of conditions as the feminizing of survival for a growing share of households, for a range of illegal traffickers, and the feminizing of particular forms of government revenue enhancement.

I THEORIZING GENDER IN THE GLOBAL ECONOMY

What are the strategic sites where the gender dynamics of current processes of globalization can be detected, studied and theorized? This is an important and difficult analytical task. As with earlier phases of economic internationalization, current scholarship on the global economy largely ignores the facts and modalities of gender dynamics.

It took a pioneering effort to begin to redress the lack of gender analysis in scholarship for earlier phases of economic internationalization.[2] The resulting scholarship shows us that in export-oriented agriculture, the strategic gender nexus is between the capitalist enterprise (the plantation or large-scale commercial agricultural enterprise) and subsistence economies (women's work in the household that takes care of the basic needs of the plantation workers (husbands, brothers, sons). In the internationalization of manufacturing production, the strategic gender nexus is that between the dismantling of an established, largely male "labor aristocracy" in major industries with shadow effects on an increasing sector of developed economies, and, on the other, the formation of an off-shore, largely female proletariat in new and old growth sectors. Off-shoring and feminizing of this proletariat (who are, after all, employed in growth industries) has kept these women workers from becoming an empowered workforce with actual union power; it has at the same time

2 Boserup 1970; Deere 1976.

also prevented existing, largely male "labor aristocracies" from becoming even stronger. Both of these features were to the benefit of employers.

These two very diverse instances where we can see that genedering functions as a strategic factor are examples of how a gendered understanding of economic processes reveals additional aspects easily hidden in conventional analysis of "development."

Among the strategic sites in today's global economy are those linked to the new organization of politico-economic power and the formation of global cities.[3] Global cities are key sites for the specialized servicing, financing and management of global economic processes. These cities are also sites for the incorporation of large numbers of women and immigrants in activities that service some of the most powerful and dominant sectors of contemporary economies, notably highly specialized services for firms and finance. This mode of incorporation renders women and immigrant workers invisible, thereby breaking the nexus between being workers in leading industries and the opportunity to become – as had been historically the case in industrialized economies – a "labor aristocracy" or its contemporary equivalent. In this sense "women and immigrants" emerge as the systemic equivalent of the off-shore proletariat. Further, the demands placed on the top level professional and managerial workforce in global cities are such that, for those professionals, the usual modes of handling household tasks and lifestyle are inadequate. This is a type of household that could be described as the "professional household without a 'wife,'", that is to say, without the traditional member of the family (the mother, the wife) in charge of doing all the housework. This is so regardless

3 For the following see Sassen 1998: chapter 1; 2007: ch 5.1

of the fact that the household may be constituted of opposite sex or same sex couples, so long as both people hold demanding jobs and neither stays at home doing the housework. As a consequence we are seeing the return of the so-called "serving classes" in all the global cities around the world, made up largely of immigrant and migrant women.[4]

But the master representations in the currently dominant account about economic globalization in media and policy circles, as well as in much economic analysis, basically elide these gendered, exploitative conditions. The emphasis within the dominant account about economic globalization is on hypermobility, global communications, the neutralization of place and distance, and the highly educated, human-capital intensive worker. This account privileges the capability for global transmission over the material infrastructure that makes transmission possible; information outputs over the workers producing those outputs, who range from specialists to secretaries; and the new transnational corporate culture over the multiplicity of work cultures, including immigrant cultures, within which many of the "other" jobs of the global information economy take place.

Detecting gender dynamics requires a shift in focus to the practices that constitute what we call economic globalization and global control: the top level firms and the top level households responsible for producing and reproducing the organization and management of a global production system and a global marketplace for finance, as well as the vast infrastructure of low-wage jobs and low-profit activities that service the former.

A focus on practices draws the categories of place and work process into the analysis of economic globalization, and allows us to recapture people,

4 Parreñas 2001; Ehrenreich and Hochschild 2003; Hirata 2006; Sassen 2001: chapter 9; Hondagneu-Sotelo 2001.

workers, communities, and more specifically, the many different work cultures, aside from the corporate culture, involved in the work of globalization. There is considerable articulation of firms, sectors, and workers who may appear as though they have little connection to an urban economy dominated by finance and specialized services, but in fact fulfill a series of functions that are an integral part of that economy. They do so, however, under conditions of sharp social divisions, low earnings, and, often, sex and racial/ethnic segmentation. The global city can be seen as one strategic research site for the study of these processes.

In the case of a city like New York City, a large share of the jobs involved in the day-to-day work of maintaining high level professions, dominated by finance, are lowly paid and manual, many of which are held by women and immigrants. Although these types of workers and jobs are never represented as part of the global economy, they are in fact part of the infrastructure of jobs involved in running and implementing the global economic system, which include highly advanced forms such as international finance. The top of the corporate economy – the corporate towers that project engineering expertise, precision, "techne" – is far more legible as necessary for an advanced economic system than are truckers and other industrial service workers, even though such workers are a necessary ingredient in the global economy.[5]

What we see at work here is a series of processes that valorize and overvalorize

---

5 For instance, with the first acute stock market crisis in 1987 after years of enormous growth, the media circulated numerous press reports about the sudden and massive unemployment crisis among high-income professionals on Wall Street. The other unemployment crises on Wall Street, affecting secretaries and blue collar workers, was never noticed by mainstream media nor reported upon. And yet, the stock market crash created a very concentrated unemployment crisis, for instance, in the Dominican immigrant community in Northern Manhattan where many of the Wall Street cleaners live.

certain types of outputs, workers, firms and sectors, and de-valorize others. We cannot take devalorization as a given: devalorization is a produced outcome. In my reading, the forms of devalorization of certain types of workers and work cultures I have described here are partly embedded in the demographic transformations evident in large cities. The growing presence of women, immigrants, and people of color in large cities, along with a declining middle class, has facilitated the operation of devalorization processes. The fact of gendering, e.g. the devaluing of feminized jobs, facilitates the devalorization of a broad range of jobs executed by the growing and mostly female "serving classes" in global cities.[6] This is significant for an analysis of globalization because these cities are strategic sites for the materialization of global processes and for the valorization of the new forms of global corporate capital.[7]

The alternative global circuits that are the focus of this paper are yet another instantiation of gendering in the global economy. But they are the circuits of people occupying disadvantaged locations (in the economy, society, culture, and interstate system) rather than the locations of power of professionals within global cities. These disadvantaged locations can involve illegal activities, such as the trafficking of women and children for the sex industry, or they can be fully legal, as in the growing dependence of many governments in poorer countries

---

6 The rapid growth of industries with strong concentrations of high and low income jobs has assumed distinct forms in the consumption structure, which in turn exercises a feedback effect on the organization of work and the types of jobs being created. The expansion of the high income work force in conjunction with the emergence of new cultural forms have led to a process of high income gentrification that rests, in the last analysis, on the availability of a vast supply of low wage workers. This has reintroduced – to an extent not seen in a very long time – the whole notion of the "serving classes" in contemporary high-income households. The immigrant woman serving the white middle class professional woman has replaced the traditional image of the black female servant serving the white master.

7 Sassen 2001.

on the remittances sent by their low-wage emigrants. Further, the decentering of the analysis of globalization contained in the global city model is grounded in two aspects. One is the presence of disadvantaged locations (workers, urban neighborhoods, firms) inside the global city. The other is the possibility of making invisble the fact that such disadvantaged locations are actually articulated with dominant sectors and dynamics; what makes this articulation invisible is that the disadvantaged locations are marked demographically: they are immigrant and minority women. The decentering of the analysis of globalization developed in this article is grounded in the presence of alternative global circuits that connect sites that we usually do not see as connected with each other.

These alternative circuits can be interpreted as constituting a counter-geography of globalization. They are deeply intertwined with some of the major dynamics constitutive of globalization: the formation of global markets, the intensifying of transnational and trans-local networks, and the development of communication technologies which readily escape conventional surveillance practices. The strengthening and, in some of these cases, the formation of new global circuits is embedded or made possible by the existence of a global economic system and its associated development of various institutional supports for cross-border money flows and markets. This constitutes a condition that reaches its most formalized version in the proliferation of free-trade agreements and in the overall structure of the WTO.[8] Positing this embeddedness has been an important element in my research on globalization: the notion that once there is an institutional infrastructure for globalization, processes which have basically operated at the national level can scale up to the global level even when this is

8 I have argued this for the case of international labor migrations (e.g. Sassen 1998: chapters 2, 3 and 4; 2007: ch 5 and 6).

not necessary for the functioning of these processes. This would contrast with processes that are by their very features global, such as the network of financial centers underlying the formation of a global capital market.

Besides being enabled by the existing infrastructure of globalization, these alternative global circuits may well be a systemic outcome that is partly constitutive of globalization. Of interest here is the fact that the WTO and major regional free-trade agreements contain specific provisions concerning the cross-border mobility of specialized professional workers in finance, telecommunications, and a broad range of highly specialized services. The North American Free Trade Agreement contains such provisions even though it was negotiated as an agreement that did not explicitly engage with cross-border flows of workers. These provisions amount to a specialized regime for the circulation of service workers, who are an integral part of the liberalization of international trade and investment in services. These provisions concern a privileged, mostly male workforce; many of the women in this category of workers are likely to function as male subjects. In contrast, the alternative circuits concern an increasingly feminized and exploited workforce. Yet some of these alternative circuits may also be an increasingly necessary component of the global economy. They all involve strategies that function on the backs of poor women: the search for new types of survival and of profit-making, and in the case of governments, new ways of securing revenue. We can see here the elements of gendering dynamics.

As with the analysis of the global city, understanding the gender dynamics is a more difficult task than detecting the presence of women in these alternative global circuits. Although the evidence for such new circuits for survival and profit-making is incomplete and partial, there is a growing consensus among experts that these circuits are expanding and that women are often a majority, including in situations that used to be mostly male. These are, in many ways, survival and profit making strategies that have existed for a long time. What is different today is their rapid growth and their rapid internationalization. The fact of gendering is easier to see in the case of trafficking for the sex industry than in the more generalized condition of profit-making and government revenue enhancement through migration for work. In my analysis the intermediation here is found in the systemic linkages between the negative impacts of globalization on male employment and government revenue based on what were predominantly male waged-employment based economies, on the one hand, and the growing pressures globalization introduced to women to ensure household survival and to offer alternative modes for profit-making and government revenue. These alternative circuits are dynamic and changing in their locational features: to some extent they are part of the shadow economy, but it is also clear that they use some of the institutional infrastructure of the regular economy.

II NEO-LIBERALISM AND DEVELOPING COUNTRIES: GENDERED OUTCOMES

Some of the major dynamics linked to economic globalization have had significant impacts on developing economies. Developing economies have had to implement a bundle of new policies and accommodate new conditions associated with globalization: Structural Adjustment Programs, the opening up of these economies to foreign firms either through free trade agreements or the provisions of the WTO, the elimination of multiple state subsidies, and, it would seem almost inevitably, financial crises and the prevailing types of programmatic solutions put forth by the IMF. It is now clear that in most of the countries involved, whether Mexico or South Korea, these conditions have created enormous costs for certain sectors of the economy and of the population, and have not fundamentally reduced government debt.

Among these costs are, prominently, the growth in unemployment, the closure of a large number of firms in often fairly traditional sectors oriented to the local or national market, the promotion of export-oriented cash crops which have increasingly replaced survival agriculture and food production for local or national markets, and, finally, the ongoing and mostly heavy burden of government debt in most of these economies.

Debt and debt servicing problems have become a systemic feature of the developing world since the 1980s. Generally, most countries that became deeply indebted in the 1980s have not been able to solve this problem. And since the 1990s we have seen a whole new set of countries become deeply indebted. Over these two decades the IMF and the World Bank launched many innovations through their Structural Adjustment Programs and Structural Adjustment Loans, respectively. The latter were tied to economic policy reform rather than the funding of a particular project. The purpose of such programs is to make states more "competitive," which typically means sharp cuts in various social programs.

Structural Adjustment Programs became a new norm for the World Bank and the IMF on the grounds that they were a promising way to secure long-term growth and sound government policy. Yet all of these countries have remained deeply indebted, with forty-one of them now considered as Highly

Indebted Poor Countries.[9] Furthermore, the actual structure of these debts, their servicing and how they fit into debtor countries' economies, suggest that it is not likely that most of these countries will under current conditions be able to pay this debt in full.[10] SAPs seem to have made entrenched indebtedness even more likely by demanding economic reforms that have added to unemployment and the bankruptcy of many smaller, national market oriented firms.

Debt service ratios to GNP in many of the HIPC countries exceed sustainable limits; many debt service ratios are far more extreme than what were considered unmanageable levels in the Latin American debt crisis of the 1980s. Debt to GNP ratios are especially high in Africa, where they stood at 123%, compared with 42% in Latin America and 28% in Asia. Many of these countries pay over 50% of their government revenues toward debt service or 20% to 25% of their export earnings.[11] Thirty-three of the forty-one Highly Indebted Countries paid $3 in debt service payments to the North for every $1 in development assistance. By 2003, debt service as share of exports only (not overall government revenue use) ranged from extremely high levels for Zambia (29.6%) and Mauritania (27.7%), to significantly lowered levels compared with 1990s for Uganda (down from 19.8% in 1995 to 7.1% in 2003) and Mozambique (down from 34.5% in 1995 to 6.9% in 2003)[12]. This debt burden

9 UNDP 2005; 1999; World Bank 2005; Pyle and Ward 2003.

10 The debt, with variations across the years, is basically held as follows: Multilateral institutions – IMF, World Bank and regional development banks – hold 45% of the debt; bilateral institutions – individual countries and the Paris group – hold 45% of the debt; and private commercial institutions hold 10% (UNDP 2006, 1999; Ambrogi 1999; see also Tables in Sassen 2001: chapter 4, and in 2008).

11 Ambrogi 1999.

12 See UNDP 2005; World Bank 2005.

inevitably has large repercussions on state spending composition.

One question running through this essay is whether there are systemic links between, on the one hand, the growing presence of women from developing economies in a variety of global migration and trafficking circuits, and, on the other, the rise in unemployment and debt in those same economies. There is a large body of data on each of these two major processes, but the data does not necessarily address and develop the connection between them[13].

It is in this context of what I would consider a systemic condition marked by high unemployment, poverty, bankruptcies of large numbers of firms, and shrinking resources in states to meet social needs, that alternative, increasingly feminized circuits for survival emerge and can be seen as articulated with those conditions. The formation of these alternative circuits for survival is, however, dependent on certain conditions, such as the existence of an infrastructure that facilitates cross-border flows described in the preceding section, and more specific linkages among particular countries, including ethnic networks. The formation of these circuits is also mediated by other conditions which can activate unemployment and reduce the options for profit-making and for securing revenue, and force a search for alternatives. Such other conditions may include the existence of older traditions of trafficking and organized crime, government initiatives to develop special programs for exporting workers, and patriarchal households that devalue women.

---

13 See Ward 1991; Pyle and Ward 2003; Cagatay and Ozler 1995; Alarcon-Gonzalez and McKinley 1999; Ehrenreich and Hochschild 2003; CIA 2000; IOM 2006; Buechler 2007; Kirsch 2006; Datz 2007.

III FEMINIZING SURVIVAL

Are there systemic links between the rise in unemployment and debt in these economies, and the growing presence of women from developing economies in the alternative global circuits discussed in section one of this article? One way of articulating this in substantive terms is to posit that the shrinking opportunities for male employment in many of these countries; the shrinking opportunities for more traditional forms of profit-making in these same countries as they increasingly accept foreign firms in an expanding range of economic sectors and are pressured to develop export industries; and the fall in revenues for the governments in many of these countries, partly linked to these conditions and to the burden of debt servicing, have all contributed to raise the importance of alternative ways of making a living, making a profit, and securing government revenue.

Research literature on women and debt exists, focused on the implementation of the first generation of Structural Adjustment Programs in several developing countries linked to the growing debt of governments in the 1980s; this literature has documented the disproportionate burden these Programs put on women.[14] And now there is a new literature on a second generation of such Programs which is more directly linked to the implementation of the global economy in the 1990s.[15]

---

14 This is by now a large literature in many different languages; it also includes a vast number of limited-circulation items produced by various activist and support organizations. For overviews see Ward 1999; Kothari 2006; Bose and Acosta-Belen 1995; Beneria and Feldman 1992; Bradshaw et al. 1993; Tinker 1990; Moser 1989.

15 See e.g. Khotari 2006; Lucas 2005; Chant and Kraske 2002; Parreñas 2001; Ehrenreich and Hochschild 2003; Cagatay and Ozler 1995; Salzinger 2003; Zlolniski 2006.

There are detrimental effects on government programs for women and children, notably education and health care – clearly investments necessary to ensure a better future.[16] Further, the increased unemployment typically associated with the austerity and adjustment programs implemented by international agencies to address government debt have also produced adverse effects for women.[17] Unemployment, both of the women themselves and also of the men in their households, has added to the pressure on women to find ways to ensure household survival. Subsistence food production, informal work, emigration, and prostitution have all increasingly expanded as survival options for women.

Heavy government debt and high unemployment have initiated the need to search for survival alternatives; and a shrinking of regular economic opportunities has created an intensified use of illegal profit-making by enterprises and organizations. In this regard, heavy debt burdens play an important role in the formation of alternative global circuits for survival, profit-making and government revenue enhancement. Economic globalization has to some extent added to the rapid increase in certain components of this debt and it has provided an institutional infrastructure for cross-border flows and global markets. We can see economic globalization as facilitating the operation of these alternative circuits at a global scale.

Prostitution and labor migration are growing in importance as ways of earning livings; illegal trafficking of women and children for the sex industry and of laborers in other industries are growing in importance as ways of making profits; and the remittances sent by emigrants, as well as the organized export

16 Alarcon-Gonzalez and McKinley 1999; Buchmann 1996.

17 Chossudovsky 1997; Standing 1999; Rahman 1999; Elson 1995. For overviews of the data see UNDP 2005; World Bank 2005a; Sassen 2001: Table 4.5; 2008.

of workers are increasingly important sources of revenue for some of these governments.[18] Women are by far the majority group in prostitution and in trafficking for the sex industry, and they are becoming a majority group in migration for labor.

The trafficking of women for the sex industry is highly profitable for those running the trade.[19] The United Nations estimates that 4 million people were trafficked in 1998, producing a profit of US $7 billion to criminal groups.[20] By 2003, the ILO estimates that criminal syndicates made over 28 billion dollars. A diversity of organizations working on trafficking estimate that in recent years several million women and girls are trafficked within and out of Asia and the former Soviet Union, two major trafficking areas. Growth in trafficking in both these areas can be linked to women pushed into poverty or sold to brokers due to the poverty of their households or parents.

---

18 The World Bank (2006) estimates remittances worldwide reached US $230 billion, up from US $70 billion in 1998; of this total amount, US $168billion went to developing countries, up 73% from 2001. The Bank also found that in 2003 for Latin America and the Caribbean as a whole, these remittance flows exceeded the combined flows of all foreign direct investment and net official development assistance (see Orozco et al. 2005).

19 Trafficking involves the forced recruitment and/or transportation of people within and across states for work or services through a variety of forms, all of which involve coercion. Trafficking is a violation of several distinct types of rights: human, civil, and political. Trafficking is related to the sex market, to labor markets, and to illegal migration. Much legislative work has been done to address trafficking: international treaties and charters, UN resolutions, and various bodies and commissions. NGOs are also playing an increasingly important role. For instance, the Coalition Against Trafficking in Women has centers and representatives in Australia, Bangladesh, Europe, Latin America, North America, Africa and the Asia Pacific region. The Women's Rights Advocacy Program has established the Initiative Against Trafficking in Persons to combat the global trade in persons.

20 For general information, see Foundation Against Trafficking in Women (STV) and the Global Alliance Against Traffic in Women (GAATW). For regularly updated sources of information on trafficking, see http://www.hrlawgroup.org/site/programs/traffic.html. See also Altink 1999; Kempadoo and Doezema 1998; Lin and Marjan 1997; Lim 1998.

The trafficking of migrants is also profitable business. According to a series of UN reports, criminal organizations in the 1990s generated an estimated US $3.5 billion per year in profits from trafficking migrants (not limited to women).[21] The entry of organized crime is a recent development in the case of migrant trafficking. Up to the 1980s, in much of the world petty criminals executed migrant trafficking. Reports also show that organized crime groups are creating intercontinental strategic alliances through networks of co-ethnics throughout several countries; these alliances facilitate transport, local contact and distribution, provision of false documents, and so on. The Global Survival Network reported on these practices after a two year investigation using the establishment of a dummy company to enter the illegal trade.[22] Such networks also facilitate the organized circulation of trafficked women among third countries – not only from sending to receiving countries. Traffickers may move women from Burma, Laos, Vietnam and China to Thailand, while Thai women may be trafficked to Japan and the US.[23]

Some of the features of immigration policy and enforcement may well contribute to make women who are victims of trafficking even more vulnerable and to give them little recourse to the law. If they are undocumented, which they

21 IOM , various years.

22 Global Survival Network 1997.

23 There are various reports on the particular cross-border movements in trafficking. Malay brokers sell Malay women into prostitution in Australia. East European women from Albania and Kosovo have been trafficked by gangs into prostitution in London (Hamzic and Sheehan 1999). European teens from Paris and other cities have been sold to Arab and African customers (Shannon 1999). In the United States the police broke up an international Asian ring that imported women from China, Thailand, Korea, Malaysia and Vietnam (Booth 1999). The women were charged between US $30,000 and $40,000 in contracts to be paid through their work in the sex trade or needle trade. The women in the sex trade were shuttled around several states in the United States to bring continuing variety to the clients.

are likely to be, they will not be treated as victims of abuse but as violators of the law insofar as they have violated entry, residence and work laws.[24] The attempt to address undocumented immigration and trafficking through greater border controls over entry raises the likelihood that women will use traffickers to cross the border, and some of these traffickers may turn out to belong to criminal organizations linked to the sex industry.

While some women are aware they are being trafficked for prostitution, for many the conditions of their recruitment and the extent of abuse and bondage only become evident after they arrive in the receiving country. The conditions of confinement are often extreme, akin to slavery, and so are the conditions of abuse, including rape and other forms of sexual violence, and physical punishment. They are drastically underpaid, and their wages are often withheld. They are barred from using protection methods against AIDS, and typically have no right to medical treatment. If they seek police help they may be taken into detention because they are in violation of immigration laws; if they have been provided with false documents then they face criminal charges.[25]

As tourism has grown sharply over the last decade and has become a major development strategy for cities, regions and whole countries, the entertainment sector has seen a parallel growth and recognition as a key development strategy.[26] In many places, the sex trade is part of the entertainment industry and has grown accordingly. At some point it becomes clear that the sex trade

---

24 See generally Castles and Miller 1998; Mahler 1995; Castro 1999.

25 A fact-sheet by the Coalition to Abolish Slavery and Trafficking reports that one survey of Asian sex workers found that rape often preceded their being sold into prostitution and that about one third had been falsely led to becoming sold into prostitution.

26 Judd and Fainstein 1999.

itself can become a development strategy in areas with high unemployment and poverty, and governments desperate for revenue and foreign exchange reserves. When local manufacturing and agriculture can no longer function as sources of employment, profits and government revenue, what was once a marginal source of earnings, profits and revenues becomes a far more important one. The increased importance of these sectors in development generates growing tie-ins. For instance, when the IMF and the World Bank see tourism as a solution to some of the development impasses in many poor countries and provide loans for its development, they may well be contributing to the development of broader institutional settings for the expansion of the entertainment industry, and indirectly of the sex trade. This tie-in with development strategies signals that the trafficking of women may well see a sharp increase.

The entry of organized crime in the sex trade, the formation of cross-border ethnic networks, and the growing transnationalization in so many aspects of tourism, suggests that we are likely to see a further development of a global sex industry. This could mean greater attempts to enter into more and more "markets" and a general expansion of the industry. It is a worrisome possibility especially in the context of growing numbers of women with few if any employment options. And such growing numbers are to be expected given high unemployment and poverty, the shrinking of a world of work opportunities that were embedded in the more traditional sectors of these economies, and the growing debt burden of governments rendering them incapable of providing social services and support to the poor.

Women in the sex industry become – in certain kinds of economies – a crucial link supporting the expansion of the entertainment industry, and through that tourism a development strategy which in turn becomes a source of government revenue. These tie-ins are structural, not a function of conspiracies.

The impact of such tie-ins on an economy will be magnified by the absence or limitations of other sources for securing livelihoods, profits and revenues for workers, enterprises and governments, respectively.

Women, and migrants generally, enter the macro-level of development strategies through yet another channel: the sending of remittances which in many countries represent a major source of foreign exchange reserves for the government. While the flows of remittances may be minor compared to the massive daily capital flows in various financial markets, they are often very significant for developing or struggling economies.

The World Bank's 2006 estimate of $230 billion in global remittances, sent by immigrants to their home countries, up from US $70 billion in 1998, assumes its full significance when we relate it to the GDP and foreign currency reserves in the specific countries involved, rather than compared to the global flow of capital. For instance, in the Philippines, a key sender of migrants generally and of women for the entertainment industry in several countries, remittances represented the third largest source of foreign exchange over the last several years. In Bangladesh, another country with significant numbers of its workers in the Middle East, Japan, and several European countries, remittances represent about a third of foreign exchange.

Exporting workers and remittances are means for governments for coping with unemployment and foreign debt. There are two ways in which governments have secured benefits through these strategies. One of these is highly formalized and the other is simply a by-product of the migration process itself. The Philippine government formalized the export of its citizens as a way of managing unemployment and securing needed foreign exchange reserves through their remittances. It played an important role in the emigration of Filipino women to the United States, the Middle East and Japan, through the

Philippines Overseas Employment Administration (POEA).[27] Established in 1982, it organized and oversaw the export of nurses and maids to high demand areas in the world. Filipino overseas workers sent home almost US $1 billion on average a year in the last few years. Confronted with a sharp shortage of nurses, who work in a profession that demands years of training yet supplies rather low wages and little prestige or recognition, the United States passed the Immigration Nursing Relief Act of 1989 which allowed for the import of nurses from abroad.[28]

An estimated 200 mail-order bride companies arrange 2000 to 5000 marriages in the United States annually. The Philippines and Russia are currently the main source countries for contract brides to the United States. The Philippines government also passed regulations that permitted mail-order bride agencies to recruit young Filipinas to marry foreign men as a matter of contractual agreement. The rapid increase in this trade was primarily due to the organized effort by the government. Among the major clients were the United States and Japan. The contract brides report many stories of abuse by foreign husbands. In the United States the INS has recently reported that domestic violence against mail-order wives has reached acute levels.[29]

Philippines, while perhaps the nation-state with the most developed program, is not the only country to have explored these strategies. Thailand started a campaign in 1998 after the 1997-8 financial crisis to promote

27 The largest number of Filipinas going through these channels work overseas as maids, particularly in other Asian countries. The second largest and fastest growing group is "entertainers," mostly to major cities in Japan (Sassen 2001: chapter 9; Yamamoto 2006).

28 About 80% of the nurses migrating under the new act were from the Philippines.

29 INS 1999.

migration for work and recruitment of Thai workers by overseas firms. The government sought to export workers to the Middle East, the United States, Great Britain, Germany, Australia and Greece. Sri Lanka's government has tried to export another 200,000 workers in addition to the one million it already sent overseas; Sri Lankan women remitted US $880 million in 1998, mostly from their earnings as maids in the Middle East and Far East. Bangladesh had already organized extensive labor export programs to the OPEC countries of the Middle East in the 1970s. This phenomenon has continued, and along with the individual migration both to these countries and to various other countries, notably the United States and Great Britain, is a significant source of foreign exchange. Its workers remitted US $1.4 billion in each of the last few years.

It is increasingly on the backs of women that these forms of securing livelihoods, making profits, and securing government revenue are realized. Thus in using the notion of feminization of survival I am not only referring to the fact that households and indeed whole communities are increasingly dependent on women for their survival. I want to emphasize the fact that governments are also dependent on women's earnings in these various circuits, and so are types of enterprises whose ways of profit-making exist at the margins of the "licit" economy. In this sense these circuits can then be thought of as indicating the growing feminization of survival. Analytically, this uncovers the systemic connections between, on the one hand, the mostly poor and low-wage women often represented as a burden rather than a resource, and, on the other hand, what are emerging as significant sources for profit-making, especially in the shadow economy, and for government revenue enhancement. To this we can add the additional government revenue through savings due to severe cuts in health care and education. These cuts are often part of the effort of making the state more competitive as demanded by Structural Adjustment Programs and other policies linked to the current phase of globalization. These types of cuts are generally recognized as hitting women particularly hard insofar as women are responsible for the health and education of household members.

IV CONCLUSION

We are seeing the growth of a variety of alternative global circuits for securing livelihoods, making profits, and securing government revenue. These circuits incorporate increasing numbers of women. Among the most important of these global circuits is the illegal trafficking of women for prostitution and other labor, organized exports of women as brides, nurses, and domestic servants, and the remittances sent back to their home countries by an increasingly female emigrant workforce. Some of these circuits operate partly or wholly in the shadow economy.

The emergence of these circuits and/or their global scale is linked to major dynamics of economic globalization in both highly developed and developing economies. The global city is one site that makes legible the formation/expansion of a demand for what these circuits deliver and hence the (relative) profitability of these circuits. In developing countries, key indicators of conditions promoting the supply of workers and the formation of these circuits are the heavy and rising burden of government debt, the growth in unemployment, sharp cuts in government social expenditures, the closure of a large number of firms in often fairly traditional sectors oriented to the local or national market, and the promotion of export-oriented growth. The growth of a global economy has produced an institutional infrastructure that facilitates cross-border flows and represents an enabling environment for these alternative circuits.

I call these alternative circuits of globalization because they are i) directly or indirectly associated with some of the key programs and conditions that are at the heart of the global economy, but ii) are circuits not typically represented as connected to globalization, and often actually operate outside and in violation of laws and treaties, yet are not exclusively embedded in criminal operations as is the case with the illegal drug trade. Linking these alternative circuits to programs and conditions at the heart of the global economy also helps us understand how gendering enters into their formation and viability.

Bibliogarphy

Alarcon-Gonzalez, Diana, and Terry McKinley. 1999. "The Adverse Effects of Structural Adjustment on Working Women in Mexico." *Latin American Perspectives* 26(3):103-117.

Aneesh, A. 2006. *Virtual Migration: The Programming of Globalization*. Durham: DukeUniversity Press.

Ambrogi, Thomas. 1999. "Jubilee 2000 and the campaign for debt cancellation." *National Catholic Reporter*, July.

Bada, Xochitl, Jonathan Fox, and Andrew Selee. 2006. *Invisible No More: Mexican Migrant Civic Participation in the United States*. Washington D.C.: The Woodrow Wilson International Center for Scholars.

Barlow, Andrew L. 2003. *Between Fear and Hope: Globalization and Race in the United States*. Lanham, MD: Rowman & Littlefield.

Beneria, Lourdes, and Shelley Feldman, eds. 1992. *Unequal Burden: Economic Crises, Persistent Poverty, and Women's Work*. Boulder, CO: Westview.

Bonilla-Silva, Eduardo. 2003. *Racism without Racists: Color-blind Racism and the Persistence of Racial Inequality in the United States*. Lanham, MD: Rowman & Littlefield.

Boserup, E. 1970. *Woman's Role in Economic Development*. New York: St. Martin's Press.

Bose, Christine E., and Edna Acosta-Belen, eds. 1995. *Women in the Latin American Development Process*. Philadelphia: Temple University Press.

Bradshaw, York, Rita Noonan, Laura Gash, and Claudia Buchmann, 1993. "Borrowing Against the Future: Children and Third World Indebtedness." *Social Forces* 71(3):629-656.

Brenner, Neil, and Roger Keil. 2005. *The Global Cities Reader*. New York and London: Routledge.

Bryson, J. R., and P. W. Daniels, eds. 2006. *The Service Industries Handbook*. Cheltenham, UK: Edward Elgar.

Buechler, Simone. 2007. "Deciphering the Local in a Global Neoliberal Age: Three Favelas in Sao Paulo, Brazil." In *Deciphering the Global: Its Scales, Spaces, and Subjects*, ed. Saskia Sassen, 95-112. New York and London: Routledge.

Buchmann, Claudia. 1996. "The Debt Crisis, Structural Adjustment and Women's Education." *International Journal of Comparative Studies* 37(1-2):5-30.

Bureau of Economic Analysis. 2004. *Improved Annual Industry Accounts for 1998-2003: Integrated Annual Input-Output Accounts and Gross-Domestic-Product-by-Industry Accounts*. eds. Brian C. Moyer, Mark A. Planting, Paul V. Kern, and Abigail M. Kish.

Cagatay, Nilufer, and Sule Ozler. 1995. "Feminization of the Labor Force: The Effects of Long-Term Development and Structural Adjustment." *World Development* 23(11):1883-1894.

Chaney, Elsa, and Mary Garcia Castro, eds. 1988. *Muchachas no more: Household Workers in Latin America and the Caribbean*. Philadelphia: Temple University Press.

Chang, Grace. 1998. "Undocumented Latinas: The New 'Employable' Mothers." In *Race, Class, and Gender*, eds. M. Andersen and Patricia Hill Collins, 311-19. Belmont, CA: Wadsworth.

Chant, Sylvia, and Nikki Kraske. 2002. *Gender in Latin America*. Rutgers, NJ: Rutgers University Press.

Chase-Dunn, Christopher, and Barry Gills. 2005. "Waves of Globalization and Resistance in the Capitalist World System: Social Movements and Critical Global Studies." In *Towards a Critical Globalization Studies*, eds. Richard Appelbaum and William Robinson, 45-54. New York: Routledge.

Chin, Christine. 1997. "Walls of Silence and Late 20th Century Representations of Foreign Female Domestic Workers: The Case of Filipina and Indonesian Houseservants in Malaysia." *International Migration Review* 31(1):353-85.

Chossudovsky, Michel. 1997. *The Globalization of Poverty*. London: Zed/TWN.

Central Intelligence Agency. 2000. *International Trafficking in Women to the United States: A Contemporary Manifestation of Slavery and Organized Crime*. Prepared by Amy O'Neill Richard. Washington, D.C.: Center for the Study of Intelligence. www.cia.gov/csi/monograph/women/trafficking.pdf.

Consalvo, Mia, and Susanna Paasonen, eds. 2002. *Women and Everyday Uses of the Internet: Agency and Identity*. New York: Peter Lang.

Datz, Giselle. 2007. "Global-National Interactions and Sovereign Debt-Restructuring Outcomes." In *Deciphering the Global: Its Spaces, Scales and Subjects*, ed. Saskia Sassen, 321-50. New York and London: Routledge.

David, Natacha. 1999. "Migrants Made the Scapegoats of the Crisis." ICFTU Online. International Confederation of Free Trade Unions. www.hartford-hwp.com/archives/50/012.html.

Deere, C.D. 1976. "Rural Women's Subsistence Production in the Capitalist Periphery." *Review of Radical Political Economy* 8(1):9-17.

Elson, Diane. 1995. *Male Bias in Development*. Manchester: Manchester University Press.

Ehrenreich, Barbara, and Arlie Hochschild. 2003. *Global Woman: Nannies, Maids, and Sex Workers in the New Economy*. New York: Metropolitan Books.

Fantasia, Rick, and Kim Voss. 2004. *Hard Work: Remaking the American Labor Movement*. Berkeley: University of California Press.

Fernandez Kelly, M. P. 1982. *For We are Sold, Me and My Sisters*. Albany, NY: SUNYPress.

______, and J. Shefner. 2005. *Out of the Shadows*. College Station, PA: Penn State University Press.

Fisher, Melissa. 2006. "Wall Street Women: Navigating Gendered Networks in the New Economy." In *Frontiers of Capital: Ethnographic Reflections on the New Economy*, eds. Melissa Fisher and Greg Downey. Durham: Duke University Press.

Froebel, Folker, Jurgen Heinrichs, and Otto Kreye. 1980. *The New International Division of Labor*. London: Cambridge University Press.

Gershuny, Johathan, and Ian Miles. 1983. *The New Service Economy: The Transformation of Employment in Industrial Societies*. New York: Praeger.

Grasmuck, Sherri, and Patricia R. Pessar. 1991. *Between Two Islands: Dominican International Migration*. Berkeley: University of California Press.

Gugler, Joseph. 2004. *World Cities Beyond the West*. Cambridge: Cambridge University Press.

Hagedorn, John, ed. 2006. *Gangs in the Global City: Exploring Alternatives to Traditional Criminology*. Chicago, IL: University of Illinois at Chicago.

Henderson, Jeffrey. 2005. "Governing Growth and Inequality: The Continuing Relevance of Strategic Economic Planning." (In *Book Title*,) eds. R. Appelbaum and W. Robinson. New York: Routledge.

Hindman, Heather. 2007. "Outsourcing Difference: Expatriate Training and the Disciplining of Culture." In *Deciphering the Global: Its Scales, Spaces and Subjects*, ed. Saskia Sassen, 153-76. New York and London: Routledge.

Hirata, Helene, ed. 2006. Special Issue, *Cahiers du Genre*, no. 40. (get details).

Hochschild, Arlie. 2000. "Global Care Chains and Emotional Surplus Value." In *On the Edge: Globalization and the New Millennium*, eds. Tony Giddens and Will Hutton, 130-46. London: Sage Publishers.

Hondagneu-Sotelo, Pierrette. 1994. *Gendered Transitions: Mexican Experiences of Immigration*. Berkeley, CA: University of California Press.

______, ed. 2003. *Gender and U.S. Immigration: Contemporary Trends*. Los Angeles: University of California Press.

International Migration Office. 2006. *Trafficking in Migrants* (Quarterly Bulletin). Geneva: IOM.

Indiana Journal of Global Legal Studies. 1996. "Feminism and Globalization: The Impact of the Global Economy on Women and Feminist Theory." Vol. 4, Issue 1.

Ismi, Asad. 1998. "Plunder With a Human Face." *Z Magazine*, February. http://www.thirdworldtraveler.com/IMF_WB/PlunderHumanFace.html.

Iyotani, Toshio, Naoki Sakai, and Brett de Bary, eds. 2005. *Deconstructing Nationality*. Ithaca, NY: Cornell University East Asia Program.

Jones, Erika. 1999. "The Gendered Toll of Global Debt Crisis." *Sojourner* 25(3):20-38.

Khotari, Uma. 2006. *A Radical History of Development Studies: Individuals, Institutions and Ideologies*. London: Zed Books.

Kirsch, Max, ed. 2006. *Inclusion and Exclusion in the Global Arena*. New York: Routledge.

Kofman, Eleonore, Annie Phizacklea, Parvati Raghuram, and Rosemary Sales. 2000. *Gender and International Migration Europe: Employment, Welfare and Politics*. London and New York: Routledge.

Koo, Hagen. 2001. *Korean Workers: The Culture and Politics of Class Formation*. Ithaca and London: Cornell University Press.

Koval, John P., Larry Bennett, Michael I. J. Bennett, Fassil Demissie, Roberta Garner, and Kiljoong Kim. 2006. *The New Chicago: A Social and Cultural Analysis*. Philadelphia: Temple University Press.

Kyle, D., and R. Koslowski. 2001. *Global Human Smuggling*. Baltimore and London: Johns Hopkins University Press.

Lardner, James, and David A. Smith. 2005. *Inequality Matters: The Growing Economic Divide in America*. New York: The New Press and Demos Institute.

Lewis Mumford Center for Comparative Urban and Regional Research. 2000. *Segregation and Income in U.S. Cities*. http://mumford.albany.edu/census/index.html.

Lucas, Linda, ed. 2005. *Unpacking Globalisation: Markets, Gender and Work*. Kampala, Uganda: Makerere University Press.

Mamdani, Mahmood. 1996. *Citizen and Subject: Contemporary Africa and the Legacy of Late Colonialism*. Princeton, N.J.: Princeton University Press.

Martin, Philip. 1997. "Economic Integration and Migration: The Case of NAFTA." In Proceedings of the Conference on International Migration at Century's End: Trends and Issues, Barcelona, Spain, May 7-10, 1997. Liege, Belgium: The International Union for the Scientific Study of Population.

Menjivar, Cecilia. 2000. *Fragmented Ties: Salvadoran Immigrant Networks in America*. Berkeley: University of California Press.

Milkman, Ruth. 1987. *Gender at Work: The Dynamics of Job Segregation by Sex During World War II*. Urbana: University of Illinois Press.

______. 2000. *Organizing Immigrants: The Challenge for Unions in Contemporary California*. Ithaca, NY: ILR Press.

Moghadam, Valentine M. 2005. *Globalizing Women: Transnational Feminist Networks*. Baltimore: Johns Hopkins University Press.

Morokvasic, Mirjana. 1984. "Birds of Passage are also Women." *International Migration Review* 18(4):886-907.

Moser, Carolyn. 1989. "The Impact of Recession and Structural Adjustment Policies at the Micro-level: Low Income Women and their Households in Guayaquil, Ecuador." In *Invisible Adjustment* Vol. 2. Santiago: UNICEF, Americans and Caribbean Office.

Munger, Frank, ed. 2002. *Laboring Under the Line*. New York: Russell Sage Foundation.

______. 1983. *Women, Men, and the International Division of Labor*. Albany: State University of New York Press.

Naim, Moises. 2006. *Illicit: How Smugglers, Traffickers, and Copycats are Hijacking the Global Economy*. New York: Anchor Books.

Nash, June. 2005. *Social Movements: An Anthropological Reader*. Malden, MA: Blackwell.

______, and María Patricia Fernández-Kelly. 1983. *Women, Men, and the International Division of Labor*. Albany: State University of New York Press.

Newman, Katherine S. 1999. *Falling from Grace: Downward Mobility in the Age of Affluence*. Berkeley: University of California Press.

Olds, Kris, Peter Dicken, Philip F. Kelly, Lily Kong, and Henry Wai-Chung Yeung, eds. 1999. *Globalization and the Asian Pacific: Contested Territories*. London: Routledge.

Ong, Aihwa. 1999. *Flexible Citizenship: The Cultural Logics of Transnationality*. Durham, NC: Duke University Press.

Orozco, Manuel, B., Lindsay Lowell, Micah Bump, and Rachel Fedewa. 2005. *Transnational Engagement, Remittances and their Relationship to Development in Latin America and the Caribbean*. Washington, D.C.: Institute for the Study of International Migration, Georgetown University.

OXFAM. 1999. *International Submission to the HIPC Debt Review*. www.caa.org/au/Oxfam/advocacy/debt/hipcreview.html.

Parnreiter, Christ of. 2002. "Mexico: The Making of a Global City." In *Global Networks/Linked Cities*, ed. Saskia Sassen, 145-82. New York: Routledge.

Parrenas, Rhacel Salazar, ed. 2001. *Servants of Globalization: Women, Migration and Domestic Workers*. Stanford, CA: Stanford University Press.

Pearce, N. 2004. "Diversity versus Solidarity: A New Progressive Dilemma?" *Renewal* 12(3). http://www.renewal.org.uk/vol12no32004diversityversussolidarity.htm.

Pessar, P. R., and S. J. Mahler. 2003. "Transnational Migration: Bringing Gender In." *International Migration Review* 37(3):812-846.

Potts, L. 1990. *The World Labor Market: A History of Migration*. London: Zed.

Pyle, Jean L., and Kathryn Ward. 2003. "Recasting our Understanding of Gender and Work During Global Restructuring." *International Sociology* 18(3):461-89.

Rahman, Aminur. 1999. "Micro-credit Initiatives for Equitable and Sustainable Development: Who Pays?" *World Development* 27(1):67-82.

Reinhardt, C. M., and G. Kaminsky. 1999. "The Twin Crisis: The Causes of Banking and Balance of Payments Problems." *American Economic Review* 89(3):473-500.

Revista Internacional de Filosofia. 2006. "Inmigracion, Estado y Ciudadania. Simposio." *Revista Internacional de Filosofia* 27 (July).

Ribas Mateos, Natalia. 2004. *Una Invitacion a la Sociologia de las Migraciones*. Barcelona: Edicions Bellaterra.

______. 2005. *The Mediterranean in The Age Of Globalization: Migration, Welfare, And Borders*. Somerset, NJ: Transaction.

Robinson, S. 2004. "Towards a Neoapartheid System of Governance with IT Tools." SSRC IT & Governance Study Group. New York: SSRC. http://www.ssrc.org/programs/itic/publications/knowledge_report/memos/robinsonmemo4.pdf, accessed 18 Mar. 06.

Roulleau-Berger, Laurence, ed. 2003. *Youth and Work in the Postindustrial Cities of North America and Europe*. Leiden, Netherlands: Brill.

Safa, Helen. 1995. *The Myth of the Male Breadwinner: Women and Industrialization in the Caribbean*. Boulder, CO: Westview Press.

Salzinger, Leslie. 2003. *Genders in Production: Making Workers in Mexico's Global Factories*. Berkeley and Los Angeles: University of California Press.

Sassen, Saskia. 1988. *The Mobility of Labor and Capital: A Study in International Investment and Labor Flow*. Cambridge and New York: Cambridge University Press.

______. 1996. *Losing Control: Sovereignty in an Age of Globalization*. New York: Columbia University Press.

______. 2001. *The Global City: New York, London, Tokyo*. Princeton, NJ: Princeton University Press.

______. 2006. *Territory, Authority, Rights: From Medieval to Global Assemblages*. Princeton, NJ: Princeton University Press.

______. 2010. "A Savage Sorting of Winners and Losers: Contemporary Versions of

Primitive Accumulation." *Globalizations* 7(1–2):23–50.

______. 2012. *Cities in a World Economy*. Thousand Oaks, CA: Pine Forge Press (4th updated edition).

Schiffer, Ramos Sueli. 2002. "Sao Paulo: Articulating a Cross-Border Regional Economy." In *Global Networks/Linked Cities*, ed. Saskia Sassen, 209-36. New York and London, UK: Routledge.

Sennett, Richard. 2003. *Respect in an Age of Inequality*. New York: Norton.

Smeeding, T. 2002. "Globalization, Inequality, and the Rich Countries of the G-20: Evidence from the Luxembourg Income Study (LIS)." Luxembourg Income Study Working Paper No. 320. Prepared for the G-20 Meeting, Globalization, Living Standards and Inequality: Recent Progress and Continuing Challenges, Sydney, Australia, May 26–28, 2002.

Silver, Beverly J. 2003. *Forces of Labor: Workers' Movements and Globalization since 1870*. Cambridge: Cambridge University Press.

Smith, Joan, and Immanuel Wallerstein, eds. 1992. *Creating and Transforming Households: The Constraints of the World-economy*. Cambridge and Paris: Cambridge University Press and Maison des Sciences de l'Homme.

Smith, Michael Peter, and Adrian Favell. 2006. "The Human Face of Global Mobility: International Highly Skilled Migration in Europe, North America and the Asian Pacific." *Comparative Urban and Community Research*. Special Issue Vol. 8.

Smith, Robert C. 2005. *Mexican New York: Transnational Worlds of New Immigrants*. Berkeley: University of California Press.

Standing, Guy. 1999. "Global Feminization through Flexible Labor: A Theme Revisited." *World Development* 27(3):583-602.

Suarez-Orozco, Marcelo M., and Mariela Paez. 2002. *Latinos: Remaking America*. Berkeley, CA: University of California Press.

Susser, Ida. 2002. "Losing Ground: Advancing Capitalism and the Relocation of Working Class Communities." In *Locating Capitalism in Time and Space: Global Restructurings, Politics, and Identity*, ed. David Nugent, 247-90.

Stanford, CA: Stanford University Press.

Tabak, Frank, and Michaeline A. Chrichlow, eds. 2000. *Informalization: Process and Structure*. Baltimore, MD: The Johns Hopkins Press.

Tait, Vanessa. 2005. *Poor Workers' Unions: Rebuilding Labor from Below*. Cambridge, MA: South End Press.

Taylor, Peter J. 2006. *Cities in Globalization: Practices, Policies, and Theories*. London: Routledge.

Taylor-Gooby, Peter. 2004. "Open Markets and Welfare Values: Welfare Values, Inequality, and Social Change in the Silver Age of the Welfare State." *European Societies* 6(1):29-48.

Tinker, Irene, ed. 1990. *Persistent Inequalities: Women and World Development*. New York: Oxford University Press.

Toussaint, Eric. 1999. "Poor countries pay more under debt reconstruction scheme?" July. www.twnside.org.sg/souths/twn/title/1921-cn.htm.

United Nations Development Programme. 2005. *A Time For Bold Ambition: Together We Can Cut Poverty in Half.* UNDP Annual Report.

U.S. Department of State. 2004. *Trafficking in Persons Report, released by the Office to Monitor and Combat Trafficking in Persons*. Washington, D. C.: U.S. Department of State.

Venkatesh, Sudhir A. 2006. *Off the Books: the Underground Economy of the Urban Poor*. Cambridge, MA: Harvard University Press.

Ward, Kathryn. 1991. *Women Workers and Global Restructuring*. Ithaca, NY: Cornell University Press.

_______, and Jean Pyle. 1995. "Gender, Industrialization and Development." In *Women in the Latin American Development Process: From Structural Subordination to Empowerment*, Chris E. Bose and Edna Acosta Belen, eds, 37-64. Philadelphia: Temple University Press.

Waters, M. C. 1999. *Black Identities: West Indian Immigrant Dreams and American*

Realities. New York and Cambridge, MA: Russell Sage Foundation.

Wilson, W. J. 1997. *When Work Disappears*. New York: Alfred A. Knopf.

World Bank. 2005. *Global Economic Prospects 2005: Trade, Regionalism and Development*. Washington, D.C.: The World Bank.

______. 2005a. "Increasing Aid and Its Effectiveness." *Global Monitoring Report: Millennium Development Goals: From Consensus to Momentum*. Washington, D.C.: The World Bank. http://siteresources.worldbank.org/INTGLOBALMONITORING/Resources/ch5_GMR2005.pdf.

______. 2006: *Global Economic Prospects: Economic Implications of Remittances and Migration*. Washington, D.C.: The World Bank.

Wallerstein, Immanuel Maurice. 1974. *The Modern World-System: Capitalist Agriculture and the Origins of the European World-Economy in the Sixteenth Century*. New York: Academic Press.

Yamamoto, Satomi. 2000. "The Incorporation of Female Workers into a Global City: A Case Study of Filipina Nurses in the Chicago Area." M.A. thesis, University of Chicago.

______. 2006. "Democratic Governmentality: The Role of Intermediaries in the Case of Latino day Laborers in Chicago." Paper presented at the American Sociological Association, Montreal, Quebec, Canada, August 13.

Yeoh, Brenda, Shirlena Huang, and Joaquin Gonzalez III. 1999. "Migrant Female Domestic Workers: Debating the Economic, Social and Political Impacts in Singapore." *International Migration Review* 33(1):114-136.

Zlolniski, Christian. 2006. *Janitors, Street Vendors, and Activists: The Lives of Mexican Immigrants in Silicon Valley*. Berkeley: University of California Press.

Analysis of Progress and Issues of Gender Equality in China

WEI Guoying

While we have achieved a great deal of progress in gender equality in various fields as a result of the state's policies and regulations and the active initiative by the government, at the same time new issues have emerged. The article discusses and analyzes the situations and issues related to progress in gender equality.

I ISSUES OF EQUAL OPPORTUNITY AND EQUAL RESULTS

Gender equality after all is an issue of social relations, with different connotations and extensions as time and place change. The currently adopted definition of gender equality in modern international society came from the

Mexico Declaration in the 1st International Women's Conference in 1975.[1] The definition covers equal human dignity and values of men and women, equal rights, opportunities, and responsibilities. This definition stresses the principles of humanism and human vision in order to examine the gender relations from a social cognitive domain. Therefore, this definition has positive epistemological impacts and practical significance since this policy has paid much more attention to equality of human dignity.

I believe that equal opportunity for men and women at critical moments of social change, gender development, and progress for survival mean that both men and women should be able to acquire accurate information, and make choices and act on their own, to the same extent. Equality of results refers to equivalent rights and interests obtained by men and women when they make similar choices and perform similar actions. However, for women's actual development in China, equal opportunity has not necessarily produced the same rights and interests for women in certain fields. This is particularly true in higher education.

Since 2000, the number of men and women receiving higher education is gradually reaching a balance. As statistics show, the number of female students has increased after the national recruitment expanded for undergraduates in 1999. According to the full data provided by the Ministry of Education, the number of male graduates in 2004 was 9% higher than that of female students, and the disparity dropped to less than 1% in 2008.[2] In 2010, female undergraduate students at school take up 49.68% of the total undergraduates,

---

1 Jinfang Zhao and Sulan Yue, eds. 2008.

2 National Center for Information Consultant and Vocational Counseling in Institutions of Higher Learning, Pedagogical College of Peking University. 2009.

and female master graduates take up 50% of the total, and the junior college female students occupy 52.41% of the total.[3] The reduced discrepancy in access to education between men and women shows that China has achieved remarkable progress in gender equality in the area of education.

Nevertheless, discrepancies in employment between men and women graduates have been increasing in recent years. A study by the College of Pedagogics of Peking University showed that there was little difference between female and male college students' scholastic attainment and wage income in 2003.[4] However, in 2009 another investigation by this College showed that there were distinct differences between female and male college graduates in actual settlement after graduation,[5] such as distribution of industries, ownership of work unit(state-owned collective or private ownership), and levels of starting salaries. A total of 21,753 graduates from 28 colleges and universities in 14 provinces responded to the survey on the graduates' studies and employment. The result showed that the employment situation had worsened for female students. First, the study shows that the rate of actual settlement after graduation for female students of various educational levels is significantly below that of male students. The higher the education levels, the greater the difference: there is a difference of 5 percentage points in the rate of actual settlement between male and female junior college graduates, 11.3 percentage points for undergraduates,

3 Data are from the 2010 educational statistics by the Ministry of Education: *http*//www.moe.gov.cn

4 Dongmao Wen. 2005.

5 Rate of settlement refers to the confirmation by graduates after graduation, which includes those who have been ensured work units, or choose to go on to study at home, or to study abroad, or choose freelance work, or to be self-employed, or to be flexibly employed. All of these options add up to the rate of settlement.

and 15.4 percentage points for postgraduates.

Second, the starting salaries for women graduates of various educational backgrounds are all lower than the starting salaries for their male counterparts: male junior college graduates earn on average 402 RMB more than female graduates, male undergraduates earn 188 RMB more than female undergraduates and male postgraduates earn 498 RMB more than female postgraduates. Third, female respondents' satisfaction with their jobs is unanimously lower than male respondents' job satisfaction: male junior college graduates' satisfaction level is 10.5% higher than that of female graduates, male undergraduates 6.9% higher than female undergraduates and male postgraduates 6.0% higher than female postgraduates. Fourth, there are also obvious gender differences in the distribution of professions and work units. More than 70% of college and university graduates work for big enterprises (such as in state-owned organizations or corporations) and 40.6% of them are male, which is 14.8% more than their female peers. At the same time, more than 36.5% of female students work for private enterprises, which is a rate 9.2% higher than male students.[6]

Generally speaking, jobseekers' competitiveness depends on his or her human capital level. It is much easier for students with broad knowledge, strong capabilities and personal qualifications to obtain jobs and earn higher wages. Does this assumption suggest that female students are inferior to their male peers in terms of knowledge, capability and personal qualifications? According to the above-mentioned investigation, female students' academic performance is distinctly better than that of male students, irrespective of the level of education:

6 Changjun Yue. 2010.

junior college graduates, undergraduates, postgraduates, and doctoral students. The proportion of male students who are members of the Communist Party and are student leaders is on par with or marginally higher than that of female students. The percentage of female students who are in the top 25% of the total class, winning scholarships, obtaining CET4 (or 6) (Certificate of English Test), acquiring computer certificates, and possessing internship experiences is higher than that of male students. Taking undergraduates for example, the ratios of female students who are in the top 25% and who win scholarships are respectively 12.9% and 19.7% higher than those of male counterparts; the ratios of female students obtaining CET4 (or 6), acquiring computer certificates, and being a minor or double degree student are respectively 7.5%, 5.7% and 3.8% higher than those of male students; the ratio of female students having internship experiences is 2.2% higher than that of their male peers.[7]

The third survey on Chinese women's social status in 2010 also showed that the proportion of female graduates acquiring excellent and good scholastic attainment was 62.4%, which was 9.7% higher than that of male graduates. There were 4.8% and 4.0% more female students than male students who took part in volunteer activities or joined the Communist Party.[8] These figures show that although women students have had equal opportunity for university/college education and have shown an evident superiority over men in their studies, this has not necessarily translated into an equality of outcome. That is, even after receiving higher education and having acquired the same scholarly attainments and capabilities as men, women have not been able to obtain professions of the

7 Ibid.

8 All China Women's Federation. 2010.

same social status, efficiency and job satisfaction as men.

The above phenomenon has drawn broad attention from the society. Investigators are aware that there is a notable gap between female and male students when it comes to obtaining top quality educational resources. The gap is evident in the percentage of women entering national key universities, which occupies only 36.6% of all the key universities which have more financial support from the state and the local governments. This percentage, as we know that nearly 50% of the total students are females, is distinctly low. In higher educational levels, the proportion of female students decrease, as documented by the percentage of female doctoral students at 35.1% of the total.[9] In our age of the knowledge economy, highly educated students will undoubtedly have an advantage in their search for jobs and career development in the future.

Researchers have found that apart from students' devotion to studies, there are other external factors that affect the students' chances of being admitted to major universities, such as the quality of elementary education and extracurricular learning. As Chinese families have long preferred boys to girls, they have invested more in sons' educations and such family decisions have severely influenced girls' educations.[10] Families invest insufficiently in girls' elementary education, and this to a certain degree affects girls' entrance examination results, which in the end will reduce girls' chances to enter key universities invested by the state and the local governments.

Other researchers have also paid attention to the fact that sexual discrimination in employment still exists. The third survey on Chinese women's

9 Changjun Yue. 2010.

10 Chunling Liu. 2009.

social status in 2010 revealed that 24.7% of those who tried to apply for jobs had been treated unfairly. As many as 10.0% of women had encountered sexual discrimination while only 4.5% of men had experienced such discrimination when applying for a job. About 19.8% of high-level female talents reported that gender discrimination had hindered their career development.[11] According to another survey by the Constitutional Research Institute of the China University of Political Science and Law, there were more than 9,762 posts in 2011 open for those who take the nationwide government recruitment exam, more than 15.6% of which were designated for or recommended to male applicants only. The number increased from 1,203 posts in 2010 to 1,519 in 2011.[12]

Therefore, the results of the national entrance examination have played an impartial role in enrolling students. This policy has granted equal opportunities for men and women before entering universities. During their studies in universities, through each individual's hardworking and diligence, the females are able to excel themselves better than the males in academic performances. However, at the "exit" of graduation, the females relying only on their own endeavor have difficulty in finding equal opportunities in workplace

Researchers have different understandings of why female graduates encounter more difficulties in finding jobs. Some suggest that the reason for the low employment rate and low starting salaries for female graduates should not be optionally attributed to sexual discrimination because there are other factors such as the variety of requirements within the labor market. While an increasing number of male graduates find jobs in the manufacturing, construction and

11 All China Women's Federation. 2010.

12 Constitutional Research Institute, China University of Political Science and Law. 2012.

energy (monopoly) industries, female graduates face a greater difficulty in finding ideal jobs. This is due to objective factors.[13]

I agree that these objective factors do exist, and that they impact employment decisions. However, the more dominating reasons are that, under the restrictions of China's mainstream ideology, namely the structural sexual caste system, gender-based separation of profession, and the established concepts of "male domination" and "male superiority", gender equality has not been truly recognized as an idea, system and mechanism, nor is practiced widely in society. Although China's college expansion plan has produced a rise in university/college enrollment for both men and women, the general equality of college entrance has not spontaneously transformed into equality of access to higher education.

The equality of results here refers to equal employment opportunity, equal professional levels and hierarchy, equal income levels and equal promotion of social status. For female college graduates, simple equal opportunity into colleges and universities is not enough, as equal opportunity does not directly translate into equality of results. We know that the prerequisite to female emancipation is women's advancement in public work fields.[14] Modern women quite reasonably expect equal posts at work, equal access to professions in knowledge-intensive and high-tech industries, and equal access to advanced administrative levels after receiving higher education. This is the foundation for development for men and women.

In the current market economy, an increase in employment disparity

13 Changjun Yue. 2010.

14 *On Women by Marx, Engels, Lenin and Stalin*. 1978.

between female and male graduates also means an increase in the cost of higher education for women, a drop of the input-output ratio, and a lower rate of return, which will undoubtedly lead to a series of negative effects including reduced investment in female education and women's lowered expectation of receiving higher education. In the long run, this will create a vicious cycle of a lower percentage of female students, and it will give rise to the mutual containment of expectations, inputs and effects by families, individuals and society on higher education of the same quality and same quantity for men and women. That is to say, it is impossible to change traditional gender values and attitudes with equal opportunity alone. The single idea of equal opportunity cannot cover all the nuanced and diverse aspects of gender equality and more should be done to think over and to solve issues such as on result equality.

Even though the increase in the number of enrollment has not changed the situations of Chinese female graduates, it is undeniable that the gender ratio of students is reaching a balance, signifying important progress toward gender equality in China. This equalizing balance should be cherished and maintained with special effort because increasing the number of female college students is prerequisite to improving female human capital, which plays an important role in the advancement of gender equality in the primary stage of socialism.

II ISSUES ON QUANTITY EQUALITY AND VIRTUAL EQUALITY

Since the end of the 20th century, the employment rate of Chinese women has been very stable. The 2003 Statistical Yearbook of Chinese Labor reveals that the proportion of female employees in cities and towns has stood around

38% of the total population from 1995 to 2002. A news report in March 2007 from the Xinhua News Network showed that the ratio of female employees reached 45% of all employees in 2007. In October 2008, Huang Tingyi, Vice Chairperson of All China Women's Federation (ACWF), stated during the 10th National Congress of Chinese Women that women had taken up 45.4% of the total employment in China. The numbers show that female employees are still occupying approximately half of the documented work in the new socialist market economy.

However, evident disparity between men and women in choices of professions, job titles, income levels and chances of promotion still exists. First, there is a gender imbalance in certain industries. The relevant data from the *2009 Statistical Yearbook of Chinese Labor* reveals that a greater percentage of female employees work in traditionally "female" industries such as health care, education, hotels, wholesale and retail, and financing, with financing as the exception as it has grown only recently in the process of the rapid development of the capital market. Career women still undertake the duties of nurturing, nursing, serving and assisting, which are arguably a social extension of women's roles in families.

Second, there are distinct differences in the types of jobs provided by the state-owned, collective or private corporations. A survey by the Research Center for Moderate Prosperity in China showed that Chinese jobs, from most to least desirable, are as follows: first, state organs (32.4%); second, state-owned enterprises (18.3%); third, government institutions (15.6%); fourth, foreign enterprises (15.5%); fifth, privately-owned enterprises (8.6%); sixth, self-employed (5.7%) and; seventh, NGOs (3.1%)[15] An investigation by the College of Pedagogics of Peking University in 2009 showed that male graduates had more opportunities to work in state organs or state-owned enterprises. The proportion of male graduates working in the state organs was 12%, 3.5% higher than that of female graduates.[16] As we know, the ownership of a corporation or an organization in China (whether state-owned, collective or private ones) is closely related to the individual's social status, career development, and income levels. The distinct differences in the property of jobs will undoubtedly have a clear impact on the job holders' career development and economic status.

Third, within the industries, women are still over-represented in occupations in the less desirable range with relatively lower labor incomes. Furthermore, women have to drop out of the labor force earlier than men in accordance with relevant regulations and system[17]. The third survey on national women's status in 2010 revealed that the average annual income of employed urban women is just 673 percent of the average annual income of men, while the average annual income of employed rural women is 56 percent of men's average annual income. This pattern was no different in the case of women from developed cities and areas such as Beijing, Tianjin, Shanghai, and eastern and mid-western China.[18]

To sum up, an equal number of jobs for men and women do not necessarily guarantee actual gender equality in the social and economic arena. Actual gender equality in the economic arena means men and women occupy equal

15 Pan E. 2010.

16 Changjun Yue. 2010.

17 Author's conclusion by analyzing relevant statistics of the structure of the employed people according to their genders and ages in the *Statistic Yearbook of Chinese Labors in 2009*.

18 All China Women's Federation. 2010.

levels and social status in terms of sharing and controlling economic resources and benefits. The actual gender equality depends on socioeconomic levels and orders both gender belong to, on what roles they play in social production, and where they locate themselves in the social wealth distribution system. In modern society, having jobs would provide women with economic incomes, and the basis for economic power while the hierarchy of employment, different levels of income, and chances of promotion would directly affect their position in socio-economic relations as well as family status, social status and political status. Hence, researchers and scholars regard virtual equality in the economic arena for men and women as the kernel of gender equality as a whole, and virtual equality has played a decisive role in measuring and evaluating women's overall social status. Although Chinese women are considered to have acquired certain basic conditions in order to survive at work, there is still a long way to go before China achieves actual equality. We should not only pay close attention to the number and proportion of women employed, but also focus on the quality and benefit of the employment so as to promote the levels of actual equality in the pursuit of quantitative equality.

III ISSUES ON EQUALITY OF FAIR COMPETITION AND EQUALITY OF SOCIAL SUPPORT

The Communist Party and the government have always been aware of the importance of educating and employing female talent since China implemented reform and open policies. However, the development of female talent has encountered new problems. First, the number of female leaders is quite low and the ratio of female talents is low compared to the ratio of male talents.

For example, in 2008, there were only 3 female ministers, or 11.1% of the 27 ministers selected by the State Department and approved by the first Session of the 11th National People's Congress (NPC).[19] In the same year, there were only 106 female leaders in provincial governments, the provincial People's Congress, and the provincial People's Political Consultative Conference (NPPCC), occupying 13.0% of the total posts. Of the 106, only 6 women were chief Party and government officials, who take up only 6.5% of the total high-level jobs.[20] As of April 2009, there has been only one female president of the 75 universities under the Education Ministry. Currently, women account for 37% of the total workforce in science and technology,[21] but the proportion of female leaders or experts in these fields is much lower. Female academics in CAS (Chinese Academy of Science) and CAE (Chinese Academy of Engineering) amount to only 5.6% of the total number of academics.[22]

Second, the pyramid-like structure of female professors and experts tends to be smaller. Generally speaking, there are only a very few people at the top of the pyramid. My research has shown that the size of the pyramid structure of male talent in universities has become larger in the past ten years, while that of female talent has become smaller and much fewer women at the top of the pyramid. The data from one famous university shows that professors constitute 38.5% of the total number of full-time teachers in the end of 2007. Male professors make up 84% and female professors occupy 16% of the total number of full-time teachers. Female professors are 22.5% below the average of the total

19 Xinhua News Agency. 2008.

20 Women's Studies Institute of All China Women's Federation. 2008.

21 *Women's Daily*. 2012.

22 This data comes from the websites of CAS and CAE.

teachers, 68% below the (something of) male professors, 10.4% lower than the proportion of all female teachers, which stands at 26.4% of the total number of teachers, and 9% lower than the rate of the retired women professors which is 25%. There are fewer women obtaining professional titles and this tendency is more obvious in Polytechnics.

Third, China faces a lack of backup talent. As of October 2010, the mathematics department of one university which ranked at the top among Chinese universities in the field of mathematical research had 98 full-time teachers, and 9 teachers, or 9% of the total full-time teachers, were female. The university employed only 2 women professors, making up 3.5% of the total number of professors. For associate professors, 3 out of 29 associate professors, or 10% of the total number of professors, were female. Even though the percentage of women professors in mathematics had always been quite low, the proportion of female talent in this department was much lower than in the previous years. For example, retired female professors constituted 21% of the total retirees, while retied female associate professors accounted for 40% of the total. As of 2012, there are more than 70 Academicians of CAS and CAE in one major university, 3 of whom are female and who are all nearly 80 years old. This indicates a lack in the reserve team of female academicians.

There are different opinions on the above-mentioned phenomenon, and many interpretations for the potential causes. I suggest one important reason is that vulnerable groups in society bear the brunt of the shocks caused by the transitions of the social strata, but these groups will in the end benefit from the rapid development of society. The socially marginalized gender is no exception. At present, as our economic system is shifting from a planned economy to a market economy, social resources will inevitably flow from those perceived as having low efficiency to putatively highly efficient people. In general, some women easily become a less efficient group because women have to undergo three periods during their lifetimes----menses, gestation, and the production and lactation period; and they have long been restricted by the established sexual division of labor in society as well as in families. Therefore, no matter what social stratum she comes from, the woman has to confront greater shocks and challenges than her male counterpart. It is true that free competition in the market economy has offered more opportunities to make independent choices and to compete on a more level playing field. Yet, as women undertake the additional responsibility of reproduction, women need not only the social environment that guarantees equality of fair competition, but also the social policies that provide equality of social support.

The so-called equality of fair competition refers to equal rights of men and women achieved with their own capabilities and endeavors without any external auxiliary conditions; the so-called equality of social support here means equal rights of men and women achieved with their own capabilities and efforts in the context of social recognition that women should be provided with corresponding social support for the specific contribution they make in reproduction. The social supportive equality seems to run counter to the spirit of gender equality, but I regard social support as indispensable for realizing true gender equality.

Throughout history, multiple factors such as the division of labor in society and families, the feudalistic convention and customs of male superiority and female inferiority, and the devaluation of women's reproductive functions have greatly influenced the systems of social economies, politics and cultures. These factors have been practical obstacles obstructing the equal competition and development of both men and women. Therefore, it is fair to say that the fair competition between men and women without any support for women is the sort of fair competition that takes gender inequality as a given. An active implementation of systems and policies for gender-specific treatment will enable women to navigate society's discriminatory structures in. This is a precondition for fair competition that guarantees an equal start for men and women.

I have noticed that in the current market economy, the state, universities, institutions of science and technology and the like have not fully taken advantage of their administrative power to support women, relying more on their individual effort, who bear the challenge of raising families and developing careers while simultaneously competing with their male counterparts. All this makes it more difficult to develop highly talented female workers. Therefore, it is necessary to modify existing policies and to introduce relevant policies in order to accelerate the increase in the number of female talent and leaders. For instance, equal gender proportions in leadership positions at different levels of administration will be better achieved with policies that guarantee women's portions of research subsidies and awards; policies that give priority to women in personal training and selection under the circumstance of equal conditions provided for men and women, and policies to use public resources and establish welfare facilities such as lactation rooms, nurseries, and kindergartens. All of the above will offer effective social support for women who choose to have children and who are primarily taking care of housework, and will create a system or a mechanism which facilitates the growth, development and success of female talent. These are necessary and important measures for the realization of equality among people and their social values and social contributions.

IV DEMAND FOR IDENTITY EQUALITY AND DEMAND FOR DIFFERENTIATED EQUALITY

In recent years, the modified proposals for same age retirement in the NPC, the NPPCC, the local People's Congress, and the local People's Political Consultative Congress have elicited different responses from both sexes and among women. In 2011, a study by the Women's Institute of ACWF on Retirement Age showed that about 74.5% of female leaders and 70.6% of female technicians asked for the same retirement age as their male counterparts, while 50.6% of female workers hoped to have a different retirement age. About 26.8% or a fourth of the total number of female workers is in favor of retiring 10 years earlier than male workers. The research group has also found that the respondents' choice between "yes" and "no" to same retirement age was related to their sex, social status (group), age, education level, household income, economic condition, family responsibility, physical condition, type of ownership of their work units, administrative ranking, position in their work units, technical titles, the economic benefits of their work units, welfare and social security, and changes in their incomes after retirement.[23]

The disagreements among women of different strata have intensified with continuous reform and opening-up. Women from different stratum have different interests, concerns, and different appeals for equality. Women from different ethnic groups, regions, educational backgrounds, ages, and social statuses have different understandings of and aspirations for gender equality. The uneven economic development has led to uneven progress in gender equality

---

23 Bohong Liu, Li Guo, and Rui Hao, eds. 2011.

between urban and rural areas, in different regions, in different industries, and in different female groups. Social transformation has produced a number of issues concerning social equity and justice, which are often mixed, and an appeal for gender equality is usually associated with less advantaged groups' interests.

While there is an obvious and increasingly diversified and complex demand for female equality in China, if we simply regard women as a homogeneous and identical entity as opposed to people with diverse realities, and ignore their internal and external differences and influences, we would not be able to achieve the goals of gender equality. Instead, such an approach will have a negative impact on women's movements, policy making on gender equality, and women's development. For example, the impact of inequality for blue-collar female workers and farmers in terms of labor and capital is much greater than that of their male counterparts. The current demand for gender equality should consider the rights and interests of all women and set the target for their overall development while at the same time setting differentiated goals for different groups of women from different social strata based on their actual needs for survival and development. For retirement age, the flexible retirement age plan proposed by the academic circle which enables individual laborers to have the right to choose retirement age would be in accordance with the realities of Chinese women while maintaining fidelity to the equal progress of women and men from various social strata.

In conclusion, the current and new issues of gender equality in China have emerged in the process of China's social transformation and development, and will only be settled through further development and progress in gender equality. In order to better cope with the new situation and issues, I suggest that the state and the government work toward deeper and more accurate understandings of the current state of gender equality, and adopt practical and effective measures to push for further progress in gender equality.

More specifically, first, the state and the government should possess the keen foresight to anticipate and identify new and emerging issues and contradictions in the process of social development and realization of gender equality. This recommendation requires special plans for early warning and reform. Second, the state and the government should seek accurate source perspectives and should bring in related leading departments and staff to formulate and implement policies, and to manage and maintain rights and interests in such a way to legally and objectively safeguard women's equal rights to and participation in the national construction and the achievement of social development. Third, they should be keenly aware of the disparities and other issues that women of different social strata face and work toward closing gaps in equality. Equality of opportunity and equality of results thus must be promoted simultaneously, as well as equality of quantity and actual equality. As women depend on the state's tendentious policies and public social resources, they should be guaranteed equal rights to participation and equal chances for social development so as to promote social progress jointly.

Bibliography

All China Women's Federation. 2010. *The Third Data Report on Women's Social Status in China*. Beijing: National Bureau of Statistics.

Constitutional Research Institute, China University of Political Science and Law. 2012. "A Survey of Gender Discrimination in Civil Service Exam." *Women's Daily*, January 10, B2.

E., Pan. 2010. "Encaged Chinese Talents." *Moderate Prosperity*, Vol. 9, 1-18.

Liu, Bohong, Guo Li, and Rui Hao, eds. 2011. *Research Report on the Retirement Age*.

Liu, Chunling. 2009. *Gender Differences Caused by Educational Status: Impact of Family Background upon Men's and Women's Educational Status*. Beijing: Collection of Women's Studies.

National Center for Information Consultant and Vocational Counseling in Institutions of Higher Learning, Pedagogical College of Peking University. 2009. *2004-2008: Employment Situation for College Graduates in China*. Beijing: Peking University Press.

On Women by Marx, Engels, Lenin and Stalin. 1978. Beijing: People's Publishing House.

Wen, Dongmao. 2005. *Gender Comparison of Opportunities of Higher Education, School Work, and Employment*. Beijing: Educational Studies at Tsinghua University.

Women's Daily. 2012. "Cohesive Teamwork: To Provide Service for the Growth and the Development of the Female Talents." February 16, A1.

Women's Studies Institute of All China Women's Federation. 2008. *Women's Studies for Internal Reference*.

Xinhua News Agency. 2008. "Name list of the 27 New Ministerial Officials of the State Department." *Xinhua Net*, March 17.

Yue, Changjun. 2010. *Gender Comparison of Higher Education and Employment*.

Beijing: Educational Studies at Tsinghua University.

Zhao, Jinfang, and Sulan Yue, eds. 2008. *Simplified Readings of the Basic State Policy of Gender Equality*. Beijing: Peking University Press.

Neoliberal Globalization and the Transformation of Women's Subjectivity: From the Perspective of Practice Theory

CHO Joo-hyun

I RAISING ISSUES: NEOLIBERAL GLOBALIZATION, LATE MODERNITY, GOVERNMENTALITY

Neoliberalism, which began to spread and accelerate since the 1970s, is the main ideological driving force that initiated most developed countries into late modernity by the end of the last century. It resuscitated the economic globalization that ended after the First World War because of political burdens incurred by deepened economic inequality. Although the present form of globalization is considered to be less intense in the economic aspect than the previous form that started at the end of the 19th century (Rodrik 1997), if we take into account the present globalization's impact on social transformations, we can justifiably call it a "thick" globalization compared to the previous "thin" globalization (Keohane and Nye 2002). One of the main contributing factors for the present "thick" globalization is the transformation of social life by revolutionary developments in information technology that also characterizes a significant part of life in late modernity (Castells 2009). Scholars such as Paul Virilio have noted that such transformations have caused an acceleration in speed, leading to an unprecedented contraction of space and time in everyday life (Virilio 1986).

However, the diverse early prognoses of political and social changes due to globalization offered by some authors (Hardt and Negri 2001; Beck and Beck-Gernsheim 2002; Friedman 2000) require major adjustments, if not the jettisoning of whole conceptual frameworks, in light of a series of global political events that have occurred after 9/11, and the re-emergence of the importance of sovereign powers in many developed countries. These events also raised serious doubts about the usefulness and appropriateness of the concept of globalization (Cameron and Palan 2004). Among the issues reexamined is the role of sovereign power in neoliberal governmentality (Dean 2008), which Giorgio Agamben tried to relocate through the concepts of "homo sacer" and the "state of exception." The understanding of neoliberal governmentality introduced by Michel Foucault captures the essential characteristics of political power operating in most developed countries and many developing countries. Foucault classified types of power according to their modes of operation into sovereign power, pastoral power, disciplinary power, and biopower; in neoliberal governmentality, these modes of power are selected and combined in variegated manners depending on spatio-temporal conditions (Ong 2005). For example, in most developed countries as represented by OECD members, neoliberal governmentality utilizes what is variously called the "technology of the self," "the conduct of conduct," or "power of freedom" to induce consent and cooperation without coercion, in a manner ever imperceptible but omnipresent, like capillaries permeating every aspect of society. This mode of power operation could be subsumed under the concept of governance in which global governance by nonstate actors, various forms of power, corporate governance and even everyday social interaction are loosely related through a family resemblance.

The underlying reason for these characteristics of power in late modernity is the rapid population growth since the 18th century with accompanying demands for higher quality of life, which led to emphasis on economic growth, hence the view that the efficiency of government is a necessary requirement. The wide acceptance of neoliberal logic as an apparently unavoidable path was shaped by the putatively effective impact of the market economy for increasing economic productivity and removing poverty in most parts of the world during the last two centuries, combined with increasing demands for the expansion of private life and freedom. Thus to many, including most economists, neoliberal governmentality is an attempt by late modern society to answer this demand by extending the economic logic to the whole socio-political area.

Neoliberalism could not have spread with little resistance in developed countries, especially at aggravating economic polarization, without implicit or explicit individual compliance to and acceptance of its logic by the majority of people in society. This acceptance was made possible because what neoliberal logic advertises as its merits, namely increasing individual freedom and its attendant creativity, efficiency, and independency, appeared to be quite obvious, whereas the necessary consequences of increasing individual freedom, such as increasing the uncertainty and inefficacy of individual action to achieve its intended goal, and the difficulty of securing the public good were comparatively less obvious (Cho J. 2012). When power employs everyday life forms of governmentality that share the same conduit with self-empowering efforts to increase individual freedom, instead of relying on sovereign forms based on laws and institutions as its predominant mode of operation, it becomes challenging to understand its operation and consequences.[1]

This paper aims to analyze the transformation of women's subjectivity in late modern Korean society which employs neoliberal governmentality as its principal mode of power operation. Our analysis will proceed in the following order. In section 2, I argue that we need a detailed theory of how social practices such as power and governmentality are constructed, maintained, transformed, or annihilated by performances of individuals in each community to reveal how transformations of operating modes of power are intertwined with issues of subjection and agency. Then I assert practice theory as the best starting point for such a philosophical framework. Section 3 addresses the problem of subjection in feminist politics from the perspective of practice theory. Section 4 starts with Brandom's theory of linguistic practice and deploys his concept of "(expressive) positive freedom" to argue for the insights it can lend to the issue of the constitution of women's subjectivity and autonomy.

Section 5 discusses the transformation of women's subjectivity in late modern Korean society and argues for the efficacy of the practice theory perspective in analyzing the problem of women's subjection and agency. This section shows agonistic politics to be an effective potential measure for resisting and transforming women's subjectivity and, more generally, neoliberal

---

1 It is due to the same underlying reason that there are so many confusing interpretations of new femininities. As will be discussed in more detail later, the problem of the constituted nature of subjectivity and agency of women is closely related to this kind of dual nature of power, as is the problem of voluntary servitude.

governmentality in Korean society. In conclusion, I claim that women in late modern Korean society have been constituted as neoliberal subjects, and that a micropolitical approach focusing on the detailed decision processes of each individual in concrete social contexts is necessary to understand both their subjection and agency. Social practice theory, developed and advocated by philosophical pragmatists and social scientists during the last century, is recommended as the best starting framework for this analysis on which further theoretical and empirical works should be built. Agonistic politics, regarded as the political implementation of practice theory, is advocated as the most effective tools for resisting domination and effecting self-transformation.

II POWER AND SUBJECT IN LATE MODERNITY

In his justifiably well-known work on power, Steven Lukes presented his three-dimensional concept of power, including the claim that the powerful can manipulate the desires of the dominated in order to affect them in a manner contrary to their interests. This concept stands in contrast to Weber's concept of power, which emphasizes the probability of realizing one's will despite the resistance of others (Lukes 2005, 110-124). According to Lukes, the third face of power operates even when there are no conflicts of interests among those involved. He also argues that "because of its links with no less contested notions of freedom, authenticity, autonomy, and real interests," no uncontested way of understanding power is possible, which implies that the concept of power is a normative one that depends ultimately on how members of each community regard power operation in consideration of normative and moral viewpoints (108). Lukes's insistence on including "the third dimension of power: the capacity to secure compliance to domination through the shaping of beliefs and desires, by imposing internal constraints under historically changing circumstances" in the concept of power implies that he regards the important instances of the third dimension of power as those deemed requiring intervention from any justice-minded reasonable members of a community (143-144). This is the main underlying reason why, against the claim that "we should speak not of my power but of my luck" in cases where "others can further my interests without my either intending or intervening to bring this about" (Barry 1989, 270-302; Dowding 1996), he insists "that such cases may, but also may not, be among the most effective and sometimes the most insidious forms of power" (Lukes 2005, 110).

There is no denying that his claim has great instinctive appeal. But his argument, similar to the claims made by his famous predecessors including Marx and Gramsci, were criticized for treating the oppressed willing subjects as dupes incapable of perceiving their real interests. In a similar vein, critics have also pointed out that these arguments will not be able to explain cases of self-organized resistance by the oppressed without external help from more intellectual but condescending elites, as can be seen in many historically successful or aborted cases of resistance. The problem Lukes's third facet of power aims to explain is part of a more general one posed by Charles Tilly and quoted by Lukes: "if ordinary domination so consistently hurts the well-defined interests of subordinate groups, why do subordinates comply? Why don't they rebel continuously, or at least resist all along the way?" (10). Tilly also provides a list of possible answers which Lukes approvingly quotes. In most actual cases, all the answers work together to explain a given case. Lukes concentrates on the subtlest one against those including rational choice theorists, claiming that there are no mysteries, but rather perfectly good explanations.

As has been acknowledged by Lukes despite his qualms against Foucault's florid rhetoric, Foucault's theory of power has a great affinity with Lukes's three-dimensional concept of power (149). In fact, Foucault sees his conception of power/knowledge working in any everyday social interaction, as exemplified by his frequently quoted remark: "everything is dangerous" (Foucault 1983, 231-232). Not surprisingly, this trait of his concept of power invites a natural question from his critics, including Habermas: if power operates everywhere, how is it possible for the dominated to resist? Though Foucault tried to complement his theory of power with a theory of resistance starting from Volume 1 of his *History of Sexuality* to the theory of the art of existence and ethics until his premature death, these efforts was never satisfactory (at least to his critics). The main cause of the theoretical lack is not difficult to recognize. Both Foucault and Lukes did not incorporate the agency of actors as an integral part of their theories. Regarding actor's agency, the approach antipodal to theirs is methodological individualism, including various versions of rational choice theory.[2]

Opponents of Foucault's and Lukes's theories, including rational choice theorist Keith Dowding, propose to avoid an infinite regression of attempts to decide the fairness of previous individual choices determining the present social norms and institutions, which in turn contributed to the constitution of the present individual preferences by regarding the social status that made possible the third facet of power to operate in the first place as luck. The backbone of his argument is the one given by the powerful in reply to the oppressed demanding

2 The relations between their concepts of power, in particular Foucault's practice theory and the problem of agency and methodological individualism in general, are a quite complicated problem and most probably require the full theory of social action and practices as will be further discussed as we go on.

justice throughout history: if you and your ancestors have made your "rational choices" from time immemorial, you should not complain even if there are some unintended consequences or inequalities. This argument, in turn, has its own problem as has been repeatedly pointed out by its critics. Rational choice theory, which in its most naive version is a favorite of neoclassical economists, neglects a whole plethora of structural factors affecting each individual choice. But we can fix this defect of rational choice theory rather easily. Simply accept the fact that the structural factors including norms and institutions can constitute the preference of each actor.[3] A more difficult problem to fix is the fact that the preferences of individual actors are not independent. In the case where this dependency is relatively weak, you can neglect it as a first approximation. But the problem is that in most important cases, including the present case we are concerned with, this dependency cannot be safely ignored.

Therefore the problem is not choosing the best theory that explains the given phenomena among contenders, but rather choosing a more fundamental and meta-theoretical one concerning the correct approach to understand complex social practices governing phenomena such as power, oppression, and domination. We suggest that practice theory is the correct philosophical framework to start with. In particular, traditions of pragmatism starting with Wittgenstein and the American pragmatists, phenomenology starting with Husserl and Heidegger, and other philosophical approaches including Otto Neurath's combined with recent progress made in cognitive sciences seem to

3 This approach was called structural rational choice theory by Ann E. Cudd (1994) in her efforts to 'tame' classical rational choice theory for feminism. Most recent scholars of rational choice theory and game theory acknowledge this effect and adopt it as an integral part of their theories (Gintis 2007; Heath 2008).

converge into a coherent framework for these phenomena.[4]

An individual in late modernity has more freedom of choices in her life and entertains much more diverse desires in general; this tendency does not show any sign of change in the near future. Therefore, any attempts to contain diverse demands and subtle differences in individual lives in late modernity within identity politics of the modernist project that relies on the strategy of identifying common rallying points in the lives of the oppressed to gain compliance from each member are no longer effective (Connolly 2002a). As discussed in section 1, power in late modernity relies on the wide acceptance and application in a society of neoliberal logic, such that the only efficient way of achieving an optimally working society is for each actor to utilize privately available knowledge and information to make the best choices in any given circumstance. Though this tenet was one of the basic intuitions of classical economists of the 18th century, the neoclassical logic underlying neoliberalism pushed it to the extreme by neglecting another important intuition that emphasized the importance of institutions such as social norms, organizations, and cultural norms among others in achieving an optimally working economy and society and providing public goods that are otherwise nearly impossible to access due to the collective action problem. The neoliberal framework means that each society has to solve its own problem of designing an appropriate system of institutions to balance the efficiency to be gained by expansion of freedom allowed to their members and the need to maintain stability necessary for such efficiency, that is, the problem of finding equilibrium points in equality-efficiency trade-off. And this problem becomes more severe as the amount of freedom allowed rapidly

4 The same comments also have direct relevance in various issues surrounding foundationalism/relativism, identity/difference, and retribution/recognition controversies.

increases as in the late modern society and the roles of institutions should be expanded to those of a whole set of social practices available and imaginable.

Since this kind of efficiency cannot be imitated by a central agency, however omniscient and omnipotent, the essential point is to minimize restrictions on individual freedom imposed by institutions, and, in case of necessary restrictions, there are all the more reasons to utilize more flexible institutions like social norms rather than tightly stipulated ones including statute laws. In deploying the kinds of loose and flexible institutions, or more generally, social practices and utilizing niche efficiency thus gained, continuous adjustments and adaptations are essential for the mechanism to continue its operation. This is because the criteria of efficiency that guide the direction the mechanism aims for are always context-dependent, hence subjected to change unless the society inhabits an improbable case of a strictly steady state.

As each agent makes a choice and acts, each practice undergoes a (small) degree of change and this, in turn, induces changes in each actor's beliefs, preferences, and constraints that determine her choices. Though the latter part of this feedback process showing how an agent decides given her beliefs, preferences, and constraints is fairly well described by rational choice theory and game theory at least to a first approximation,[5] there are almost no theoretical tools with a modicum of reliability in the former part that concern how each action by an agent transforms, creates, and annihilates social practices. This is in spite of the fact that most traditional sociological works have been concerned with this problem. This is because this part of the feedback process involves the most complicated characteristics of complex adaptive systems; in this case,

5 For a recent exposition of rational choice theory and game theory, see Gintis (2007).

dynamics of social practices including emergent phenomena among others.

Basic philosophical insights essential to understanding the whole mechanism is provided in century-long efforts by many philosophers, mainly in pragmatic and naturalistic traditions, as mentioned above. But they remain at the level of understanding the general structure and do not even indicate what direction to take for their formalization. What is necessary is the kind of effort shown by Robert Brandom in his work on linguistic practices. The efforts made by these philosophers combined with the works contributed by diverse groups of social scientists are called practice theory. These social scientists, including Bourdieu, Foucault, Garfinkle, and Latour among others, reveal the gritty and mundane details of everyday social interactions where actions by each agent are performed and transform relevant social practices in various contexts. Though their works lack the kind of systematic thoroughness of pragmatic philosophers, they serve as good antidotes for the latter's tendency for the rather clear-cut, hence too reductive, treatment of performances that constitute practices.

The practical theoretical approach to power regards those approaches that assume the concept of power as fixed and attempt to elaborate its operational processes in details, then to classify and interpret the cases to be analyzed according to determined rules as approximate at best, certainly not generally applicable in every possible case. In practice theory, power that operates in the context determined by various social practices including institutions and norms can never work in predetermined manners. Only in special cases does power function in fairly specified and classifiable ways. In most cases, especially in a period of late modernity deeply submerged under neoliberalism, its characteristics continuously undergo transformation at each action performed by agents participating in its operation. Or more precisely, its characteristic space is never completely closed, and remains ever open to new interpretations. At each moment of performance in social practices, a participating agent evaluates social practices based on a whole set of criteria including beliefs, preferences, and constraints, the result of such evaluation in turn transforming her and other agents' criteria. This process usually results in the fine-tuning of some aspects of social practices. But at each moment of evaluation, there is always a possibility of initiating a drastic refurbishment of the whole structure of social practices and power which might be, for instance, a moment of revolutionary change of paradigm in Kuhn's theory of scientific practices. It is also the moment of reflective judgment in Arendt's theory of action and judgment and is called the predicative moment of politics or the world-building practice of judging by Linda Zerilli (2012). At such a moment, each agent confronts the possibility of new interpretations of performances and practices.

III PROBLEM OF SUBJECTIVITY IN FEMINIST POLITICAL THEORY

Critical theorists, including feminist political theorists, tend to oversimplify theoretical frameworks dealing with relations between social practices and each agent's actions in efforts to concentrate and resolve obvious and serious social problems in capitalism or patriarchy. In their descriptions of how institutions and norms constrain freedoms of individuals, each individual is usually treated as slavishly passive. More importantly, an inverse process of creating social consequences or changes by the actions of individuals is described as the results of a simple agglomeration of rather homogeneous effects from each individual action, which largely misses an important part of the creative dimensions of each action and accompanying possibilities of resistance.

At each moment of performance, an individual actor does not simply follow the rules prescribed by institutions and norms; rather, she is "the subject of normative attitudes, to be capable of acknowledging proprieties and improprieties of conduct, to be able to treat a performance as correct or incorrect" (Brandom 1994, 32). When feminist political theorists search for the cause of women's seemingly voluntary subjection from the constituted nature of women's subjectivity under patriarchy (Allen 2009), and critical theorists explain the cause of workers' voluntary servitude in a capitalist system as due to false consciousness and ideological indoctrination (Rosen 2000), they are missing this important aspect of each performance and accompanying deontic score-keeping.

According to Amy Allen, "feminist theory has been obsessed with the so-called problem of the subject" for more than three decades (2009, 1). As explained before, many have frequently noted that the theory of subjection proposed in social constructivist approaches to the relations of subject and power, though very successful in explaining women's subjection, reveals a peculiar incapability for explaining how the gendered subject constituted by power can initiate resistance against it. Feminist theorists in the Foucauldian framework have inherited this problem of the subject, especially the framework proposed by Butler . In short, how is it possible for the subject constituted by intersectional power relations of race, class, and sex to reveal self-transforming agency in order to resist and transform those structures?

The issue of the constituted subject and agency of women is central for feminist political theories that comprise women's experiences and prospects for its main terrain. Understanding this issue is the most important task for contextualizing various feminist positions in contention and proposing appropriate political prescriptions. As an example, we could cite two opposing feminist approaches to the issue of interpreting pornography in Allen's discussion of the topic. Both Dworkin and MacKinnon's viewpoint that regards all forms of pornography as tools for male domination and the radical feminist viewpoint that stresses pornography's character of resistance against the subjection of women and its subversive potential to undermine dominant power relations overemphasize the dominating and empowering aspects of power respectively. However, as we can glimpse in both Williams's proposal to interpret the consumption of pornography as an interrelation of power and pleasure (Williams 1999), rather than regarding it either as exclusively contributing to the consolidation of women's subjection or to empowering women, and Butler's attempts to refine the theory of subjection that emphasizes the entwined nature of these two aspects of domination and empowerment and suggest that empowering women's subjectivities does not necessarily imply resistance against domination, these two aspects cannot be so cleanly separated.

The main problem for feminist political theory is detailing the entwined operating modes of domination and empowerment of the gendered subject (Allen 2001, 521-528). In order to begin this task, as explained in section 2, we need to introduce social practice theory. In her attempt to construct such a theory, Zerilli first pointed out that in the subject-centered frameworks of Foucault and Butler, we see there are inherent limits to incorporating truly revolutionary transformations or a liberatory political agency. Instead, she proposed to change the whole paradigm to one of political practices that emphasizes the predicative moment of politics initiated by women subjects and the ensuing responses by members of a community, leading to transformations of social practices and power relations (Cho J. 2010a). Whereas Butler regarded the frontline of contention to reside in the political structure of dominant discourses and disciplinary power that determine meanings of "women" and attempted to overthrow existing political foundations by re-describing and realigning the intelligible and unintelligible in the current cultural and political terrain (Butler 1999, 189), Zerilli regarded the construction of feminist communities to respond to political actions proposing these attempts of subversion as the core practices essential for their success. That is, each agent's performance initiating the constitution of a new identity or world-building practice of judging can lead to the displacement of social practices that have been serving dominant discourses and disciplinary power, eventually to their demise. Zerilli's claim that these overthrowing attempts cannot be effected by politics of the subject only but should eventually rely on social interaction among community members for its success gains strong philosophical support from practice theory, which argues that social practices undergo transformations including their creation and demise by performances and their interactions, and they in turn serve as the matrices constraining and controlling the performances of each member.

Allen points out that Zerilli's proposal is exposed to the danger of obfuscating the dominating role of power in the constitution of political agents. Allen starts by admitting that collective political engagements may be, as Zerilli suggested, the very moment for women to reject their constituted subject and move toward their emancipation. However, she claims that Zerilli (and for that matter, Arendt, too) should be able to answer following two questions. First, contrary to Zerilli's criticism of the subject-centered framework adopted by Foucault and Butler, the constituted subject could utilize such a collective engagement as a moment of revealing and acting out wounded attachments to its ascribed identity (Brown 1995). Second, how would it be possible for the dominated to engage in collective politics without re-inscribing the current dominant power structure, hence reproducing social inequalities, starting from their social context constrained by structural dominance and oppression (Allen

2009, 10-11)?

Though Allen's critique reveals her underestimation of Zerilli's efforts for the solution of these problems, as shown in Zerilli's analysis of the Milan Women's Bookstore Collective (Cho J. 2010a), I suggest that Zerilli could have avoided the main part of the critique if she had more actively accepted the framework of practice theory. As we can see from Allen's analysis above, the problem of the constituted subject and agency which has preoccupied feminist politics is the one at the heart of both practice theory and methodologies of social sciences (Cho J. 2010b, 2012). Recent work in practice theory is moving in the direction of constructing the models and theories that try to "make explicit" processes of transformations in social practices effected through performances of each actor and the accompanying deontic scorekeeping, including commitment, entitlement, and acknowledgement (Heath 2008; Rouse 2007). In the next section, concepts of freedom and subjectivity which are closely related to the problem of the subject and agency discussed in this section will be analyzed in the framework of practice theory to gain better understandings of the latter problem.

IV FREEDOM AND SUBJECTIVITY IN PRACTICE THEORY: AGONISTIC POLITICS

There are two perspectives on rational acts. One regards the action that an actor performs to achieve her desires or utilities as rational. The other regards the action of a person performing her abilities to constitute and transform herself self-consciously as rational (Brandom 2009, 130-155). These two concepts of rationality translate into two corresponding concepts of freedom: negative freedom from varied social and natural constraints, and positive freedom to do something . The latter is "obtainable only by constraining oneself by the conceptual norms implicit in discursive social practices." The first perspective is based on instrumental rationality and regards the legitimacy of each individual's desire as beyond rational analysis or out of intelligent discussion, thus insisting on concentrating the issues of choosing the most efficient way to satisfy desire. On the other hand, in the second perspective, each individual is regarded as the subject of discursive practices and each individual's performances and accompanying responsibility, commitment, entitlement, and acknowledgement collectively determine meanings of rational acts. And it accepts "the capacity to *bind* oneself by conceptual norms, to undertake responsibility, to make commitments, to exercise and acknowledge authority as the core of the freedom" (Brandom 2009, 143). Brandom claims that Hegel transformed this Kantian concept of positive freedom into "expressive positive freedom," adding the following three aspects: normative status as essentially social status, the importance of discursive practices as the paradigmatic exercise of Kantian positive freedom, and the possibility of "self-conscious self-constituting self-transformation," that is, making themselves be different by taking themselves to be different. Following Kant and Hegel, Brandom emphasized "expressive positive freedom," the enabling aspect of positive freedom made possible by social practices and the possibility of "self-conscious self-constituting self-transformation."

An important point to note is that it is possible to transform social practices through expressive positive freedom allowed to us by linguistic practices. Though social practices are sources for positive freedom, they can also serve to sustain "wrong" or "inefficient" practices. Both the possibility of problematic social practice and the creativity of positive freedom through social practice are ineluctable twin aspects of the same origin: the absence of objective criteria or God's point of view. The absence of a freestanding foundation means that each new performance in social practice could be either a predicative moment of politics or a retrogressive moment of deterioration, with no comprehensive doctrines that can guarantee the better world. Foucault's all too famous remarks are perspicuous comments on this point:

> My point is not that everything is bad, but that everything is dangerous, which is not exactly the same as bad. If everything is dangerous, then we always have something to do. So my position leads not to apathy but to a hyper- and pessimistic activism. I think that the ethico-political choice we have to make every day is to determine which is the main danger. (Foucault 1983, 231-232)

The fact that there are no comprehensive and algorithmic doctrines that allow "to determine which is the main danger," thus guaranteeing a better world, implies that neoliberal governmentality with its capillary manners of power operation and expressive positive freedom share social practices as their networks of channels and conduits for operation, making neoliberal governmentality all the more difficult to resist. For instance, as Butler has stated, psychic attachments that contribute to the perpetuation of relations of domination and subordination originate from a desire for recognition. But this desire for recognition emerges from the social interactions women are engaging in, which in turn are determined by social practices forming basic frameworks to interpret and assign meaning to individual lives. Thus social practices serve as resources for the self-empowerment of female subjectivity as well as causes for continuing its subordination. An important point is that social practices enable expressive positive freedom through linguistic practices, offering valuable tools for transforming social practices that originally made such freedom possible. Although this approach may not seem to be much, and may exasperate foundationalists and those in support of identity politics, this framework actually offers both the most efficient and creative tools, and is moreover the only one available to us, as practice theorists have reminded us.

Practice theory does not only point out possibilities of resistance that the concept of positive freedom offers, but also emphasizes the fact that an individual enjoying expressive positive freedom can create and transform a new language and recreate herself through that language. As discussed in the previous section, Zerilli argued that in feminist politics aiming for the emancipation of women through political practices, the agency of the feminist subject emerges not through holding on to a specific identity and claiming for its justification to speak out, but only through anticipatory discourses which is exactly what we would expect to happen when transformations of social practices through expressive positive freedom occur according to practice theory.

If Foucault's practice theory articulated the constituted character of subjectivity through his concept of power, Brandom's theory tried to reveal the twin aspects of the constitution and agency of the subject residing in each performance through the concept of positive freedom. Viewed from the perspective of positive freedom, social practices working through operations of power reveal their positive role of enabling women to live as social beings and to serve as sources for creative self-constitution and self-transformation. This aspect implies ample possibilities to overcompensate the loss of negative freedom from complying with institutions and norms by increasing positive freedom (Brandom 2009, 52-77). Of course, the similarity of these concepts to those of the market economy is not accidental, and both cases will be seen as manifestations of one common basic phenomenon when a general theory of social practices is completed.

Facing no comprehensive prescriptions for political decisions, what will be the most "efficient" procedure for political decision? We have already seen Zerilli's proposal for political action to initiate transformations of "anomalous" social practices or to overthrow domination. We can generalize and formalize her strategy to deal with the problem of political decision procedures. An agonistic politics willing to lay down everything on the table, including the rules of the game and decision procedures, and to question them will arguably be the best bet. In liquid modernity, where each individual cannot be sure of what she desires, only agonism as a sublimation of antagonism can hope to satisfy each desire efficiently by opening up creative space in politics. Raising issues, arguing for her claims, endeavoring for clarification, and raising objections in confrontation, with no consensus or conclusion enforced, will provide eventually "optimal" political results if successful. Practice theory, which forms the theoretical foundation for agonistic politics, suggests there are no predetermined criteria allowing people to classify each performance as an instance of subjection or self-transformation. This fact reveals the necessity of a more detailed theory of action and decision process comprising practice theory (Brandom 2009, 144-146).[6]

Perhaps a comparison of agonistic politics and deliberative politics will bring the issue into relief. Though deliberative politics shares many characteristics with agonistic politics, such as an emphasis on political deliberations, it refuses

6 This last point is what was missing in Foucault's early works on power and the subject as its effects, and what Foucault tried to incorporate in his theory with his aesthetics of existence or ethics to reintroduce possibilities of resistance against power. This is also the point on which Foucault and other practice theorists including Brandom could successfully compromise.

to give up the idea of public reason as a final arbitrator to lean on. It agrees implicitly or explicitly that the political issues on the table for deliberation should be restricted to "reasonable" claims and procedures and that methods of deliberation should be based on some forms of criteria agreed upon by "reasonable" members of communities. Agonistic politics rejects these hopes as impossible since "agreement on procedures or a public conception of justice (and hence what counts as a 'reasonable' claim) is made possible only insofar as members of a society already share a common 'form of life,'" (Schaap 2006, 264) as Wittgenstein taught us. This is especially conspicuous when we are involved in fundamental political conflicts, as we see in the cases of controversies surrounding the activities of the Truth and Reconciliation Commission (TRC) in post-apartheid South Africa (Schaap 2006) and ex-slave abolitionists such as Frederick Douglass (Zerilli 2012). As we can see in these cases, the "reasonableness" requirement can serve as a regulative idea and as tools of exclusion. Of course, in "normal" situations, this requirement works as tools to increase efficiency in political deliberations and decisions, but there is absolutely no way of judging when a given situation is normal or abnormal prior to the context of the event. As noted above, we cannot have both efficiency and justice.

In late modernity, where the desires of each individual changes in fleeting ways and you cannot be sure of what you desire by yourself without a cue from commercial advertisements, setting the political goals that most reasonable members of a community agree upon and settling on the prescriptions that can achieve those goals through the procedure of reflexive equilibrium (Rawls 1971) may not always be practicable. Even in "normal" situations they will remain as "a boundary-securing activity" and will surely miss many creative aspects of "democratic world-building" political practices (Zerilli 2012). From the perspective of practice theory, whether an individual's performance is preconstituted or is a result of her agency depends on how members of a community judge the performance and the social practices that the performance is a part of. This is because the social practice that affects each performance --whether it is a norm, convention, or ideology-- is determined and transformed by the scorekeeping activities of each member of the community. Agonistic politics helps each member become aware of this fact consciously or unconsciously by offering public agons for political issues.

Accepting the arguments of practice theory and agonistic politics, that subjection and agency are not determined by predetermined rules, naturally leads us to the conclusion that the concept of power based on the dichotomy of domination/subordination is incapable of understanding the diverse actions of women in late modernity in all dimensions. For better theoretical tools to work through Butler's so-called paradox of subjectivation or the possibility of agency for women in subjection, it might be helpful to start with introducing two concepts of power: "power of," denoting the power of domination/subordination and "power to," denoting the power to empower (Butler 1997; Allen 2001, 527).

In the next section, we will examine what kinds of insights the perspective of practice theory and agonistic politics offers on the current issues of feminist practices in Korean society.

V LATE MODERN KOREAN SOCIETY AND THE TRANSFORMATION OF WOMEN'S SUBJECTIVITY

Korean society experienced widening social and economic gaps caused by unemployment and labor flexibility after the Asian Financial Crisis in 1997. The neoliberal restructuring of the labor market not only transformed traditional gender relations but also deepened economic polarization among women. As the unemployment rate rose, women were the first to get laid off, the proportion of non-regular employment among female wage workers increased rapidly, and officials acquiesced to the labor flexibility policy as a normal part of everyday life in labor market, especially for women. Neoliberalism, in conjunction with patriarchy, began to make asymmetrical impacts on gendered workers.

During this period, the divorce rate and average age at marriage began to rise and the birth rate renewed its record low, leading to a diffusion of "family-in-crisis discourses" throughout Korean society. Meanwhile, consumerism intensified and an interest in body practices began to grow. These phenomena prompted feminist gender politics to actively create diverse counter-discourses, with most efforts concentrated on resisting the influences and effects of a rapidly encroaching neoliberalism and continuing patriarchy on women. Women's movements and women workers' movements continued to resist and protest against the practices of laying off female workers first or turning them into non-regular workers first (Cho S. 1998). Feminist activists and scholars raised counter-arguments against family-in-crisis discourses, then prevalent in Korean society, claiming that this was not a crisis of the family but a crisis of the patriarchal family, and that this was the proper time to acknowledge diversity in families (Lee J. 2004). Feminist activists and scholars also argued that low fertility rates were not a symptom of family disintegration, but a result of strategies by families seeking upward social mobility by investing in the education of children (Hwang J. 2005). Finally, feminist activists and scholars interpreted women's heightening interests in bodies, love, and sex as one escape route to ascertain their agencies as women relocated as individualized subjects in the era of neoliberal high competition (Kim E. 2006).

However, with the return of the Global Financial Crisis in 2008, this time originating from developed countries, there appear to be no significant efforts within feminist politics, though women have been hit hardest by this economic crisis (Bae E. 2009). No collectively organized voices have been raised against gender discrimination from women's groups. Since the Asian Financial Crisis, the neoliberal restructuring process of Korean society has already progressed well beyond any further resistance, at least for most Koreans who have grown accustomed to the neoliberal logic.[7] With the neoliberal social welfare regime permeating every aspect of Korean society, the "male breadwinner model" has been rapidly replaced by the "dual-earner family model," and with motherhood and maternal rights denied the status of civil rights and endowed with derived rights only, the status of mothering has grown increasingly precarious (Bae E. 2009, 66).

The most conspicuous result of the neoliberal restructuring process is the impoverishment of maternal rights. Though the national welfare policy has been improved since the Asian Financial Crisis, it still does not acknowledge motherhood as a social right (Ma K. 2005). The right to maternal benefits, a concept introduced to remunerate income losses incurred due to motherhood, was only selectively acknowledged through paid maternity leave and paid child care leave and by supporting only a modicum of total child care and education costs. This means that a woman cannot expect protection from the social welfare system in late life unless she is eligible for retirement pension

7 Of course, the full impacts of this economic crisis may be yet to come in Korea where the decade-long housing bubble has not completely burst compared to developed countries, including the United States. Thus its influences are slowly beginning to be felt especially among low-income families. But this can explain the current "complacency" only in a very limited sense.

as a regular worker, or from surviving spouse pension benefits guaranteed by derived rights in programs for male breadwinners' dependents. Thus, after the Asian Financial Crisis, the only socially acceptable ways for a woman to support herself are to survive as a regular worker in fiercely competitive labor markets or to become through a marriage a full-time housewife for a male bread-winner in at least a middle class or upper class family. Simply serving faithfully as a wife and mother in a patriarchal family does not guarantee a woman any protection from the market, state, or patriarchy in late life. The status of women faithful to the patriarchal family system as full-time care workers has become increasingly perilous. Thus cornered, women considering motherhood responded with increasingly delayed marriages and childbirth. Delayed marriages and the rising mean age at first childbirth played major roles in driving fertility rates into a free fall. However, the falling fertility rate is more conspicuous among college-educated women than among women overall (Choi K. 2004). On the other hand, delayed marriage and plummeting fertility rates led to an increase in Korean men marrying non-Korean migrant women, with the percentage of international marriages among the marriages in Korea reaching 10.5% in 2010.[8] Motherhood in the Korean patriarchal family increasingly seems to be realized in these "new" families.

Along with and as consequences of these transformations of the Korean family, prospects for a stable life for women underwent enormous diversification in ways never previously experienced. Polarization deepened between regular and non-regular workers in the women's labor market in Korea (Kim Y. and Kim K. 2004); "professional" full-time housewives willing to devote themselves

8 http://www.mogef.go.kr/korea/view/policyGuide/policyGuide04_03_01.jsp

and all the available traditional and nontraditional capital for the classed reproduction of family began to appear among middle- and upper-class families (Park H. 2009); and an increasing number of alpha girls intent on overcoming gender inequalities in the labor market through their abilities and talents entered the professional job market. The differences and differentiation among women led to the disintegration of "women" as a single collective entity. It is no longer easy to imagine gender inequality operating uniformly on a single homogeneous group of "women." Diverse identities of women emerge from intersections among race, class, gender, sexuality, and family systems, and each individual woman continues the political processes of (re)constructing her identity through her performances. One example is the case of transformation in the modes of self-subjectivity formation among runaway girls from low-income families. These girls no longer resort to families or men to ascertain their values, but instead choose to rely on establishing contacts with society in varied, other direct manners (Min K. 2009). However, their decision to confront the market face-to-face, rejecting the traditional gender roles and family norms that have been constraining them, drove them to an all the more subordinated status contrary to their initial high hopes (Kim Y. 2011).

On the other hand, in neoliberal Korean society, women are allowed to or decide to lead diverse forms of lifestyles in an unprecedented fashion. The traditional, exclusive identity of "Korean women" is being replaced by multifarious forms of identities, and women began to initiate the political processes of reconstituting their own identities. Self-empowerment discourses of women governing their own selves and making the most of their abilities have begun to spread widely and incessantly.

With over 80% of secondary school graduates entering colleges, college students and colleges are no exception to neoliberal competition. Already in their freshman year, many students start to amass various certificates and skills that will help them attain their ideal jobs after graduation. Of course, the private institutes professing to help students in need are also in full blossom with high profits, resulting in heavy costs for students already under burden from rising tuitions. For female college students, the issues of body practices including cosmetic surgeries are unavoidable (Lim 2004). Although it is forbidden by law to discriminate against women based on their appearance, almost every woman believes it is still one of the most important factors in job interviews (Lim 2003).

Interest in the body contributed to widespread dieting and cosmetic surgery booms among women from every class. In Korea, with high numbers of cosmetic surgeons per capita and cosmetic surgeries per year in Asia, the woman's body is no longer an integral whole, but instead is classified into over 150 categories of minute parts requiring various remedies or improvements (Choi O. 2005, 90). The meticulous classifications of "defects in need of remedies" reappear with a vengeance in the private marriage-matching service market. Indices, which quantify one's value as a future spouse and assigned to each client by flourishing marriage-matching service companies, include a "body index" category (based on height, weight, attractiveness, etc.) without fail. Furthermore, the "body index" and "social capability index" (based on education, occupation, and annual wages) are given greater weight for female and male clients respectively (Kim H. 2006; Lee Y. 2008). Although the commercial intentions and motives underlying these kinds of consumer strategies are all too obvious, the intensity and starkness of body practices in Korean society urge us to reexamine the problem of the constitution of women's subjectivity and agency with the greatest care.

Whether to understand booming body practices, including cosmetic surgery, solely as due to dominant patriarchal norms under the influences of patriarchy,

Confucian or not, or to acknowledge at least some part of it as a realization of women's agency as new feminists have insisted, will depend on how much of the changes in body practices can be argued to be an outcome of the influence of women's movements of past decades. Flourishing body practices among Korean women are interpreted as actions subordinate to ongoing Confucian norms in a mainly androcentric Korean society, and as internalizations of the idea of self-sacrificing women for family in altruistic self-development, or in other words as an acquiescence to dominating patriarchal norms (Park S. 2007, 64). In addition, queer or feminine images appearing in body practices among young men are regarded only as instances of consumerism intent on commercializing even sexual and gender differences in Korea is claimed to still maintain stronghold (Lim 2008). These claims all tend to emphasize the overwhelming influences of patriarchal norms on choices made by women in body practices, and deny or completely neglect possible roles of agency.

Indeed, above researchers all appear to underestimate the general tendency for neoliberal governmentality to destabilize the patriarchal family and society, and reconstitute neoliberal female subjects though variegated forms of neoliberalism which shows diversity and a wide range of variation in their impacts. As Fraser once pointed out, capitalism is very adroit in maneuvering resistant discourses to adopt and incorporate them into its own strategic discourses (2009). It is obvious that consumerism is the main workhorse for this kind of suave and sophisticated maneuvering capability, which in its neoliberal version reached its zenith as eloquently described by Bauman (2000). They also miss the point of the claims raised in new femininities : that these body practices could also be self-empowering moments where self-control and self-management by each individual woman play important roles, and the fact that perceptions, meanings, and evaluations of beauty, success, and recognition in society are undergoing rapid and fundamental transformations in character and context due to the ongoing neoliberal restructuring of Korean society and responses to the restructuring.

We can summarize the discourses on cosmetic surgery produced in advertisements as emphasizing self-management in order to achieve outward beauty and social success. Moralizing discourses including self-reliance, the willingness and fortitude to give your best effort, social courtesy and responsibility, and others are imported into the body practice industry and used to coerce women to make efforts and investments for external beauty. Because individuals require endurance and abstinence to maintain a well-kept body, the latter is regarded as reflecting her character and self-restraint. Previous opinions of cosmetic surgery in early days as requiring no significant efforts on the part of a woman in contrast to, for example, fitness training, began to change to opinions about demanding descriptions in moralistic terms, capable of reflecting a woman's agency which involves visualizing the experiences of pain that she had to undergo (Tae 2011).

Women who choose cosmetic surgery are no longer assigned to a single common identity. Rather, as subjects actively opting for cosmetic surgery, they enter into intersubjective processes with the discourses produced in the cosmetic surgery industry, in which they are both subjected to and are actively transforming dominant discursive systems, hence continuing entangled processes of constituting both the subject and agency (Chun 2010; Tae 2011). In distinguishing the "correct" practice of cosmetic surgery from the "incorrect" one and claiming the former as a practice in which the subject is not addicted to cosmetic surgery but is rather revealing her own agency by containing it within the limits of rational choices, this new type of discourse reflects the awareness that it is possible for each woman to reconstitute herself through her own decisions and efforts, and that she should take responsibility for the results of cosmetic surgery (Chun, 2010). Thus body practices, including cosmetic surgery, have been transformed into potential tools for self-empowerment, and the logic of appearance as reflecting the essential part of each woman has gained further support in late modern Korean society.

Whether to regard the flourishing phenomena of body practices such as cosmetic surgery exclusively as subjection to dominant norms under the influence of a patriarchal system, or to acknowledge at least in some cases as a manifestation of women's agency in action, will have to be decided only after detailed studies on the impacts of women's movements over the past few decades on these body practices. This means acknowledging the insufficiency of relying solely on concepts such as subjection and agency to reflect the complexity of contexts in a late modern terrain where these social phenomena, including body practices, occur. The latter complexity induces complex responses from each actor which, in turn, complicates the meanings and interpretations of these responses and contexts.

There are always chances for social practices, including body practices, either to regress or degenerate into anomalous practices losing their subversive or revolutionary potentiality or, depending upon changes in consciousness, the perception or recognition of these practices among members of a society, including women, to start creative transformations. Of course the former case of anomalous change could be mistaken for the successful stabilization into "efficient" social norms or institutions contributing to the improvement of the quality of life in a society. Furthermore, in the latter case we could be cajoled into believing, through a new spirit of capitalism or the cunning of consumerism, subjection to dominant discourses or, in our case, neoliberal governmentality as a creative transformation into "better" social practices. As in the case of epistemology, in which we have to steer through treacherous straits between foundationalism and relativism without colliding against either side, we could be lost on the dangerous roads of misunderstanding. There are no convenient and comprehensive recipes to follow in order to avoid mishaps. The only way to deal with this difficult task of choosing the optimal path is the laborious way of deploying agonistic politics. After all, to fend off anomalous practices subordinating women and secure possibilities of creative practices is possible only through the operation of an agonistic politics that proposes diverse interpretations of these phenomena and produces objections against and responses for such interpretations. When there are no criteria for correct interpretations that can be comprehensively implemented, in other words formulated in terms of "the social," including identity politics among others, agonistic politics serves as simulating tools for predicting and searching for "optimal" directions for changing or improving social practices.

Though traditional interpretations pointing out the subordinating character of practices of managing women's bodies are still legitimate and are a necessary part of preventing degenerate regression as ever-present dangers, it seems necessary and vital to maintain the possibility of new interpretations.[9] Both "complaints" against late modern practices, including flourishing body practices, and the eulogies for creative room offered by late modernity reveal two simultaneously opposing and inseparable aspects of late modern society

9 As is mentioned by Allen, rational choice theorists point out without missing a beat that the mechanism underlying the collective action problem operates in the case of body practices of women, and for that matter, those of men refusing to invest in body practices is an optimal choice for women collectively but investing in body practices is a rational choice for individual woman since the benefits of collective action are shared by all women whereas the benefits from investing go to individuals (Allen 2008, 182).

(Connolly 2002b, 179; Cho J. 2012).

VI CONCLUSION

Neoliberal rationality, in enforcing economic logic over the socio-cultural areas, tends to solve individuals' social problems through individual and subjective measures rather than through a social structural approach. Thus, when women in late modern Korean society pursue self-confidence and self-empowerment, they usually rely predominantly on easily quantifiable, hence convenient, self-evaluation tools rather than unquantifiable ones such as self-respect and self-confidence. This is because each individual woman has to be constantly measured, judged, and trained to easily tune and interlock self-empowerment to collective measures. As we have seen in cases of the cosmetic surgery industry and the marriage-matching service industry, turning each problem into exquisitely classified and quantified data is to make efficient self-evaluation as a basis for self-respect and self-empowerment. However, even though these quantified criteria make self-confidence and self-empowerment possible and efficient, the criteria in turn serve as essential means in late modernity to control each individual as analyzed in detail by Foucault in his archaeological and genealogical works. Of course, as we have seen above, this unquenchable appetite for quantified criteria is one of the principal tools for rampant consumerism in late modernity to perpetuate its existence, hence the rampant consumerism serving as quantified criteria's primary provider. The constitution of women's subjectivity and agency proceeds in these entangled ways. Consequently, the estimation and interpretation of the performances of each female subject can be properly accomplished only in the framework comprising the whole spectrum of social practices.

If the defects and problems of neoliberalism originate mainly from ignoring the positive roles of social practices such as norms, institutions, and conventions, namely the possibility of positive freedom to transform social practices themselves, we can argue that their resolution will only be possible through reinvigorating these channels for the annihilation and transformation of current practices and the creation of new practices. For this prescription to work properly, it is essential to maintain open attitudes to the performances of each individual member of community that can serve as starting points of the whole process of transforming social practices. In order to achieve this goal, the social awareness and recognition of the creative role of "deontic scorekeeping" processes should spread widely among community members. We claim that this is possible through the implementation of agonistic politics in everyday social and political life, which is the only viable tool.

The basic unit in late modernity that is deepening in Korea is an individual actor self-managing as an entrepreneur in whole matters of her life. Women in Korea are doing their best to make choices to maximize total future incomes and human capital in the social space framed by "suboptimal" social practices, including a rapidly disintegrating but still ongoing Confucian patriarchy. Efforts of body practices, including cosmetic surgery, are tuned to the purposes of getting good jobs, searching for husbands capable of providing the best material and cultural satisfaction, or gaining recognition from others. As this phenomenon becomes prevalent and intensifies, these efforts and choices in themselves can provide confidence and satisfaction.

The most successful individual in the neoliberal system will be the one that best internalizes and conforms to neoliberal logic without any intention to exercise her own agency. However, it does not seem possible for neoliberal rationality to establish its strongholds without incurring significant transformations in Korean society. For instance, interpretations of body practices are undergoing transformations among young women and, in these transformations, agency in action that cannot simply be explained away as effects of simple consumerism and commercialism can be palpably noticed. Though maybe somewhat distorted and tainted by capitalism, lessons from feminism are already forming embodied experiences, and the evaluation of capitalistic logic does not seem to lead to simple acquiescence without resistance.

The eventual purpose of any type of governmentality remains making sure the population is safe, happy, and maintaining the state (Foucault 1991, 100). The main peculiarity of neoliberal governmentality is its mode of operation, which works in a microscopic and unavoidable manner. It is microscopic in that, instead of directly enforcing each individual under control, it induces an internalization of its logic under the disguise of self-empowerment across whole societies. It is also unavoidable in that this self-empowerment seems to be a result of free and rational choices based on her pure self-interests and appeals to such an instinctual human desire for freedom. The "crisis" of feminist politics emerged as a result of neoliberal globalization and governmentality, the reflexivity of women's actions is strengthened, leading to a weakening of the explanatory power of gender politics that has served quite well as effective identity politics. It is time for a more fundamental reconstruction of conceptual framework of feminist politics. The prospect and strategy of feminist politics could be actualized through understanding the dynamic relations between political and economic circumstances, on the one hand, and the subjectivity of women taking shape in new discursive terrains in formation on the other. The perspective of practice theory promises to be essential in this search for alternative strategies for feminist politics.

Bibliography

Allen, Amy. 2001. "Pornography and Power." *Journal of Social Philosophy* 32:512-531.

______. 2008. *The Politics of Our Selves*. New York: Columbia University Press.

______. 2009. "Feminism and the Subject of Politics." In *New Waves in Political Philosophy*, eds. Boudewin de Bruin and Christopher Zurn, 1-18. New York: Palgrave Macmillan.

Bae, Eun-Kyung. 2009. "Gyeongje wigi-wa hanguk yeoseong – yeoseong-ui saengaejeonmang-gwa jendeo/gyegeub-ui gyocha" ('Economic Crisis' and Korean Women: Women's Vision-of-Life and Intersection of Class and Gender). *Peminijeum Yeongu* (Issues in Feminism) 9(2):39-82.

Barry, Brian. 1989. *Democracy, Power and Justice*. Oxford: Clarendon Press.

Bauman, Zigmunt. 2000. *Liquid Modernity*. Cambridge: Polity.

Beck, Ulrich, and Elisabeth Beck-Gernsheim. 2002. *Individualization: Institutionalized Individualism and Its Social and Political Consequences*. London: Sage.

Brandom, Robert B. 1994. *Making it Explicit: Reasoning, Representing, and Discursive Commitment*. Cambridge, MA: Harvard University Press.

______. 2009. *Reason in Philosophy: Animating Ideas*. Cambridge, MA: Harvard University Press.

Brown, Wendy. 1995. *States of Injury*. Princeton, NJ: Princeton University Press.

Burchell, Graham, Colin Gordon, and Peter Miller, eds. 1990. *The Foucault Effect: Studies in Governmentality*. Chicago: University of Chicago Press.

Butler, Judith. 1997. "Introduction." In her *The Psychic Life of Power: Theories in Subjection*, 1-30. Stanford, CA: Stanford University Press.

______. [1990] 1999. *Gender Trouble*. New York: Routledge.

Cameron, Angus, and Ronen P. Palan. 2004. *The Imagined Economies of Globalization*. London: Sage Publications.

Castells, Manuel. 2009. *Communication Power*. New York: Oxford University Press.

Cho, Joo-hyun. 2010a. "Saheojeogin geosui wigi-wa peminiseuteu jeongcheseong-ui jeongchi: linda jerilri-ui daean" (The Crisis of the Social and Feminist Identity Politics: Linda Zerilli's Proposal). *Saheo-wa Iron* (Society and Theory) 17:53-83.

______. 2010b. "Silcheoniron-euro bon bipansahoehak-gwa peminiseuteu jeongchihak-ui munje" (The Problems of Critical Sociology and Feminist Politics: From the Perspective of Practice Theory). *Gyeongje-wa Sahoe* (Economy and Society) 88:68-93.

______. 2012. "Hugi geundae-wa sahoejeogin geosui wigi: agonizeum jeongchi-ui ganeungseong" (Late Modernity and the Crisis of the Social: The Possibility of Agonistic Politics). *Gyeongje-wa Sahoe* (Economy and Society) 95:163-189.

Cho, Soon-Kyoung. 1998. "Gyeongje wigi-wa yeoseong goyong jeongchi" (Economic Crisis, Women's Work and Employment Politics). *Hanguk Yeoseonghak* (Korean Journal of Women's Studies) 14(2):5-33.

Choi, Kyungsoo. 2004. " Chulsanyul harak chui-e daehan bunseok" (Causes of the Recent Fertility Drop in Korea). *Hanguk Inguhak* (Korea Journal of Population Studies) 27(2):35-59.

Choi, Ok Sun. 2005. "Yeoseong-ui mom damron-gwa seonghyeongdamron-ui sanghotekseuteuseong-e gwanhan yeongu: yeoseongjapji-ui gisa-wa seonghyeong uiryogwanggo-reul jungsim-euro" (A Study on Intertextuality between Discourses on the Female Body and Plastic Surgery: Focusing on Female Magazine Articles and Medical Advertisement). PhD dissertation, Sungkyunkwan University.

Chun, Bohkyung. 2010. "Mom-jaa tekeunoloji-roseoui miyong seonghyeong-e daehan gyebohakjeok damron yeongu" (A Genealogical Study on the Discourse of Cosmetic Surgery as Technologies of the Body-Self in Korean Society). MA thesis, Ewha Womans University.

Connolly, William E. 2002a. "Confessing Identityl Belonging to Difference." In his *Identityl Difference: Democratic Negotiations of Political Paradox*, xiii-xxix.

Minneapolis: University of Minnesota Press.

______. 2002b. *Neuropolitics: Thinking, Culture, Speed.* Minneapolis: University of Minnesota Press.

Cudd, Ann E. 1994. "Oppression by Choice." *Journal of Social Philosophy* 25:22-44.

Dean, Mitchell. 2008. "Governing Societies: the Story of Two Monsters." *Journal of Cultural Economy* 1:25-38.

Dowding, Keith. 1996. *Power.* Minneapolis: University of Minnesota Press.

Foucault, Michel. 1983. "On the Genealogy of Ethics: An Overview of Work in Progress." In *Michel Foucault: Beyond Structuralism and Hermeneutics*, eds. Hubert L. Dreyfus and Paul Rabinow, 229-252. Chicago: University of Chicago Press,

______. 1991. "Governmentality." In Burchell, Gordon and Miller 1991, 87-104.

Fraser, Nancy. 2009. "Feminism, Capitalism and the Cunning of History." *New Left Review* 56:97-117.

Friedman, Thomas L. 2000. *The Lexus and the Olive Tree: Understanding Globalization.* New York: Anchor Books.

Gintis, Herbert. 2007. "A Framework for the Unification of the Behavioral Sciences." *Behavioral and Brain Sciences* 30:1-61.

Gordon, Collin. 1991. "Governmental Rationality: An Introduction." In Burchell, Gordon and Miller 1991, 1-52.

Hardt, Michael, and Antonio Negri. 2001. *Empire.* Cambridge: Harvard University Press.

Heath, Joseph. 2008. *Following Rules: Practical Reasoning and Deontic Constraint.* New York: Oxford University Press.

Hwang, Jung-Mee. 2005. "'Jeochulsan'gwa hanguk moseong-ui jendeojeongchi" ('Low Fertility' and Gender Politics of Motherhood in Korea). *Hanguk Yeoseonghak* (Korean Journal of Women's Studies) 21(3):99-132.

Keohane, Robert O., and Joseph S. Nye Jr. 2002. "Governance in a Globalizing

World." In *Power and Governance in a Partially Globalized World*, ed. Robert O. Keohane, 193-218. New York: Routledge.

Kim, Eun-Shil. 2006. "Jiguhwa sidae hanguk sahhoe seongmunhwa-wa seongyeongu banbeop" (Research Methods on Sexuality and Sexual Culture of Korean Society in the Era of Globalization). In *Seksyueolliti Gangue, Du beongjjae* (Lectures on Sexuality, Vol. 2), ed. Hyejeong Byeon, 18-49. Seoul: Dongnyeok.

Kim, Hyun-Soo. 2006. "Wanbyeokhan sinlang-sinbukkam? kkumeseona chajaboseyo!" (Perfect Groom and Bride? Only in Your Dreams!). *Dong-A Ilbo* (Dong-A Daily), December 29.

Kim, Yeonju. 2011. "Seongmaemae gyeongheom-i itneun sibdaeyeoseongdeul-ui saheojeog baeje-e gwanhan yeongu: pyeswaejeoggin sahoegwangyemang-eul jungsimeuro" (A Study on the Social Exclusion of Teenage Women Engaging in Prostitution: Focusing on Closed Social Network). *Peminijeum Yeongu* (Issues in Feminism) 11(2):239-274.

Kim, Youngock, ed. 2004. *Hangug Yeoseong Jeongchaeg-ui Nyu Paereodaim Jeongrip* (Founding a New Paradigm of Women's Policy in Korea). Seoul: Ministry of Gender Equality & Family.

Kim, Youngock, and Kyunghee Kim. 2004. "Yeoseong nodongjeongchaeg-ui hangye-wa saepaereodaim mosaek" (Limits of Women's Labor Policy and Search for a New Paradigm). In Youngock Kim 2004, 105-138.

Lee, Jae Kyung. 2004. "Gongsa yeongyeog-ui byeonhwa-wa 'gajog'-eul neomeoseoneun gajokjeongchaek" (The Transformation of the Public and Private Spheres and the Family Policy Going beyond 'the Family'). In Youngock Kim 2004, 79-104.

Lee, Yunju. 2008. "Dangsin-ui baeuja jisu-neun myeoch deunggeub imnikka?" (What level does your spouse index belong?). *Juganhanguk* (Hanguk Weekly) Vol. 2227, June 24.

Lim, In-Sook. 2003. "Yeoseong-ui chwieop-gwa yongmochabyeol: gieob-ui yongmochabyeol-jeok mojipchuse-wa teukseong-ui byeonhwa" (Women's Employment and Appearance-Discriminatory Selection). *Hanguk Yeoseonghak*

(Korean Journal of Women's Studies) 19(1):113-144.

______. 2004. "Oemochabyeol sahoe-ui seonghyeong gyeongheom-gwa uihyang" (The Experience and Intention of Cosmetic Surgery in the Looks-Discriminatory Society). *Hanguk Yeoseonghak* (Korean Journal of Women's Studies) 19(1):95-122.

______. 2008. "The Trend of Creating Atypical Male Images in Heterosexist Korean Society." *Korea Journal* 48(4):115-146.

Lukes, Steven. 2005. Power: *A Radical View*, 2nd edition. New York: Palgrave.

Ma, Kyoung-Hee. 2005. "Sahoegweon-euroseo dolbom-ui jedohwa-reul wihan paereodaim-ui mosaek" (A Search for an Alternative Paradigm to Institutionalize Care as Social Right). *Yeoseong-gwa Sahoe* (Women and Society) 16:35-66.

Min, Kayoung. 2009. "Sinjayujuui jilseo-ui hwaksan-e ttareun sipdae yeoseong-ui jucheseong byeonhwa-e gwanhan yeongu" (A Research of Subjectivity which is Being Performed by Teenage Girls from Poverty Families Based on the Context of Neoliberal Milieu). *Hanguk Yeoseonghak* (Korean Journal of Women's Studies) 25(2):5-35.

Ong, Aiwa. 2005. "Graduated Sovereignty in South-East Asia." In *Anthropologies of Modernity: Foucault, Governmentality and Life Politics*, ed. Jonathan Xavier Inda, 83-104. Oxford: Blackwell.

Park, Hye Gyong. 2009. "Hanguk jungsancheung-ui janyeogyoyuk gyeongjaeng-gwa 'jeoneop eomeoni' jeongcheseong" (Competition over Children's Education and the 'Full-Time Mother' Identity in Korean Middle Class Families). *Hanguk Yeoseonghak* (Korean Journal of Women's Studies) 25(3):5-33.

Park, Sang Un. 2007. ""Beauty Will Save You": The Myth and Ritual of Dieting in Korean Society." *Korea Journal* 47(2):41-70.

Rawls, John. 1971. "Original Position and Justification." In his A *Theory of Justice*, 17-21. Cambridge, MA: Belknap Press of Harvard University Press

Rodrik, Dani. 1997. *Has Globalization Gone Too Far?* Washington, D.C.: Institute for

International Economics.

Rosen, Michael. 2000. "On Voluntary Servitude and the Theory of Ideology." *Constellations* 7(3):393–407.

Rouse, Joseph. 2007. "Social Practices and Normativity." *Philosophy of the Social Sciences* 37(1):46-56.

Schaap, Andrew. 2006. "Agonism in Divided Societies." *Philosophy and Social Criticism* 32(2): 255-277.

Tae, Hee-Won. 2011. "Miyong seonghyeonguiryo neteuwokeu-ui jaeguseong-gwa sobija/hwanja juche-ui hyeongseong" (The Formation of the Consumer/ Patient Subject and Cosmetic Surgery Network in Korean Society). PhD dissertation, Yonsei University.

Virilio, Paul. 1986. *Speed and Politics*, trans. Mark Polizzotti. New York: Semiotext(e).

Williams, Linda. 1999. *Hard Core: Power, Pleasure, and the "Frenzy of the Visible."* Berkeley: University of California Press.

Zerilli, Linda. 2012. "Value Pluralism and the Problem of Judgment: Farewell to Public Rrteason." *Political Theory* 40(1):6-31.

East Asian Gender in Transition

PART II

Women and Family in Transition in East Asia

II WOMEN AND FAMILY IN TRANSITION IN EAST ASIA

The Logics of Family and Gender Changes in Early 21st-Century East Asia[1]

Emiko OCHIAI

Everybody says that families and gender in East Asia are changing. But how? Are the changes in East Asia the same as the changes in Europe and North America? Are the changes just delayed in comparison to these places? Or, do the changes have salient differences? Another question concerns the causes of changes. Are the causes of changes in East Asia the same as those in Europe and North America, or are they different?

The first half of this chapter reviews current changes in the family and gender in East Asia, focusing particularly on East Asian characteristics. The latter half of the chapter is devoted to a discussion of the factors that create such East Asian

---

1 This chapter is based on a conference presentation at Keimyung University, which aimed to provide an overview of my recent thoughts developed in the projects and activities of the Global Center of Excellence on "Reconstruction of the Intimate and Public Spheres in 21st Century Asia" and published in recent works including Ochiai (2010, 2013 forthcoming) and Ochiai and Johshita (2013 forthcoming).

characteristics, in the hope that this chapter may contribute to the construction of a theoretical framework that will do justice to East Asian realities instead of simply applying Western theories or merely providing an ad hoc list of various phenomena.

I EAST ASIAN REALITIES REGARDING FAMILY AND GENDER CHANGES

1. Demographic and Family Changes in East Asia

1) Lowest-low and Ultra-low Fertility

First, let us take a demographic view at the current state of East Asian societies[2]. In the contemporary moment, East Asia is the region most associated with very low fertility. The latest total fertility rates (TFR) for Taiwan, Hong Kong, South Korea, Singapore, Japan and China are 1.03 (2009), 1.06 (2008), 1.19 (2009), 1.33 (2009), 1.39 (2010), 1.8 (2009), respectively (WHO 2011; NIPSSR 2012). In the 1990s, Southern and German-speaking European countries recorded fertility levels below 1.3, which was described as the "lowest-low fertility" (Kohler et al. 2002), but several East Asian societies, with the exception of China, have broken through that level. The societies like Taiwan, Hong Kong and South Korea are termed "ultra-low fertility" societies

2 The geographical tag "East Asia" has, in recent years, been used in two ways. The first is the traditional way of referring to the countries of China, South Korea, Japan, and Taiwan, in a more restricted sense of the term. The second is a more encompassing use that includes both East Asia in the narrow sense in addition to Southeast Asia. This paper covers the societies in East Asia in the wider sense.

(Straughan et al. eds. 2008).

A historical look at the five ultra-low and lowest-low fertility societies in East Asia shows that all these societies except Japan had TFRs above 3.0 in 1970. In the 1970s, these societies were in the stage before the fertility transition that is a component of the demographic transition. Governments started family planning programs as part of national policy, spurring the fertility transition. Japan reached replacement level fertility in 1956, Singapore in 1975, and South Korea and Taiwan in 1984 (Suzuki 2010, 20). Hong Kong reached the replacement level in 1980. After reaching the replacement level, Japan's fertility rates remained steady for about twenty years, and then in 1974 started dropping below replacement level. This phenomenon immediately followed the second fertility decline, a part of the second demographic transition, which began in Europe around 1970. In contrast to Japan, there was no stable period in the other four societies where fertility continued to drop to below the replacement level.

In the 1990s, while Japan's fertility level continued to drop, that of Singapore, South Korea, and Taiwan steadied temporarily, holding at between 1.6 and 1.8. A new trend in fertility started after the Asian Financial Crisis in 1997-98, and became clearer once the 21st century started. The TFRs for Taiwan, Singapore, and South Korea dropped sharply. In 2001, South Korea fell below the 1.3 level, and in 2003 Japan, and Singapore followed suit.[3] After 2003, fertility levels in South Korea, Taiwan, and Singapore dropped below Japan's fertility levels, and while Japan and Singapore showed either a slight improvement or held steady, South Korea and Taiwan continued dropping along with Hong Kong, dropping

3 Hong Kong has occupied a level below 1.3 since the 1990s, but since it was handed over to China in 1997, the political situation at the time must be considered in the analysis of fertility levels.

below 1.1 and reaching a new global low in fertility levels. The lowest levels each society reached were 1.05 in South Korea in 2008, 1.03 in Taiwan in 2009, and 0.98 in Hong Kong in 2007. This group, termed "ultra-low fertility societies," started showing its unique trends beginning from this period. Scholars are just beginning to provide explanations for this trend. Considering the timing of trend change, the Asian Financial Crisis in 1997-98 seems to have played a critical role in altering the trends.

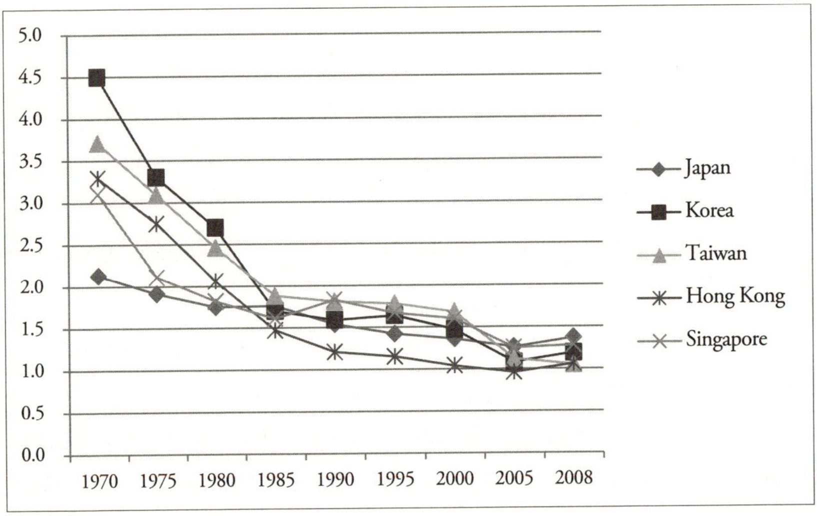

Figure 1. Trends in TFR in Five East Asian Societies
Source: Cabinet Office (2010)

2) Divorce, Late Marriage, Celibacy

Scholars consider the fertility decline to sub-replacement level to be a part of the second demographic transition in Europe. However, in the second demographic transition in Europe, it was not just fertility, but marriage-related indicators that contributed to major changes (Lesthaeghe 1991). These indicators included an increase in divorce rates, a decrease in marriage rates, an increase in age at first marriage, an increase in the proportion never married, an increase in cohabitation rate, and an increase in births out of wedlock. In East Asia, which has plummeted to historically extreme levels of low fertility, changes related to marriage are relatively moderate compared to Europe.

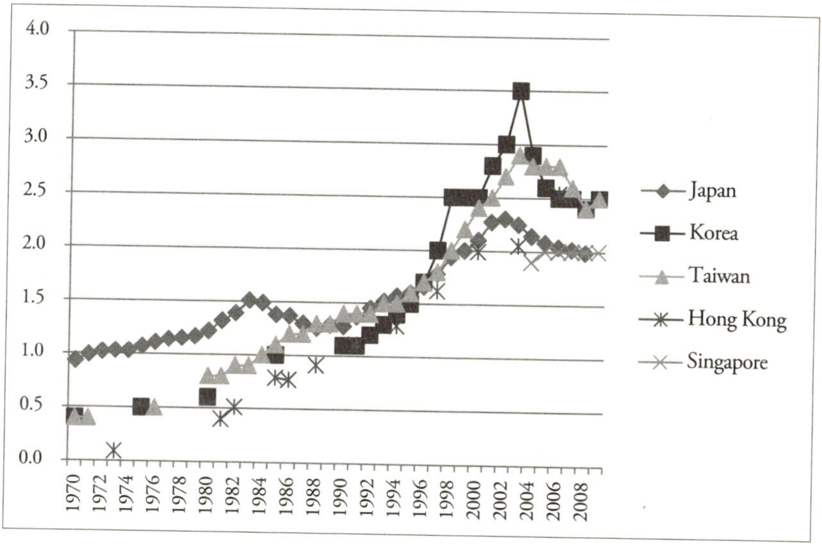

Figure 2. Trends in Crude Divorce Rates in Five East Asian Societies

Source: Japan: NIPSSR (2010), Korea: Chang (2010a) and Statistics Korea (2008), Taiwan: Ito (2010), Hong Kong: Census & Statistics Department (2002)(2007a)(2007c), Sigapore: Singapore Government, Department of Statistics (2009)

Divorce rates in East Asia are also notably increasing (Figure 2). After the late 1960s, when the divorce rate in Europe started rising, a similar increase began in Japan, which by the 1980s spiked at a crude divorce rate of 1.50, and in 2002 recorded an all-time high of 2.30. This is the same level as European nations like the United Kingdom, Germany, Sweden, and France. In Taiwan and South Korea, divorce rates started rising from the 1980s. By the start of the 1990s the divorce rates in Taiwan and South Korea reached the level in Japan, passing it during the Asian Financial Crisis, with South Korea's 2003 record level of 3.50 almost the same as the U.S.'s 3.60.

Table 1. Crude Marriage Rate, Crude Divorce Rate, The Ratio of Divorce and Marriage in Selected Societies

Area	Year	CMR	CDR	div/mar
Uruguay	(2007)	3.84	4.33	1.13
Belgium	(2007)	4.29	2.83	0.66
Spain	(2007)	4.49	2.80	0.62
Hungary	(2007)	4.06	2.50	0.62
Cuba	(2007)	5.05	3.08	0.61
Austria	(2007)	4.33	2.47	0.57
Czech	(2007)	5.53	3.01	0.54
Russia	(2007)	8.90	4.83	0.54
France	(2007)	4.33	2.22	0.51
Germany	(2007)	4.48	2.27	0.51
Switzerland	(2007)	5.34	2.63	0.49
USA	(2005)	7.50	3.60	0.48
UK	(2007)	5.14	2.37	0.46
Taiwan	(2007)	5.8	2.6	0.45
The Netherlands	(2007)	4.42	1.95	0.44
Sweden	(2007)	5.24	2.26	0.43
Hong Kong	(2007)	-	-	*0.39
S. Korea	(2007)	7.10	2.57	0.36
Japan	(2007)	5.70	2.02	0.35
Macao	(2007)	3.90	1.30	0.33
Singapore	(2007)	5.22	1.48	0.28
Poland	(2007)	6.50	1.75	0.27
China	(2007)	7.50	1.58	0.21
Italy	(2007)	4.21	0.84	0.20
Iran	(2007)	11.80	1.40	0.12
Mongol	(2007)	15.70	0.67	0.04
Vietnam	(2007)	5.70	0.20	0.04
East Asian societies				

*Calculated from numbers of marriage and divorce.

Source: Hong Kong, Macao, Vietnam; United Nations Statistics Division (2008), Taiwan: Ito (2010), Other: NIPSSR (2010),

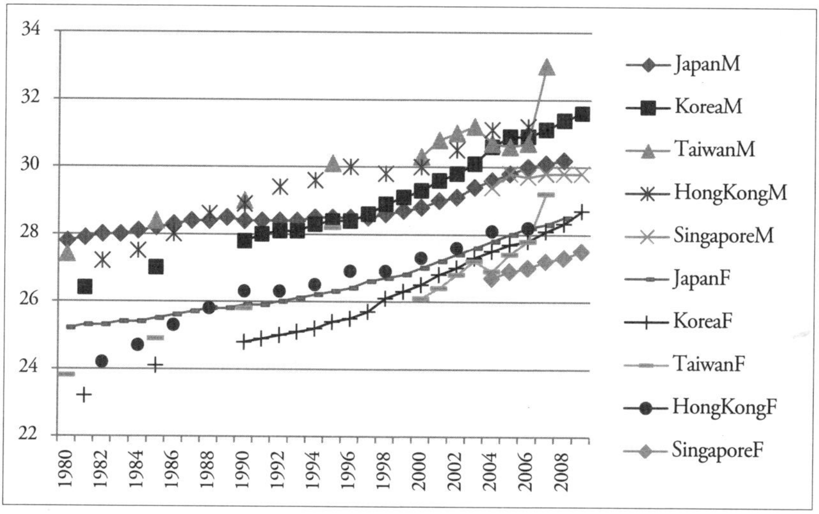

Figure 3. Trends in Age at First Marriage in Five East Asian Societies

Source: Japan: NIPSSR (2010), Korea: Chang (2010a), Taiwan: Suzuki (2010), Sun (2009), Taiwan Ministry of Interior (2010), Hong Kong: Census & Statistics Department (2001)(2007a)(2007b), Singapore: Singapore Government, Department of Statistics (2009)

However, East Asian and European divorces are not equally comparable. In Europe, marriage has become an option rather than a necessity, which contributes to the decrease in marriage. In East Asia, the marriage rate itself is not significantly lower. So when we look at the ratio of marriage and divorce, North and South American and European countries dominate, with East Asia's highest figures remaining at 0.45 for Taiwan, 0.39 for Hong Kong and 0.36 for South Korea. Marriage in East Asia is changing, but for the moment marriage is still relatively common, and once a couple is married, they are less likely to divorce than in Northwest Europe or North and South America.

The increases in age at first marriage, and, in proportion never married are also clear in East Asia. Figure 3 shows the changes in age at first marriage in Japan, South Korea, Taiwan, Hong Kong and Singapore. Japan was the first to demonstrate an increase, but Hong Kong, Taiwan and South Korea also demonstrate steep curves. Changes in age at first marriage for men in Hong Kong, Taiwan and South Korea outpaced Japan in the 1990s, while for women, the age at first marriage showed almost no difference by the 2000s. The age at first marriage in these societies in 2005 and 2006 was 30-31 for men and approximately 27-28 for women, close to Western European levels.

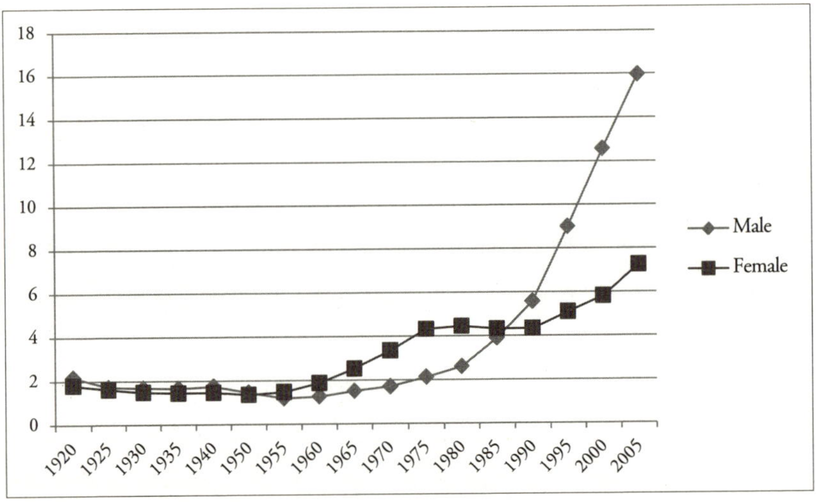

Figure 4. Trends in Proportion of People Never Married in Japan
Source: NIPSSR (2010)

The proportion never married cannot be calculated until the relevant cohorts are 50 years old, so Figure 4 only shows Japan, which was the first one to show changes. The proportions of both men and women who never married at all increased[4], leading to a society in which one in six men and one in thirteen women would never experience marriage. When we look at the proportions of women aged 35-39 who are unmarried in Japan, Taiwan, Singapore, and Taiwan for comparison, the levels are 19%, 16%, 15% and 8% respectively, showing that there is a considerable gap from the "early marriage and universal marriage that marked the marriage patterns of mid-20th century Asia" (Suzuki 2010, 21). South Korea is an exception in this regard. South Korean marriage is still close to universal marriage.

3) Cohabitation and Births Out of Wedlock

There is another point we need to focus on here. In Europe, these phenomena – the increase in age at marriage and the proportion never married – occur in line with the increase in cohabitation and births out of wedlock. In other words, even if Europeans may marry later, they still have sexual liaisons and cohabit, causing a "transformation of intimacy" (Giddens 1992).

In contrast, there is no such clear increase in either cohabitation or births out of wedlock for people in Asia, and this point has been termed the greatest difference from the European second demographic transition. According to a survey of unmarried people in Japan, the ratio of those aged between 18 to 50 who responded that "there is no one of the opposite sex I am involved with" was 52.2% for men and 44.7% for women, and there is even a slight increase in the trend since the 1990s (NIPSSR 2005). Japan's increase in age at marriage and the proportion never married does not seem to emerge from a "transformation of intimacy" but, rather, represents a "lack of intimacy."

---

4 The rise in the 1970s in women who never married was due to eligible men having died during the war.

Indeed, in just the past few years there have been reports of increasing numbers of people who cohabit without marrying. A Cabinet Office survey carried out at the start of 2009 (Cabinet Office 2009) compared the ratio of those who had experience cohabiting in each age group in Japan, South Korea, and Singapore. Those results are shown in Table 2, along with results from a 2005 survey (Cabinet Office 2005) covering the same topic in the U.S., France, and Sweden for comparison (Kojima 2010a, 2010b). In contrast to Europe and North America, especially Sweden, where cohabitation before marriage is the norm, it remains less common in East Asia, but is spreading, starting from Japan, then Singapore, then South Korea. As there are large differences in the ratios of men and women who have experienced cohabitation in South Korea, it has been suggested that female respondents are concealing their experience (Kojima 2010a). South Koreans seem to be the most conservative in their outlook about marriage.

Table 2. Proportions of people who have experienced cohabitation

	Japan 2009		Korea 2009		Singapore 2009	
Age	male	female	male	female	male	female
20-29	19.4%	19.5%	10.1%	2.0%	12.7%	9.3%
30-39	33.0%	25.8%	11.1%	1.8%	12.6%	9.2%
40-49	20.8%	12.5%	3.4%	0.6%	8.9%	7.0%

	USA 2005		France 2005		Sweden 2005	
Age	male	female	male	female	male	female
20-29	48.1%	51.2%	39.1%	53.0%	54.8%	69.0%
30-39	62.0%	61.7%	61.0%	66.1%	80.8%	87.2%
40-49	66.1%	60.5%	51.4%	45.9%	80.8%	77.5%

Source: Kojima (2010) Table 3 based on Cabinet Office(2009) and (2005).

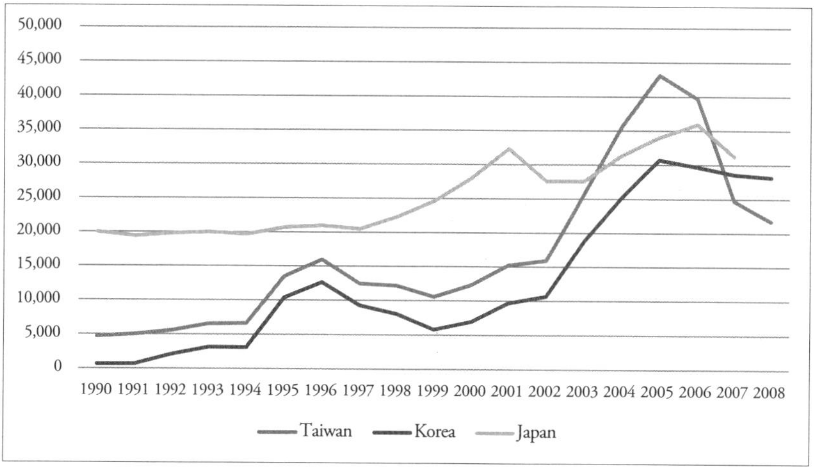

Figure 5. Marriage Migration of Women in East Asia, 1990-2008
Source: Lee (2010)

Despite spreading cohabitation, however, births out of wedlock are still extremely rare in East Asia. The ratio of births out of wedlock in 2005 was 2.0% in Japan, 1.5% in South Korea, 4.0% in Taiwan, and 1.3% in Singapore (Suzuki 2010). In Europe, births out of wedlock count for more than half of all births in Northwestern Europe, and the rate rapidly increased even in Southern Europe (20.7% for Italy, 28.4% for Spain, and 31.6% for Portugal), which presents a great contrast with East Asia (Suzuki 2010). Instead, what we find is an increasing number of so-called "shotgun marriages," or to be more faithful to the Japanese expression, "oops marriages."[5] In Japan, the number of marriages due to pregnancy increased from the second half of the 1990s, and

5 This type of marriage is called "*dekichatta kon*" in Japanese, which can be translated loosely as "Oops, we've done it! marriage." These are not "forced marriages" in the sense of "shotgun marriages."

the proportion of cases in which the birth of the first child was less than nine months after the wedding was 10.6% in 1980, but had increased to 20.9% in 1999, 25.6% in 2005, and 25.3% in 2009 (MHLW 2010). The gap between the frequency of premarital sex and the contrasting conservative standards has presumably been responsible for this increase in "oops marriages."

Cohabiting before marriage is possible, but must be concealed; pregnancy before marriage is possible; but birth out of wedlock must be avoided: marriage and other intimate relationships are still completely different things in East Asia. Unlike in Europe, where cohabitation is replacing marriage and the institution of marriage has weakened, in East Asia the institution of marriage, while shaky, is nevertheless solid. This is the most notable difference between families in Europe and East Asia.

4) International Marriages and High Sex Ratio at Birth

When we talk about recent demographic changes in East Asia, we cannot ignore international and cross-border marriages. Kojima Hiroshi includes these phenomena in the elements that make up the "East-Asian model of second demographic transition" (Kojima 2010b). The increase in international marriages is once again led by Japan ahead of the other East Asian societies, starting back in the 1980. In order to solve the problem of the lack of women for rural men to marry, a number of local authorities started government-led match-making projects, encouraging marriage with women from Asian countries including, for instance, the Philippines and Sri Lanka. In other words, rather than more organic marriages, this growth in international marriage was propelled by an extension of arranged marriages, the traditional way of mate selection. In short order, marriage brokers jumped on the international marriage promotion bandwagon. In the 2000s, international marriage began to increase in urban areas and industrial regions as well as in rural areas (Liew, Ochiai, and Ishikawa 2010).

South Korea and Taiwan started showing increased numbers of international or cross-border marriages from the 1990s, a little later than Japan, but both countries' international marriages rapidly increased in number, soon growing to exceed Japan's rates. The proportions of international or cross-border marriages[6] are 5.1% in Japan (2008), 11.0% in South Korea (2008) and 12.2% in Taiwan (2008) (NIPSSR 2010; Yamaji 2010; Ito 2010). In 2003 nearly one in three marriages in Taiwan was a cross-border marriage.[7]

In South Korea and Taiwan, as in Japan, the factor behind cross-border marriages was the lack of women in rural areas and for lower-income men, but another factor, one not found in Japan, was the high sex ratio (male/female) at birth. A high sex ratio has been prevalent in East Asia (in the narrow sense of the term) and South Asia for the past 30 years, since the start of the first fertility decline, with the exception of Japan which does not prioritize patrilineal kinship groups and preferences for sons. Kojima considers a high sex ratio to be another formative factor in the East Asian model of second demographic transition (Kojima 2010b). The sex ratio at birth in 1990 was 117 in South Korea and 110 in Taiwan (Suzuki 2010). Ironically, the late start of the fertility decline enabled the people of these societies to use the emerging technologies of checking the sex of fetuses and of sex-selective abortions. This is a typical example of compressed modernity, which we will discuss later in the article.

The husbands of foreign wives usually present the following reasons for

6 The term "cross-border marriage" is used in Taiwan to include marriages with mainland Chinese.

7 28.0% of brides in 2003 were non-Taiwanese.

choosing international marriages: the need to have a son to inherit the family name, the need for people to care for elderly parents, and to ensure a labor supply for the farms (Ochiai 2007). This data suggests that the increase in international and cross-border marriage in East Asia occurs to maintain the traditional family structure.

2. Gender Role Changes in East Asia

1) Housewifization and De-housewifization in Western Countries

An analysis of gender is critical for this study. Capitalist countries such as those in Western Europe and North America have experienced the era of the modern family and a decline in female labor force participation rates. This latter phenomenon refers to what can be called the "housewifization" of the woman (Mies 1986). The Indian economist J. N. Sinha (1965) analyzed data collected by the United Nations and hypothesizes a U-shaped relationship between economic development and the labor force participation of married women. Since the 1970s, the labor force participation rate for women in Western Europe and North America has increased. The ascent along the right-hand side of the U-shaped pattern is symptomatic of what can be called the "de-housewifization" of women (Ochiai 2008a, 4–5), in a reverse movement to "housewifization."

In Western Europe and North America, the deep and long-term economic recession that started with the 1973 Energy Crisis precipitated the weakening of gender-based divisions of labor. Since employment was uncertain for both men and women, people who could find jobs worked, and there was no room for "luxuries" such as a gender-based division of labor. Of course, value changes forged by youth and women's movements in the 1960s and authorized by international organizations[8] were effective in making gender equality a cosmopolitan value, but it is likely that the main reason for the weakening of gender-based divisions of labor was economic necessity. We can also assume that demographic conditions also demanded a weakening of gender-based labor divisions. In Europe and North America, where the demographic change took place early, population ageing also happened earlier than in East Asia. Since the 1970s, the proportion of the elderly has topped 10% of the population, and in the 1980s there were countries where it topped 15%. The labor mobilization of women in their productive years is also necessary as a countermeasure to an aging population.

2) Diversity in Gender Roles in East Asia

When we widen our focus to include other Asian societies, we can discover surprising data on the amount of diversity. Figure 6 shows the labor force participation rate for women by age, according to official statistics for six societies in East and Southeast Asia. We can note that the patterns for age-specific rates of female labor force participation in these societies can be classified into three types. We define Type 1 societies as those in which high participation rates are maintained throughout the productive years. China and Thailand belong to this type. In Type 2 societies, women's rates of labor force participation gradually decline beginning in the 30s age brackets. Singapore and Taiwan belong to this type. Type 3 is where, after a temporary decline from the late twenties, the rate begins to climb again, thus showing an M-shaped curve. South Korea and Japan belong to this type.

8 The International Women's Year in 1975 and The United Nations Decade for Women, which started in 1976, were both important.

Women living in societies belonging to the first two types continue to work during the period of childbirth and childcare. This holds true not only for China and Thailand but also for Singapore and Taiwan, where female labor force participation rates remain high for age groups likely to be mothers of infants (until the early 30s) but begin to decline for age groups likely to have somewhat older children.

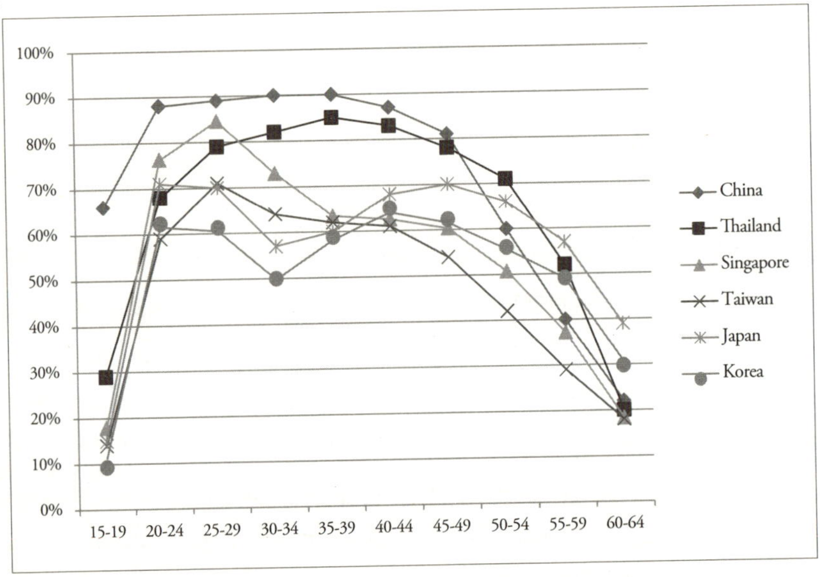

Figure 6. Female Labor Force Participation Rates by Age

* As of 2000 except for South Korea which figures are as of 2002.

Source: China: National Bureau of Statistics, 2000 Census; Thailand: National Statistical Office, Report of the Labor Force Survey; Singapore: Dept. of Statistics, Cnsus of Pupulation 2000; Taiwan: Executive Yuan, Human Resource Survey; Korea: National Statistical Office, Economically Active Population Survey; Japan: Statistics Bureau, Labor Force Survey.

The diversity we currently observe is the outcome of diversity regarding traditional patterns and the paths to modernity. Thailand has shown no change; it had the same table-shaped pattern in the 1960s as it does now. This phenomenon is not unique to Thailand, however; in Southeast Asia, women's active roles in working and their strong position in owning assets is an old tradition, one that was commented upon by explorers from Europe in the Age of Exploration (Reid 1993). In the rice-growing regions of southern Asia, female labor has been important (Sechiyama 1996, 2013). Southeast Asian societies have kept the same pattern during the modernization process, with women in urban areas continuing to work in small businesses, factories and modern offices.

It is important to note that Japan was indeed a society of this type. Women's labor force participation in Japan had been higher than European countries until the beginning of the 1970s, although it had declined since the modernization process started in late 19th century.

China took a socialist policy that emphasized productivity and therefore promoted the labor mobilization of women; in this case, then, rather than housewifization, we see a change in terms of labor mobilization after the socialist revolution. Similarly, in Singapore—which is not a socialist state—the state promoted the labor mobilization of women, due to that country's developmentalist policy of prioritizing economic development in line with strong state leadership.

South Korea after the 1960s showed an M-shaped pattern very similar to that of Japan, but prior to that time, it is not certain whether it was experiencing the decline in female labor force participation rates as in Japan. Due to the influence of Confucianism, it is likely that the labor participation of women was not as high in South Korea as in Japan or Thailand.

Taiwan is a difficult case because its population has diverse backgrounds. The aborigines and Taiwanese who are the descendants of intermarriage between aborigines and Chinese have a Southeast Asian background, while the

Chinese who moved to Taiwan after World War II have a more East Asian and Confucian background.

3) Trends in Gender Role Changes in East Asia

There are no simple answers to questions about the impact of modernity on gender in East Asia. Modernization/modernity contributed to housewifization in Japan, de-housewifization in China and Singapore, and no changes in Thailand. In very recent years, there have been further changes in societies like Thailand, China, and Singapore, where women continue to work following childbirth. Whether due to job losses, a lack of childcare facilities, or parental focus on children's education, more women are voluntarily or involuntarily becoming housewives (Ochiai 2008b). It seems that admiration for the "housewife life" is emerging in these countries. On the contrary, South Korea, Japan, Taiwan and Singapore demonstrate trends of de-housewifization. In the East Asian context, the trends of housewifization and de-housewifization did not occur separately in different time periods as in Western societies, but they occurred and are occurring simultaneously, while also displaying patterns of reversal.

The results of value surveys on gender demonstrate interesting contradictions. Women in many Asian countries respond differently than do women in Western countries to the question on whether they agree with a gender-based labor division where the man works and the woman stays at home (Figure 7). In Western countries, gender-based labor division has become old-fashioned, but in Asia, intriguingly, the higher the current labor force participation, the stronger the converse support for gender-based labor division as in the cases of China and Thailand. On the other hand, there are societies like South Korea where thoughts and ideas on this matter are on par with those of the West, while the actual labor participation rate for women does not correspond to the beliefs.

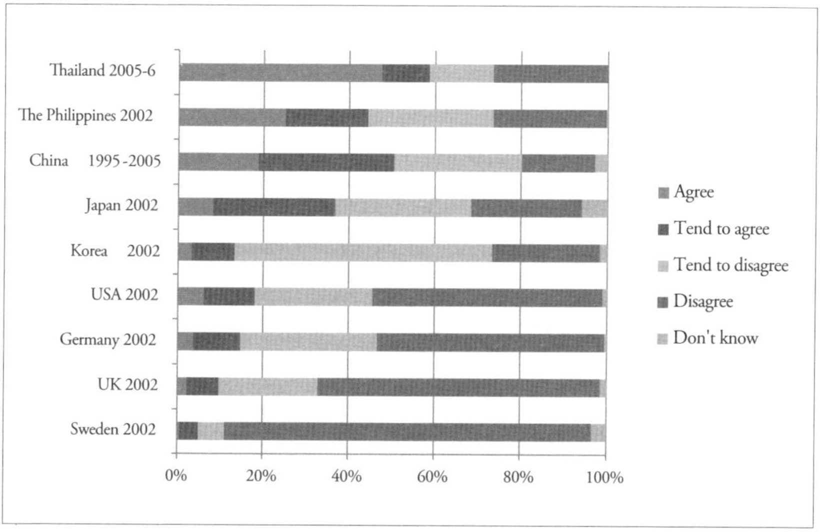

Figure 7. Women's Attitude Toward Gender Division of Labor

Source: China: 中国性别平等与妇女発展報告1995-2005; Thailand: International Comparative Research on "Home Education," National Women's Education Center, Japan; Other: International Comparative Survey on Gender Equality, Cabinet Office, Gender Equality Bureau, Japan.

II THE LOGICS OF ASIAN MODERNITY

A review of current trends in family and gender changes in East Asia reveals two major differences from Western countries. The first point is moderate changes regarding marriage, in contrast to extreme fertility decline, which suggests that the institution of marriage has not weakened significantly. The second point is complex trends in gender role changes; at the moment, the trends of housewifization and de-housewifization occur simultaneously.

The latter half of the chapter will discuss the causes that have generated these East Asian characteristics, and will examine three hypotheses.

1. Confucianism

1) Shallow Influence of Confucianism on non-Confucian Societies

The first hypothesis about the influences on the institution of marriage and gender roles is the impact of culture. People may surmise that the family in East Asia is relatively stable and that gender role change does not follow the Western path because of the influence of Confucianism in the region as a common cultural heritage.

However, as a researcher of the family sociology and political history of Japan, I feel uneasy whenever I come across a description that lumps together East Asian societies as Confucian societies. It is a common understanding in Japanese academia that the penetration of Confucianism into traditional Japanese society was shallow, compared to the other countries of East Asia. "Shallow" here means two things. One is that, in terms of social class, Confucianism only affected the higher strata, the *samurai* or warrior class. The other meaning of "shallow" is that the influence of Confucianism stopped at the ideological level, and everyday life was not actually affected.

To give one example, in Confucian teachings, there is the saying "a virtuous woman does not take a second husband." Young widows who did not remarry and continued to serve their parents-in-law and, in extreme cases, women who followed their husbands into death, were praised as "heroines" and valorized by the state in China and South Korea. However, in Japan, with its high rates of divorce, not only was remarriage common after the death of a husband, it was also common after divorce. Historical demographic studies indicate that the divorce rate in the north-eastern part (Tohoku) of Japan in the 18th and 19th centuries was as high as current US levels (Ochiai 1999; Kurosu, Tsuya, and Hamano 1999). On the other hand, in the south-western part of the country, freer attitudes toward sexual relations, known as *yobai* or "night calling," were widespread among young men and women—and sometimes not-so-young married ones were also involved— (Akamatsu 1994; Ochiai 2011) and resulted in around 10% of births out-of-wedlock (Ochiai and Nakajima 2010). It means that the Confucian teaching that "Boys and girls should be separate after age seven" was not observed.

In order to learn why the effects of Confucianism on Japan were so shallow, we need to be aware that Confucianism reflected the social structure of China, from which Confucianism emerged, and in particular, Chinese kinship structure. China is a society with exogamous patrilineal kinship groups, and such societies determine attribution to kinship group through ties with the father. This means, in general, women's sexuality is strictly controlled, and women's inheritance rights are limited. In contrast, Japan, like much of Southeast Asia, has a bilateral kinship structure, so women occupy a relatively higher social position, with relatively greater sexual freedom.

Agricultural technology also affects the division of labor by gender. In the rice belt, from Southeast Asia to southern China, women make considerable contributions in agricultural production, but in northern China, in the wheat belt where agricultural workers use cattle, men tend to take the central role in agriculture (Sechiyama 1996, 2013).

The basic structure of Japanese society shared a great deal with Southeast Asia both in terms of kinship structures and agriculture technology. Confucianism arrived in Japan in the 5th or 6th century, but its influence was limited. The Chinese civil service examination system (*keju*) did not take root and the legal code (*luling*) was modified. The situation changed somewhat in the 17th century, when the fledging Tokugawa Shogunate drew on neo-Confucianism for the core of its governing ideology; however, Japanese Confucian scholars had to struggle to apply the Confucian concepts to everyday life in Japan (Watanabe 2010) and political and social institutions were less affected by the ideology.

The influence of Confucianism in Japan only reached the whole population once the modern period had started after the 1868 Meiji Restoration. The Meiji Government spent its first decade following strong Westernization policies, but later initiated a movement to return to a traditional Eastern cultural background, and Meiji leaders promoted the use of Confucian moral education texts. Nevertheless, the Meiji Confucianism that filtered into modern Japanese society was too complex to be categorized as merely a return to tradition. Confucianism was modified and mobilized in a number of ways in order to create an ideology to support the modern Japanese state.

Countries like South Korea experienced a similar history. In South Korea, although there was a system of partible inheritance among sons and daughters until the 17th century, women later lost their inheritance rights and the state's glorification of chaste women increased. In Vietnam, although women have been economically quite active throughout its history, it was considered a virtue for women to sacrifice themselves for their husbands and families (Pettus 2003; Ochiai and Aoyama 2013 forthcoming). We must not be naïve when it comes to using Confucianism as a factor to explain the contemporary state of East Asia. Confucianism is not simply traditional, but has been imported, reshaped and used to suit the aims of the rulers of the era.

2) Traditionalization of Modern Gender Roles

The intellectual history behind the concept of "ryōsai-kenbo," the concept of the "good wife and wise mother," provides us with a good example of the intertwined relationships between Confucianism, modernity and gender. This phrase was often used in Japan to model the ideal role for women, as well as in China (where it is "wise wife and good mother") and in South Korea (where it is "wise mother and good wife") and has generally been thought of as an ancient precept that came from Confucianism and other traditions (Jin 2006).

However, research in the 1980s corrected this view. Koyama Shizuko discovered that the phrase "ryōsai-kenbo" was not to be found anywhere in records from the Tokugawa Shogunate. Its first appearance was at the end of the 19th century and actually emerged due to the influence of European ideas about women in the early Meiji period (Koyama 1991, 2012).

One of the key roles of the good wife and wise mother was to take the lead in educating her children. In contrast, the Confucian view of women in the Tokugawa Period did not rate the intelligence of women highly, and there was no expectation that mothers would actually educate their children. The details of the role of the good wife and wise mother were actually closer to the role models promoted in modern Europe (Koyama 1991, 2012). Girls who were educated to become good wives and wise mothers in girls' high schools at the time were proud to fulfill their new role of contributing to not just the family but also to the formation of the state. The role of women as good wives and wise mothers was also exported to nearby countries in Asia from the late 19th to early 20th centuries. In these societies, the concept of the "good wife and wise mother" was accepted as a modern, advanced role for a woman (Jin 2006; Ochiai and Aoyama 2013 forthcoming)

The intellectual history of the good wife and wise mother does not end here. The educational ideal informing the "good wife and wise mother" showed some changes following World War One. There was an increased emphasis on the concept of building the nation and strengthening Confucian women's values, which made the good wife and wise mother concept more conservative.

In China, the impact of the May Fourth Movement (1919) meant people focused on a new image of women as "independent individuals," along the lines of Nora in Ibsen's play 'Doll's House" (Jin 2006: Ch.6). The late 1920s saw increasing criticism of the unthinking Westernization of China, and the wise wife and good mother made a comeback, but its contents had changed, with a new emphasis on the woman's role in the household, and in addition, connections with traditional Chinese Confucian ideas (Jin 2006: Ch.7).

In this way, both China and Japan enacted what could be called a "traditionalization" of the good wife and wise mother by the period following World War One. The force acting here was what we may call the cultural geopolitics of "Asia." The putative superiority and threat of the West led to the introduction of the European good wife and wise mother idea, but at the same time the spirit of resistance to the West required the creation of an Eastern image of women. As the "new woman" appeared as an individual who was equal to a man, "new woman" was recast as a Western image of women, and the "good wife and wise mother" idea was recast as part of Eastern tradition. This shift was perhaps not so much due to shared traditions such as Confucianism as to a sort of identity politics based on the mechanism we can name "Self-Orientalism." In fact, the modern domestic role of women was made into an "Asian tradition." Through this very complicated process, Asian people started to justify the modern division of labor by gender in the name of "our cultural tradition," or sometimes, Confucianism.

Given the challenges outlined above, how can we assess the validity of the first hypothesis? It is difficult to say that Confucianism is the cause that has generated the East Asian features of family and gender changes today, because, to begin with, Confucianism is not a common tradition in the wider East

Asian region. There are at least two different social and cultural traditions in this region. One is the tradition based on a society with exogamous patrilineal kinship groups and another has its roots in a society with bilateral kinship groups. Confucianism is only related to the former.

However, due to the mechanism that we can call "traditionalization of modernity" that functioned in many of Asian countries, Asian people often believe that the modern gender role division is a part of their tradition and sometimes misunderstand that it originated in Confucianism. This is why many people mistakenly consider the first hypothesis plausible.

2. Paths to Modernity

1) Compressed Modernity and Semi-compressed Modernity

The second hypothesis is related to the different paths to modernity. In contrast to the assumptions of the modernization theory in the 1960s that all societies follow the same path to modernity, resulting in convergence at the end, the idea of "multiple modernities" assumes that societies follow different paths. Different paths might create longstanding differences in the future due to the effect of path dependency.

Earlier, I noted how we need to focus on the fact that, in the process of declining fertility, Asian societies other than Japan never had a period where fertility stayed at the replacement level, an argument I would like to develop further. When we take another look at long-term trends in declining fertility in different regions of the globe from a macro perspective, we can gain a theoretical idea for considering social change in East Asia.

Figure 8 shows the long-term trends in TFR for a number of East Asian countries, including Japan, as well as those of Europe and the United States. The first thing we should notice, at least in Europe, is that there were two declines, one as part of the first demographic transition and the other as part of the second.

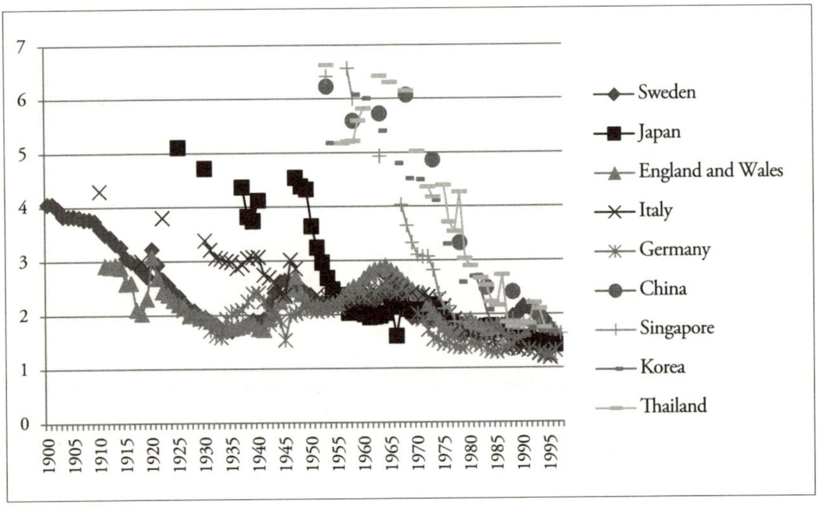

Figure 8. Long-term Trends in TFR in Europe and Asia
Source: UN, Demographic Yearbook

An interesting fact is that, with very few exceptions, societies within one region—i.e., Europe or Asia—experienced their fertility declines almost simultaneously. In those two regions—with the exceptions of France in Europe and Japan in Asia—there is a gap of about half a century in the timings of first fertility declines. The first fertility decline occurred in most European societies between the 1870-80s and 1920-30s, and in most East Asian societies in the 1970s-80s. Japan experienced it in the 1950s, exactly halfway between the time of most European countries and that of most East Asian countries.

Next, when did the second fertility decline take place? In Europe and the

U.S., it started at the end of the 1960s, and from the mid-1970s in Japan. Thus while there was a quarter-century gap between Japan and most countries in Europe for the first fertility decline, for the second fertility decline, the gap was only several years. Latecomers thus had their modernity not only delayed but "compressed," as the South Korean sociologist Chang Kyung-Sup has noted based on the experience of his country (Chang 1999).

When, then, did the second fertility decline take place in Asian countries other than Japan? In Asian countries, the fertility decline is continuing as shown in Figure 8; we cannot see any boundary between the first and second fertility declines as we could for Europe, the United States, or Japan. We need to operationally define a decline below replacement levels as a second fertility decline, which means that in Singapore the second fertility decline started in the mid-1970s, only a few years after Japan. Meanwhile, the second declines in South Korea, Thailand, and China started, respectively, at the beginning of the 1980s, in the second half of the 1980s, and in the 1990s.

If we think of the period between these two fertility declines—when fertility was stable and at around the replacement level—as the "golden age" of modernity, then the length of this period was about 50 years in Europe and America, 20 years in Japan, and almost nonexistent in the rest of East Asia. As Asian societies with the exception of Japan have not experienced a stable period of modernity, they have plunged headlong and directly into "late" or "second" modernity.[9]

---

9 The term "second modernity" was coined by Ulrich Beck to explain the fact that a modern society with distinctly different attributes to the previous modern society had emerged in Europe in the 1970s. Beck defines the previous classical modernity as "first modernity." Beck did not define these two modernities in relation to the two demographic transitions, but I believe they should be understood in relation, so at times I shall refer to the society created by the first demographic

From the demographic point of view, we can see very clearly the compression of modernity that Chang Kyung-Sup points out. Areas in Asia outside Japan have gone through this "compressed modernity," while Japan has had a "semi-compressed modernity," and this phenomenon provides an explanation for the experiences these regions would later undergo. Chang Kyung-Sup defines "Compressed modernity [as] a social situation in which economic, political, social and/or cultural changes occur in an extremely condensed manner with respect to both time and space, and in which the dynamic coexistence of mutually disparate historical and social elements leads to the construction and reconstruction of a highly complex and fluid social system" (Chang 2010a, 24).

2) Familialism and Risk-aversive Individualization

Chang Kyung-Sup employs the concept of "compressed modernity" to explain the gap between the extreme low fertility and moderate changes regarding marriage in East Asia. He notes that "South Koreans ... have led highly family-centered social and personal lives under what may be called familist[10] compressed modernity" (Chang 2010a, 24; Chang 2010b). This is due to the insufficient development of social security in compressed modernity, as the family is the only social resource that can support individuals exposed to capitalist industrialization, urbanization, proletarianization, extreme competition in the pursuit of education, and privatized welfare protection in rapid modernization. However, "the institutional weakening of families induced family relations to turn from social resources into risks." In other words, people

---

transition as the "first modernity" and the society created by the second demographic transition as the "second modernity" (Ochiai 2010).

10 "Familialism" and "familism" are used in the same meaning.

might be obliged to help their family members and relatives who have fallen behind in this competitive world, rather than being able to receive support from them. So, "Risk-aversive individualization is defined as a social tendency of individuals trying to minimize the family–associated risks of modern life by extending or returning to individualized states of life" (Chang 2010a, 25). We can observe this pattern in operation after the 1997-98 Asian Financial Crisis in ultra-low fertility societies. People decided to postpone marriage or having children or divorce to avoid the risks these situations might create for them. Furthermore, as Kojima suggested, cohabitation, which has started increasing in East Asia, is related to the "social exclusion" of people with less education and unstable employment (Kojima 2010a), rather than by individualistic choices to free themselves from the institution of marriage.[11]

Chang's key point is that these tendencies are "not necessarily symptoms of individualization, because they seem to reflect the ever intensifying significance of family relations and values in South Korean life" (Chang 2010a, 24). Chang also notes that these trends are not restricted to South Korea, but are shared by Japan and Taiwan, summing up the situation by stating: "The apparent convergence of capitalist East Asia in individualization without individualism is a historical outcome of the condensed modernization and second modernization of the latecomers" (Chang 2010a, 35).

Compressed modernity also at least partially explains complex and confusing trends in gender role changes. The two phases of gender role change in Western modernity – housewifization and de-housewifization – do not happen separately in order in Asian modernity. The two trends sometimes occur

11 However, Kojima also found a new tendency for highly-educated women in Japan to cohabit after 2000, which might be interpreted as the birth of a new lifestyle (Kojima 2010a).

simultaneously. However, compression in time does not explain everything. In some societies, the original point is different from that in Europe; if women did not work in a traditional society, there is no room for housewifization. Other societies took a completely different path, which is called socialist modernity.

3) Socialist Modernity in Transition

The East Asian region includes societies with another path to modernity. This is socialist modernity. The experience of socialist modernity has left clear effects even to the present time particularly with regard to gender.

Socialist ideologies included women from the emergence of the ideas. Socialist thought regards "reproductive labor" as vital for reproducing a society, so the labor was not exclusively associated with the household. Indeed, reproductive labor became socialized, or turned into social labor, thus liberating women from domestic tasks. Socialism proposed a contrasting path to Western European capitalism, which promoted the modern gender role division through housewifization.

At present, the former socialist countries in Europe are termed "post-socialist societies" or "transitional societies," and are experiencing major changes in a number of fronts. In terms of family and gender, Saxonberg and Sirovatka have noted the trends of "retraditionalization" and "refamilialization" (Saxonberg and Sirovatka 2006). Along with the transition to a free market, public childcare facilities have been closed, and the "traditional" household role of women has been emphasized, leading to a decline in their workforce participation. The only social institution which people can rely on, if any, is the family, so familialism is strengthened, and feminism is forced into the background (Dupcsik and Tóth 2008). Without public support and social safety nets, people's lives became harder, and this hardship is evident in the ultra-low fertility rates in this area.

The current state in Asia shares some similarities with the European case, but the differences are also significant. The biggest difference is that there are a number of countries in the region that are still socialist. Nevertheless, these countries are also changing economically while professing to be socialist market economies. In terms of gender, the female labor participation rate remains high, and while the ideological changes are not as far-reaching as in Europe, the image of women created during the peak of socialism is nevertheless showing some cracks.

The changes in gender roles in China, which are demonstrated by Mao's famous phrase that "women hold up half the sky," started with the "women return home" debates in the 1980s. To solve the problem of excess labor that Chinese companies faced, certain economists urged women to leave work and stay at home (Ochiai 1989). This shift never happened at the time because the All-China Women's Federation (Zhōnghuá Quánguó Fùnǔ Liánhéhuì) opposed the change, and the tide of "reform" was suspended with the 1989 Tiananmen Square Incident. Actual changes have surfaced from the middle of the 2000s as China's economic growth continued.

A study conducted in Wuxi, Jiansu province, in 2002 has shown that middle-aged women who had lost their jobs by regime change called themselves housewives to accept their fate (Ochiai 2005). In 2004, women in Fushun, Liaoning province, said that when they had enough economic leeway, they would devote themselves to educating their children, but in actuality there were few such cases (Ochiai 2005). However, in 2007, a newspaper company in Harbin organized a group of full-time housewives to form the "Good Wives

Club" (Hao Taitai Julubu: 好太太倶楽部).[12] Compared to the total population, the number of housewives is a tiny fraction, but the "housewife" (in Chinese: 全職太太 quanzhi taitai or 家庭主婦jiating zhufu) is turning to reality. The closing down of daycare facilities attached to workplaces in the 2000s is another change that is making it harder for women to balance work and home (Zhang and Maclean 2011).

If we look at the results of comparative family surveys conducted in 2006 in four East Asian societies, China, South Korea, Taiwan, and Japan, we can see that although the rates of both husband and wife participating in the labor force is the highest in China (nearly 80% among the 20 to 40 age group), and the proportion of men doing housework is also the highest in China, China also had the highest ratio of people in the 20 to 40 age group who agreed with the statements that "The husband should work outside the home, and the wife should look after the home" or "For a wife, it is more important to help your husband's work than to do your own job." In the other three countries, the ratios agreeing with the above statements were smaller in younger age groups, but in China, there was almost no variation by age. So we see a reverse phenomenon that Chinese are the most pro-gender equality for the age group over 50, but for below 40, they are the least (Iwai and Yasuda 2009: 21, 22, 25, 63).

The current changes are followed by the revisions in discourse regarding history. The liberation of women during the peak of socialism has come to be reinterpreted as hurting women by giving them a double burden. In other words, the idea is now that it is better to allow women to have the choice of becoming housewives. The past tends to be recast as a mirror of the present,

12 See the chapter by Zhang Yang in Ochiai and Aoyama (2013 forthcoming).

and these days we can observe a use of the "politics of memory" for the socialist era. The Confucian view of women and the modern gendered division of labor (good wife and wise mother) have been combined in a harmonious way, and have now once again resurfaced.

The Asian "socialist modernity" is not simply rejected as in Europe, but has been transformed. Therefore, the ideal of gender equality has not been clearly denied, but gradually combined with a Confucian view of women and a modern gender norm, widening the gender gap in reality. Will the ideal of gender equality be inherited by the next generation in the era of transition? Or, will it be the start of modern gender division, merely delayed half a century? History is being created right now.

How do we assess the second hypothesis? Asian modernity is much more diverse than European or Western modernity. Various paths to modernity—compressed modernity, semi-compressed modernity, and socialist modernity—and diversity within the region explain the difference between Europe and Asia. People have to stick to the family under compressed modernity because the compression in time does not allow the state to develop a social security system that reduces the family responsibility. However, for the same reason, people avoid having a family to escape from family responsibilities. The apparent contradiction of extremely low fertility, high divorce rates, high age at marriage and relatively moderate changes in the family institution can be explained by this contradiction.

Complex trends in gender role change are also explained by the different paths to modernity and regional diversity. There are two types of society in terms of traditional gender roles; those with higher labor force participation by women and those with lower participation. The ones with higher participation, which belong to the Southeast Asian tradition like Thailand and Japan, can follow the same process as European countries, i.e., housewifization and de-housewifization. Japan experienced the phase of housewifization from the beginning of the 20th century to the 1960s, while Thailand has kept a high participation rate until recently and is currently at the crossroads of whether it will start housewifization or not. In both societies, the phase of de-housewifization has already started if we define it by the increasing number of educated women in employment. The two phases are overlapped.

On the other hand, there are societies with a tradition of lower labor force participation rate of women, like China, South Korea, and perhaps Singapore and Taiwan. Among them, the countries where the government promoted women's employment as state policy, i.e., China (socialist modernity) and Singapore, experienced de-housewifization earlier, while others experienced it later. However, the countries that experienced the state-driven de-housewifization are now facing the reversed trend of housewifization. The process China is facing might be called "re-housewifization" which is in the same continuum with the refamilialization and retraditionalization that have occurred in post-socialist countries in Europe, although the change in China is much more subtle.

3. Policy Decisions

1) Varieties of Familialism

Policy decisions play an important role in determining the path society takes. The future of a society depends on the paths it has taken but society can also choose its own paths. This is the idea implied by the concept of the welfare regime. Esping-Andersen argues that Europe has progressed in three or four different directions through its policy choices. In contrast, East Asian policy is usually called a "familialist welfare regime" based on the idea that the family should have the greatest welfare responsibility towards its members, both in income distribution and care provision. We should pay more attention to the policy decisions East Asian governments have made and are making under the conditions of compressed modernity.

An empirical look at the welfare regimes in Asian societies reveals a diverse reality. The results of our international joint-research project were presented in the form of a diagram called a "care diamond" (Ochiai 2009); it depicts patterns of care provision in each society, assuming that care is provided by four different sectors: the state, the market, family (and relatives), and the community (Razavi 2007).[13]

What strikes us first are the diverse patterns among different societies in spite of the commonality that the family and relatives sector is large. Familialism is not uniform. Patterns also differed according to the type of care that was under observation. For example, the state plays a significant role in childcare provision in China and Singapore, in order to promote female employment; such is not the case with elderly care provision in those same societies. Another impressive feature is the importance of the market sector in some societies—especially for childcare and elderly care in Singapore and for elderly care in Taiwan—which reflects the employment of foreign domestic and care workers in the home. The transnational migration of domestic/care workers within the Asian region is becoming increasingly common. We can call the welfare regime of East Asian societies with a particularly strong market sector "liberal familialism."

13 The comparison of care diamonds among Asian societies, as quoted here from Ochiai (2009), is based on the results of a research project that has been conducted by Japanese, South Korean, Chinese, and Thai social scientists since 2002. The outcomes of the research have been published as Ochiai and Molony (2008); Ochiai, Yamane, and Miyasaka (2007); Ochiai and Ueno (2006); and Ochiai, Miyasaka, Zhou and Yamane (2010).

Among the societies with a strong state sector, China can be called "socialist familialism."[14] Then what can we name Singapore? Singapore is a society with a strong state and market, just like social democrat countries in Scandinavia. However, the Singaporean political system is different from the political systems of Scandinavian countries in many ways. It would be more appropriate to call it "developmental familialism." Compared to other East Asian countries, Japan seems to be the closest to the genuine familialism without strong state or market sectors. With the combined effects of compressed modernity and the policy decisions made under the social conditions created by the former, East Asia has developed a stronger familialism than in Europe, while at the same time creating varieties of familialism (Ochiai 2010b).

2) Familialist Reform in Japan

Then, how are the policy decisions made? For Japan, we should understand the importance of the policy reform made in the 1980s. Prior to that period, until the High Growth period of the 1960s, the Japanese government was still following developmentalist policies. We may grant that Japan was ahead, in the Asian context, in the construction of a social security system. However, the role of social security still remained peripheral in the 1960s, because growth was considered to be the best way to improve people's well-being. We can call this system a sort of "workfare." It was only when substantial economic growth had been achieved in the late 1960s and early '70s that the government recognized the need to revise the existing welfare system to construct a more appropriate

14 The Chinese regime has dramatically changed in the first decade of the 21st century. For example, the closing down of public nurseries attached to state-owned companies pushed it toward the direction of "liberal familialism."

welfare state. The year 1973 was named "Welfare Year 1."

However, ironically, "Welfare Year 1" was hit by the Energy Crisis. The government became wary and set a new agenda called the "Japanese-style welfare society" that emphasized "traditional" Japanese virtues of "self-help and mutual support within the family and the community." What the government tried to promote was not actually a welfare "state," but instead a welfare "society." People might find an early example of welfare retrenchment in this idea[15] but the level of welfare state already achieved prior to the change was different. Japan did not have a developed welfare state to retrench. Rather, the size of social expenditure was increased from the 1970s on. Under the conditions of compressed modernity, the development and retrenchment of welfare state happened at the same time.

Actually, economic and demographic conditions made the simultaneous development and retrenchment of welfare state possible. Growth rates remained high even after the Energy Crisis. Compared to Europe and North America, "the affluent society" lasted 20 years longer in Japan. Also, with an already low number of children and an even lower number of elderly people, Japan was still enjoying a "demographic dividend" in the 1970s. Under these favourable conditions, the Japanese society was able to continue "workfare" for two more decades.

In 1980s, the government made the "family" a policy issue to create the foundations of a "Japanese-style welfare society." Flattered by the cultural explanations of Japan's economic success, the government and their ideologues

15 Prime Minister Nakasone Yasuhiro who promoted this idea in 1980s was proud of his close relationship with President Reagan of the United States and Prime Minister Thatcher of the United Kingdom, the leaders of neo-liberalism (Ochiai and Johshita 2013 forthcoming).

tried to create a unique policy direction, not imitating any policies in the West. They were also irritated by the changes in the family already becoming visible in social statistics, such as increasing divorce rates and age at marriage, and decreasing fertility. The Ohira Cabinet's policy agenda on "Enrichment of Family Foundations" (1979) as well the so-called "Whitepaper on the Family" (a special issue of the "Whitepaper on National Life") were produced from this fear of a "family crisis" and a strong desire to protect the Japanese family, the core of national identity, from contamination by Western culture. In other words, these policies were a reaction to the second demographic transition that started from Europe and North America. Laws known as the "protection of the housewife's throne" were implemented in 1980s, including an increase in the legal inheritance amount for the wife (1980), pension reform that waived premiums for the wives of employees of large companies (1985), and the creation of a special tax deduction for those with dependent spouses (1986).

The effect of this anachronistic familialist reform was enormous. Increase in the full-time employment of women since the 1950s ceased by the Energy Crisis and the only expansion in women's employment from the latter half of the 1970s to the present has been in part-time employment (Tanaka 1999; Ochiai 2010a). This was because the wives of large company employees restricted their working hours to adjust their income within the amount that would be recognized as "dependent" on their husbands. This new gender division of labor—what Jane Lewis calls a "one-and-a-half earner model" (Lewis 2001)—was created during the recession, became fixed by the law, and remained entrenched for decades.

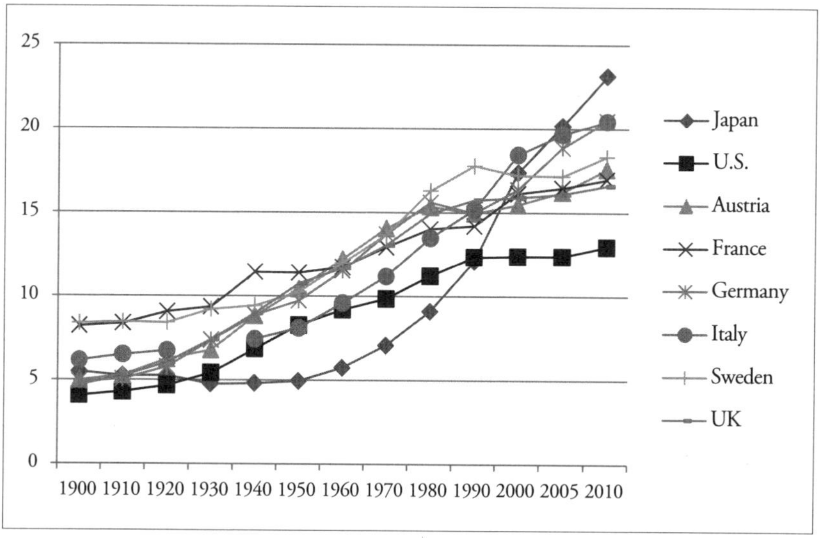

Figure 9. Trends in Proportion over 65 in Selected Countries
Source: NIPSSR (2010)

In 1970, in contrast to expectations, the rate of female labor force participation was higher in Japan than in most European countries (Ochiai 2010a, 12). However, in the three decades that followed, Europe and North America each saw big jumps, while little change has been observed in Japan. Women's participation rates by age still reveal an M-shape pattern in Japan. The gender role change that occurred in most European and North American countries at the same time as the second demographic transition did not occur in Japan because the gendered division of labor was consolidated by the familialist reforms of the 1980s.

In the 1990s Japan lost the economic and demographic conditions it had held in 1980s. When the bubble economy finally burst in 1991-92, the Japanese economy entered a long period of stagnation. The favourable demographic state also did not last. The proportion of the elderly population skyrocketed in 1990s, reaching 22.1% in 2008 (NIPSSR 2010), the highest rate in the world (Figure 9).

In spite of these drastic changes in economic and demographic conditions, the familialistic structure consolidated in the 1980s resisted change, resulting in the "lost decades." The government introduced new policy measures beginning in the late 1990s, allegedly aiming for the socialization of care, but those policies were still heavily reliant on familialistic ideas. For example, the LTCI (Long-term Care Insurance), which was introduced in 2000, is designed to promote home-based care, not institutional care. Family caregivers can hire "home helpers" for a number of hours a day with subsidies from this insurance, but they still bear responsibility for care for the rest of the day and also for the economic burden of having to partially pay for this care (co-payment) (Ochiai, Abe, Uzuhashi, Tamiya and Shikata 2012).

3) Liberal Familialism in Other East Asian Societies

Other East Asian societies had different experiences compared to Japan. Modernity was even more compressed in these other societies, forcing them to undertake the paradoxical task of constructing a welfare state while simultaneously retrenching welfare (Miyamoto, Peng, and Uzuhashi 2003, 301). For example, South Korean President Kim Dae-Jung (1998-2003) was faced with this contradiction despite the forced application of neo-liberalism and globalization after the IMF Crisis, which created a concept of "productive welfare" that would construct social welfare as a social investment, or in other words, the foundation of economic growth.

One significant finding in our field research on the patterns of care provision mentioned above was the key role the market sector played in certain societies, especially for childcare and elderly care in Singapore and for elderly care in

Taiwan (Ochiai and Molony 2008; Ochiai 2009). This reflects the employment of foreign domestic workers and care workers in the home. Interestingly, those families who hire care services from the market usually profess the familialistic idea that a family should take care of its elderly parents at home. Yet the reality is that it is migrant care workers who perform these care tasks. To put it another way, these families outsource their filial piety (Lan 2002). We call this approach "liberal familialism."

Compared with societies like Singapore or Taiwan, the complete lack of a solution that involves hiring foreign workers in Japan is striking. Japan's immigration policy does not provide visas for unskilled foreign workers, so there are almost no foreign domestic or care workers in the country (Liew, Ochiai, and Ishikawa 2010).[16] Just as in the case of the consolidation of the family, Japan sticks to its 1960s system and resists changes in numerous aspects in spite of the thorough transformation of the society. In its "semi-compressed modernity" Japan barely managed to build a structure resembling European modernity in the 1960s. However, there was not enough time to mature the system and reconstruct it according to changing circumstances. In contrast, other East Asian societies had even less time in their much more "compressed modernity" to achieve stability, which functions as a positive factor to promote constant change. For example, the hiring of domestic workers was a normal habit in an earlier stage of modernity. Before losing their collective memory of hiring domestic help, other East Asian societies started accepting domestic workers with foreign nationalities, while carefully-constructed private sphere or

16 Japan has recently begun accepting care workers as candidates to become nurses based on agreements with Indonesia and the Philippines, but their numbers are still few and the program has a lot of problems (Asato 2009).

modern family works as an obstacle in Japan's case.

Asian familialism is diverse. However, even in the case of liberal familialism in which the family receives care services from the market, the responsibility to finance the cost of care is usually borne by the family. This is why liberal familialism is still called familialism, and why fertility in these societies is also low. The economic burden is particularly heavy for people who occupy an economically disadvantaged status. The impact of the economic crisis in and after 1997-8 was severe, because in liberal familialist societies, people who occupy a lower economic status are more vulnerable to economic stress.

III CONCLUDING REMARKS

A review of current trends in family and gender changes in East Asia in the first half of this chapter reveals that East Asian societies also observe the features of the second demographic transition, but maintain a few significant differences from Western countries. Moderate changes regarding marriage, in contrast to extreme fertility decline, suggest that the institution of marriage in East Asia has not weakened in spite of demographic changes. Another significant point is the complex trends in gender role changes; in the contemporary moment, the trends of housewifization and de-housewifization occur simultaneously. Given these facts, some might conclude that East Asians carry a relatively conservative attitude toward marriage and gender. But it is too early to rely on this conclusion.

The latter half of the chapter discusses the causes of these East Asian characteristics, and examines three hypotheses. The first hypothesis gauges the impact of culture, particularly Confucianism. It sounds plausible that the common cultural tradition in East Asia, which has roots in Confucianism, has generated the conservative attitude toward marriage and gender in this region. However, such a simplistic view is not acceptable, because the cultural traditions of the East Asian region are diverse and the levels of the influence of Confucianism also differ. Instead, we must be attentive to the process of what we call "traditionalization of modern gender roles" or "traditionalization of modernity," which functions in many Asian countries. Asian people often believe that the modern gender role division is a part of their tradition due to an ideological mechanism that can be described as self-Orientalism.

The second hypothesis is related to the different paths to modernity. The relatively stable institution of family in East Asia can be explained by the paths toward modernity taken by the societies in this region. Due to the insufficient development of social security in "compressed modernity," the family is the only social resource East Asians can rely on. East Asians have to stick to the institution of family not because they are conservative but because they have no alternative. Compressed modernity also explains the simultaneous occurrence of opposite trends in gender role changes. Socialist modernity, another path in East Asia, also influences gender role changes. The trend of housewifization is observed as a new trend in transitional socialist countries.

The third hypothesis is the importance of policy decisions. Even with the same social conditions created by the same path, space for decision-making exists. The difference between Japan and other East Asian societies is an example of the effect of policy decisions. Constructed "East Asian tradition" is sometimes utilized to justify policy decisions.

The three factors proposed by the three hypotheses are combined and work together to generate the current reality of family and gender in East Asia.

Bibliography

Akamatsu, Keisuke. 1994. *Yobai no Minzokugaku* (Folklore of Night Calling). Tokyo:Akashi Shoten.

Asato, Wako. 2009. Gaikoku karano jinzai ukeire no ronten (Issues regarding human resources from abroad). In *Shido suru gaikokujinzai niyoru kango kaigo* (*Cross-cultural care in globalization*), ed. Wako Asato and Noriko Maekawa, Sasakawa Foundation, Tokyo.

Chang, Kyung-Sup. 2010a. "Individualization without Individualism." *Journal of Intimate and Public Spheres*, 0: 23-39.

______. 2010b. *South Korea under compressed modernity: familial political economy in transition*. London: Routledge.

Cabinet Office Director-general for Policies for Cohesive Society. 2005. *Shoshika shakai ni kansuru kokusai ishiki chosa* (*International value survey on low-fertility society*).

______. 2007. *Kodomo, kosodate hakusho 2007* (*White paper on child and childrearing 2007*). http://www8.cao.go.jp/shoushi/whitepaper/w-2007/19webhonpen/html/i1431200.html

______. 2009. *Asia chiiki ni okeru shoshika taisaku no kokusai hikaku kenkyu* (*International comparative survey on low fertility policies in the Asian region*).

Dupcsik Csaba and Olga Tóth, 2008, "Feminizmus helyett familizmus" (Familism instead of feminism), *Demográfia* 5-4:307-328.

Giddens, Anthony. 1992. *The transformation of intimacy*. London: Polity Press.

IMF (International Monetary Fund). 2004. *World economic outlook database 2004*.

Ito, Seiichi. 2010. Taiwan niokeru kazoku hendo no genjo to seisaku (The state of family changes in Taiwan and policy). In *Higashi Asia no kazoku-jinkogaku-teki hendo to kazoku seisaku ni kansuru kokusai hikaku kenkyu* (*An international comparison of family demography and family policy in East Asia.*) ed. Suzuki

Toru, 99-135. MHLW Grant Research Report.

Jin, Jung-won. 2006. *Higashi Ajia no Ryosai Kenbo Ron: Tsukurareta Dento* (Debates over Good Wife and Wise Mother in East Asia: An Invented Tradition). Tokyo: Keiso Shobo.

Kohler, Hans-Peter, Francesco C. Billari, and Jose Antonio Ortega. 2002. "The emergence of lowest-low fertility in Europe during the 1990s." *Population and Development Review*, 28-4:641-681.

Kojima, Hiroshi. 2010a. Higashi Asia ni okeru dosei to sono kanren yoin (Cohabitation in East Asia and its related factors). *Jinko Mondai Kenkyu (Journal of Population Problems)*, 66-1:17-48.

______. 2010b. Higashi Asia, Obei shokoku ni okeru dosei to sono kanren yoin (Cohabitation in East Asia, Europe and North America and its related factors). In *Higashi Asia no kazoku-jinkogaku-teki hendo to kazoku seisaku ni kansuru kokusai hikaku kenkyu (An international comparison of family demography and family policy in East Asia.)* ed. Suzuki Toru, 99-135. MHLW Grant Research Report.

Koyama, Shizuko. 1991. *Ryosai Kenbo toiu Kihan* (The Norm of Good Wife and Wise Mother). Tokyo: Keiso Shobo.

______. 2012. *Ryosai Kenbo*. Leiden: Brill.

Kurosu, Satomi, Noriko Tsuya, and Kiyoshi Hamano. 1999. "Regional Differentials in the Patterns of First Marriage in the Latter Half of Tokugawa Japan." *Keio Economics Studies*, 36-1:13-38.

Lan, Pei-Chia. 2002. "Subcontracting Filial Piety: Elderly Care in Ethnic Chinese Immigrant Households in California." *Journal of Family Issues* 23:812-35.

Lesthaeghe, Ron. 1991. The second demographic transition in Western countries: An interpretation. IPD Working Paper. Interuniversity Programme in Demography.

Liew, Kao-Lee, Emiko Ochiai, and Yoshitaka Ishikawa. 2010. "Feminization of immigration in Japan: marital and job opportunities." In *Asian cross-border marriage migration* ed. Yang Wen-Shan and Melody Lu. Amsterdam: Amsterdam University.

Mies, Maria. 1986. *Patriarchy and accumulation on a world scale: Women in the international division of labor*. London and New York: Zed Books.

NIPSSR (National Institute of Population and Social Security Research). 2005. Shussei doukou kihon chosa (Basic survey on birth trends).

______. 2012. *Jinko tokei shiryoshu 2012* (*Demographic statistics 2012*).

Ochiai, Emiko. 1989. "Chūgoku Josei ha Ie ni Kaeru ka: Gendaikan Rosen to 'Fùnǚ Huíjiā' Ronsō no Yukue." *Kindai Kazoku to Feminism*, Keisō Shobo.

______. 1999. *Kindai Kazoku no Magarikado* (The Modern Family at a Cross Road). Tokyo: Kadokawa Gakugei Shuppan.

______. 2007. Gurobaruka suru kazoku: Taiwan no gaikokujin kaji rodosha to gaikokujin tsuma (Globalising families: foreign domestic workers and foreign wives in Taiwan). In *Gurobaruka jidai no jinbungaku* (*Humanities in the era of globalization*), ed. Eisaku Kihira.,Kyoto: Kyoto University Press.

______. 2008a. "Researching gender and childcare in contemporary Asia." In Asia's new mothers, ed. Emiko Ochiai and Barbara Molony. Folkestone: Global Oriental, pp. 1–30.

______. 2008b. "The birth of the housewife in contemporary Asia: Globalization and the modern family." In *Asia's new mothers*, ed. Emiko Ochiai and Barbara Molony. London: Global Oriental, pp. 157–180.

______. 2009. "Care diamonds and welfare regimes in east and southeast Asian societies: Bridging family and welfare sociology." *International Journal of Japanese Sociology* 18: 60–78.

______. 2010. "Reconstruction of intimate and public spheres in Asian modernity: familialism and beyond." *Journal of Intimate and Public Spheres* 0: 2-22.

______. 2011. "Love and Life in Southwestern Japan: The Story of a One-hundred-year-old Lady." *Journal of Comparative Family Studies* 42-3: 399-409.

———. 2013 forthcoming. "Intimate Work and the Construction of Asian Women." In Emiko Ochiai and Kaoru Aoyama (ed.). *Asian Women and Intimate Work*, Leiden: Brill.

———, and Kayoko Ueno, eds. 2006. *21st century Asian Families*, Tokyo: Akashi Shoten.

———, Mari Yamane, and Yasuko Miyasaka, eds. 2007. *The Asian family and gender.* Tokyo: Keisō Shobō.

———, and Barbara Molony, eds. 2008. *Asia's new mothers: Crafting gender roles and childcare networks in east and southeast Asian societies.* Folkestone: Global Oriental.

———, Yasuko Miyasaka, Weihong Zhou, and Mari Yamane, eds. 2010. *The Asian family and gender: Empirical and comparative studies in China, Japan, Korea, Singapore and Thailand (5 countries, 6 areas).* Shijie Zhishi Chubanshe.

———, and Mitsuhiro Nakajima. 2010. Children out-of-wedlock in a Japanese seaside village, 18-19th centuries. Presented at the annual meeting of the Social Science History Association, Chicago.

———, Aya Abe, Takafumi Uzuhashi, Yuko Tamiya, and Masato Shikata. 2012. The struggle against familialism: reconfiguring the care diamond in Japan. The political and social economy of care: research report 5, UNRISD.

———, and Kaoru Aoyama (ed.). 2013 forthcoming. *Asian Women and Intimate Work*, Leiden: Brill.

———, and Kenichi Johshita. 2013 forthcoming. Prime Ministerial Discourses in Japan's Reforms since the 1980s: Traditional Confucianism or a Traditionalization of Modernity. Sung, S. and Pascall, G. eds, *Gender and Welfare State in East Asia: Confucianism or Equality?*, Palgrave.

Pettus, Ashley. 2003. *Between Sacrifice and Desire: National Identity and Governing of Femininity in Vietnam.* London and New York: Routledge.

Razavi, Shahra. 2007. "The political and social economy of care in a development context: Conceptual issues, research questions and policy options." Gender and development programme paper number 3. Geneva: UNRISD.

Reid, Anthony. 1993. *Southeast Asia in the age of commerce, 1450–1680*. New Haven: Yale University Press.

Saxonberg, Steven, and Tomas Sirovatka. 2006. "Failing Family Policy in Post-Communist Central Europe." *Journal of Comparative Policy Analysis* 8-2: 185-202.

Sechiyama, Kaku. 1996. *Patriarchy in East Asia: The comparative sociology of gender*. Tokyo: Keisō Shobō.

______. 2013. *Patriarchy in East Asia*. Leiden: Brill.

Sinha, J. N. 1965. Dynamics of female participation in economic activity in a developing economy. United Nations World Population Conference, Document WPC/285.

Straughan, Paulin, Angelique Chan, and Gavin Jones, eds. 2008. *Ultra-low fertility in Pacific Asia: trends, causes and policy issues*, London: Routledge.

Suzuki, Toru. 2010a. Post kindaika to higashi Asia no kyokutei shusseiryoku (Post-modernization and lowest-low fertility in East Asia). *Jinko Mondai Kenkyu (Journal of Population Problems)*, 66-1: 1-7.

______, ed. 2010b. *Higashi Asia no kazoku-jinkogaku-teki hendo to kazoku seisaku ni kansuru kokusai hikaku kenkyu (An international comparison of family demography and family policy in East Asia.)*. MHLW Grant Research Report.

Tanaka, Shigeto. 1999. *Seibetu bungyo no bunseki* (Analysis of sexual division of labor). Ph.D diss. Osaka University.

Watanabe, Hiroshi. 2010. *Kinsei Nihon Shakai to Sougaku (Early-modern Japanese Society and Neo-Confucianism)*. Tokyo: University of Tokyo Press.

Yamaji, Kumiko. 2010. Kankoku shakai no tabunka kazoku to shien seisaku (Multicultural families and their support policies in South Korea). In *Higashi Asia no kazoku-jinkogaku-teki hendo to kazoku seisaku ni kansuru kokusai hikaku kenkyu (An international comparison of family demography and family policy in East Asia.*) ed. Suzuki Toru, 41-63. MHLW Grant Research Report.

WHO. 2011. *World Health Statistics 2011.*

Zhang, Yanxia, and Mavis Maclean. 2011. "The Rolling Back of the State?: Multiple Roles the State Played in Child Care in Urban China." Presented at 'Conference on Shifting Boundaries of Care Provision in Asia' held at Asia Research Institute, National Singapore University on March 14 and 15.

Zheng, Yang. 2013 forthcoming. "The Gender Norms of Chinese Women in the Market Economy in China: Research interviews with wives in three urban centers." In Ochiai Emiko and Aoyama Kaoru (ed.). *Asian Women and Intimate Work*, Leiden: Brill.

Negotiating Between Cultures: Chinese Women Making Muslim Families in Hong Kong

WONG Wai Ching Angela

I INTRODUCTION

The conflict among cultures and religions was particularly heightened after 9/11 when the United States launched its unilateral "War on Terror" in Afghanistan (2001) and Iraq (2003). Samuel Huntington's proposition of the "clash of civilizations" turned into a self-filling prophesy when American foreign policy targeted, both ideologically and strategically, non-Western cultures as "enemies." U.S. supported military insurgency against Islamic extremism has since further instigated the Islamic extremist call for a global jihad against the infidels of the West. Media reports of ongoing conflict and escalating casualties in many locations with multicultural populations soon dominated the world.

In the shadow of widespread violence, religious identities and traditions have increasingly in importance for the communities concerned. The issues of peace and conflict among people of different ethnic, religious and cultural backgrounds have since emerged as one of the most significant contemporary concerns.

The prevailing portrait of the world conflict between religions and cultures outlined above is unfortunately over-represented in the mainstream media. In Hong Kong, partly due to British colonial policy and partly because of the political sensitivity of the religious communities caught between Communist-ruled China and Kuomintang (KMT) governed Taiwan until the nineties,[1] Hong Kong had no official religious policy before the handover in 1997. Except for Christian churches, which were privileged with specific social and educational resources because of British colonialism, religious communities and organizations have kept very low profiles and have been highly cooperative with the government as well as with one another. During this time, while social unrest because of anti-colonial sentiments and patriotic support for political movements in China have played a significant part in Hong Kong history, conflicts among communities of different religions and cultures is almost unheard of. In contrast to the persistent, emphatic attention paid by the Chinese central government to

1 Despite the fact that most of the religious institutions in Hong Kong, including those of Christianity, Buddhism, Daoism, and Islam, were cut off from their affiliations to their respective Chinese national headquarters after the Communist closure of China in the fifties, personnel and informal organizational ties between Hong Kong and China remain. At the same time, before China opened up again in the late seventies, a relationship between the religious institutions in Hong Kong and those who settled down with KMT in Taiwan after 1949 has steadily developed. As a result, just like the general social sector of Hong Kong before its return to China in 1997, the religious sector had implicitly become a contested ground for political influence among Communist China, the KMT of Taiwan, and the anti-communist Western forces represented by the British Colonial government.

building "harmony" among the different ethnic groups in the mainland, ethnic communities practicing various cultural beliefs and customs has rarely been a problem in Hong Kong. In the case of Islam, despite a strong Christian presence in the public, Muslims, the small community of mixed cultural traditions in Hong Kong have been living in peace with their neighbors through the century of colonial history.[2] Whereas the colonial government worked closely with the South Asian Muslims, whom they recruited from India for the force of security and defense in the territory, the colonial government has largely left alone the Chinese Muslims, a mixed group constituted of migrants, local births and families of interracial marriages. In other words, rather than fitting in with the American ideological representation of the "clash of civilizations," Chinese Muslims in a British Protestant-led Hong Kong generally succeeded in the negotiation and accommodation of various aspects of Islamic teachings and practices with the surrounding cultures including Western modernity and colonialism and Chinese pragmatism prevailed in the community in everyday life.

In the interest of space, this paper will focus on Chinese Muslim women and their experiences of negotiating between cultures in their conduction of families in Hong Kong. I focus on Chinese Muslim women not only because women have always played a significant role in preserving cultural traditions and resolving

---

2 In a 2001 study, Ho Wai Yip documents a case of initial community resistance to the expansion of some Islamic social service facilities to include the setting up of a mosque in Yuen Long. The local community, comprised primarily of Chinese residents, raised the concern about the noise that could be generated from the mosque's call to prayers five times a day, and the possible decline of estate value as a result. However, at the time of the conclusion of the study, conversations seeking mutual understanding between the Islamic organization and the community had already been underway. Cf. Ho Wai Yip, "Historical Analysis of Islamic Community Development in Hong Kong: Struggle for Recognition in the Post-colonial Era," *Journal of Muslim Affair* 21, 1 (2001): 63-77.

conflicts among religions, but also because the question of Islam for women and family values has been particularly caught up in the polemic between a modern, democratic West and an archaic, autocratic Islamic world. The issues impacting women, including veiling, polygamy, and gender equality, have fueled intensive debate among humanitarians and feminists alike. Feelings of resentment and distrust are generated and heightened on the sides of both the liberal campaign for universal women's rights and the resistance movement against the exercise of Orientalism toward non-Western and nonChristian women. In fact, with the fervent Islamic fundamentalist sentiment around the world, there is a voluntary revival of veiling among Muslim women in many countries, including some Chinese Muslim women in Hong Kong. However, is the meaning of the veil the same in Hong Kong as it is portrayed in the "worldwide" picture? How have these minority Chinese Muslim women negotiated their religious enthusiasm with the modern role and place of women in a highly "westernized" society of Hong Kong? In what ways have they been successful in upholding their faith and raising families in the midst of the strong presence of Western education and Chinese customs in the society? A careful case study of women in the small but highly complex Chinese Muslim community in Hong Kong will shed light on unmasking the monolithic representations of Islamic religion and culture in the media, and will reconstruct a discursive space for the meeting of traditions and values in women's practical living.

II LIVING MULTICULTURALISM: CHINESE MUSLIMS IN HONG KONG

The complex ethnic and cultural backgrounds of the Muslim community in

Hong Kong became quite evident as I interviewed five Chinese Muslim women in 2010. Amazingly, in the family lineages of these five women, there are at least twelve nationalities and or ethnicities represented. Among the five women, only Man Kei was married to a Chinese person. Yasmin is now remarried to a Chinese but had first married and divorced a South Asian.[3] Yasmin herself was born to a "traditional" Chinese family who practiced folk religion. Three other women, Zameena, Aleeza and Rania, are married to South Asian Muslims, and except for Rania, all including Yasmin converted to Islam either before or after marriage. Both the former husband of Yasmin and the husband of Aleeza are "local boys" (本地仔),[4] and Aleeza's father-in-law is an Indian born in Burma. While Zameena's husband is a new arrival from Kashmir, the northwestern India-administered region, her natal family is Hakka. She was originally baptized into Catholicism by her mother, and her father was a dedicated communist. Among the five, Rania's ancestry, together with her husband's ancestry, are the most telling. Rania mentioned three nationalities in her immediate family line. Her maternal grandfather was an Afro-Arabian and her mother a Xinjiang-Chinese who was married to a Malaysian Chinese. And Rania's husband's lineage has more racial and national diversity: his ancestry consists of six nationalities, including Turkish, Arab, Pakistani, Indian, Malaysian and Urgur. Both Rania and her husband are mixed blood from long legacies of interracial marriages in

3 In the context of Yasmin's narrative, the ex-husband was most likely a Pakistani. She only referred to him as a South Asian throughout her interview and made no distinction of his nationality. And yet in her comments on the difficulties of interracial marriages, she mentioned a few times the problems of being married to Pakistani men.

4 Indian or Pakistani men who were born in Hong Kong, grew up in Hong Kong, and speak fluent Cantonese, the local dialect. The prior generations of their families have settled in Hong Kong for many years, for different reasons. More details will be explained below.

their families. Among my interviewees, Man Kei is the only Chinese Muslim by birth, and she has a relatively straightforward Chinese lineage. She is now a widow but both she and her deceased husband came from very prominent Chinese Muslim families in Guangdong; there had been several generations of Chinese officials in both families. Despite Man Kei's family members all being Chinese, her maternal grandfather was a diplomat stationed in Korea, where her mother grew up and learnt to speak fluent Japanese.

Table 1. Family Trees of Participants

Name[5]	Natal family lineage	Marital family lineage
Man Kei (born Muslim)	Prominent Chinese Muslims in Guangdong; maternal grandfather a diplomat in Korea	Prominent Chinese Muslims in Guangdong
Yasmin (converted Muslim)	Chinese practicing traditional folk religion	Current husband: Chinese Former husband: South Asian, probably Pakistani, family settled in Hong Kong for generations
Zameena (baptized Catholic at birth; converted Muslim)	Chinese Hakka; Catholic mother, Communist father	Muslims in Kashmir, Northwest India
Aleeza (converted Muslim)	Chinese family	Indian family settled in Hong Kong for a long time; husband's father was born in Burma
Rania (born Muslim)	Maternal side: Afro-Arabian grandfather, Xinjiang Chinese mother and Malaysian Chinese father	Family lineage includes Turkish, Arab, Pakistani, Indian, Malaysian and Urgur members

In sum, with family lineages interwoven through multiple generations of marriages, the five women interviewed had reported cross-fertilization of Muslims across regions and continents, representing families of an unusually complex tapestry of cultural, ethnic and religious mixture. In short, the focus

5 Only Pseudonyms are used throughout the paper

on Chinese Muslim women in Hong Kong serves as a window to the world of people practicing and living multiculturalism in everyday life.

When and how such a fascinating history and "hybrid" makeup of the Muslim community in Hong Kong began has been a subject of debate. In fact, except for a few sporadic studies on its individual aspects,[6] the history of Muslims in Hong Kong has not been documented. Due to the colonial policy of not including religious affiliation in the census, there are no official statistics about the religious composition of the Hong Kong population and hence no systematic calculation of the Muslim population in Hong Kong until the contemporary moment. The number of 100,000 Muslims listed in the *Hong Kong Yearbook* in 2010 is only an estimate offered by the Incorporated Trustees of the Islamic Community Fund of Hong Kong (the Trustees).[7] There are no details about who these Muslims are, where they come from, and what racial or ethnic composition they constitute in the larger population. And except for the stylish Moorish mosque at Tsimshatsui, the centre of the business district on the Kowloon Peninsula, and the growing presence of the veiled Indonesian domestic workers in the public areas on Sundays, Muslims are generally invisible as a religious community because of the low profile it adopted over the years.

Unlike the demographic organization in China, Muslims are not

---

6 Existing topics of study include Indians as an overseas community in Hong Kong, the history and organization of the main Islamic organizations in Hong Kong, and the growth of the Indian group called "local boys" (本地仔). Respective studies will be alluded to in the paragraphs below.

7 This number has not included the estimation of about 120,000 Indonesian domestic workers who are untable and staying by permission of working visas. The number in the *Hong Kong Yearbook* varies slightly from 70,000 to 90,000 from the late nineties to 2006 and remains the same at 220,000 (including 120,000 Indonesian domestic helpers) from 2007. These estimations, according to an interview with the Secretary of the Trustees, have been provided to the government annually based on their "impression." Interview on 10/9/2010.

categorized as a "nationality" of *hui* (回族) by religion in Hong Kong. Rather, due to the colonial introduction of Indians to Hong Kong for military and disciplinary measures, the identity of Muslim almost overlapped with that of Indian and Pakistani (after the independence of Pakistan in 1947) in the public acknowledgement of the British Hong Kong government before 1997. Indeed, despite the general recognition of the fact that the majority of Muslims are Chinese,[8] for a long time, the Trustees, the stipulated Muslim representative body overseeing the mosques (and related buildings) and cemeteries in Hong Kong, is consisted of largely South Asian organizations. Except for the Islamic Union who has grown into a mixed ethnic body comprising of a large percentage of "local boys" (本地仔) and Muslim Chinese by intermarriage,[9] the other three constituent members of the Trustees include the Pakistan Association, the Indian Muslim Association, and the Dawoodi Bohras, all of which have clear South Asian ethnic affiliations.[10] Due to a disagreement with the Trustees' stipulations that all members are required to surrender all organizational properties to the Trustees, the Chinese Muslim Cultural and Fraternal Association (Chinese Muslim Association, 中華回教博愛社), the principal coordinating body for

---

8 The estimates of Chinese Muslims in the *Hong Kong Yearbook* had been "more than half" when the total was estimated to be 70,000 and 80,000 throughout the years until a more concrete number of 30,000 has been given since 2004 when the total was estimated to rise above 90,000. Other studies have also referred the same observation. Cf.

9 The mosque, the Masjid Amar & Osman Ramju Sadick Islamic Center situated in Wan Chai, in which the office of the Islamic Union is based, is also the first mosque initiated to be built by a "local boy." In 1967, Ramju Sadick, whose father was Indian and mother was Chinese, donated one quarter of his assets to building the mosque. Different from the first two mosques in Hong Kong, the Shelly Street Mosque and Kowloon Mosque, the Wan Chai Mosque attracts large numbers of local boys and Chinese Muslims. There is even a Chinese restaurant integrated in its eight-storey complex. Cf. Ho, 67.

10 The historical background and evolvement of these South Asian organizations are explained in details in several works. See Joel Thoraval (1991) and Caroline Pluss (2000).

social and religious services for Chinese Muslims in Hong Kong, have refused to be its official member until today. As a result, except for the purpose of convenience of colonial governance, the organization of the Trustees is hardly representative of Hong Kong Muslims beyond the South Asian and the Sunni community.[11]

The dominant representation of the South Asian Muslims in Hong Kong is attributed largely to its colonial history. The earlier Indian groups came as sailors for the East India Company, or were migrants from the Straits who were sailors, or were traders who originally settled in Hong Kong. Since the colonized people were free to travel around the British Empire until the 1930s, there were Malays who joined the move as well. From the beginning of the twentieth century, a much larger number of Indians arrived for the posting of security staff in the military, police force, and prisons in Hong Kong. The reasons for the migrations were also largely colonial: first, it had been an intentional practice of the British Empire to set up an Indian military for deployment throughout the Empire to maintain law and order. Second, there was the concern of Chinese corruption. Indians who had no local contacts were believed to be less susceptible to bribery or illegal deals in their occupations as police or prison guards. As a matter of fact, Indians were placed immediately in the border skirmishes, putting down resistance from local inhabitants when the New Territories were ceded to Britain on lease in 1898.[12] Third, there was the convenience of language since

11 Weiss, 441.

12 Weiss, 427. Pakistanis were intentionally recruited to join the Emergency Unit of the government specifically for riot control in the late nineteenth century. During one of the most violent riots in Sham Shui Po in 1967, despite the government's order not to shoot the protesters, many protesters were killed by the automatic machine guns used by the Emergency Unit on the rioters. As a result, the Pakistani unit was severely criticized in the press for excessive

many Indians were educated in English and spoke the language fairly well.[13] To a much lesser extent, the colonial government also recruited Indians to staff postal, health and educational services, for which the government believed there were no qualified Chinese with the required knowledge of the English language and skills.[14] After the wars in the mid-twentieth century, many more traders and individual Indians came to Hong Kong for its thriving economic opportunities, which include the posting of private watchmen and security guards by foreign banks and companies.[15]

Intermarriages between Indians and Chinese took place as early as the late nineteenth century. In her essay, Anita Weiss presented two figures of the family lineages of Haji Ahmad Rumjahn from Calicut and El-Acrulli from Tamil Nadu up until the mid-twentieth century, in which each generation had a son or two who married Chinese wives.[16] And yet for the policemen and prison guards, there was a rule in the early period that forbade them to marry local women.[17] These early migrants mostly married back home and retained familial relations with the subcontinent. When the ban was finally lifted with the Japanese occupation in 1941, and as many Indian Muslims settled down in the colony and began to build their businesses and families in Hong Kong, interracial marriages became more common. When Indian men intermarried with Chinese women (who then converted to Islam), and the parents raised

brutality. Cf. Weiss, 434.

13 Weiss, 419-420.

14 Vaid, 17.

15 Weiss, 426.

16 Weiss, 421, 429.

17 Weiss, 431.

their children as Hong Kong natives, new generations of "local boys" emerged, who would refer to the "home based" South Asians as "visitors."[18]

The pre-existence of a Chinese Muslim community before British colonization was referred to by Caroline Pluss as not sufficiently grounded.[19] Weiss notes that there was probably a Muslim community that existed in Guangdong since the eighth century when Islam was introduced by Arab, Persian and Indian traders, but this had little to do with the South Asian Muslims who came to Hong Kong in the wake of the British Empire. She argues that only when the Muslim seamen and traders arrive did there emerge a sense of identity for the Islamic community.[20] However, Tang Kaijian (湯開建) and Tien Yingxia (田映霞) suggest that rather than coming from the north, the beginning of Muslim settlement in Hong Kong began via the trade route by sea from Arabia to China along its eastern coast. According to the scholars, those Arabian traders by-passed Tuen Mun (屯門) of Hong Kong before they reached up to Quanzhou (泉州), Fujian province, in the seventeenth century during the Ming dynasty.[21] According to Liu Suying (劉淑英), the former vice-president of Guangzhou Muslim Fraternity Association, it was only during the later time before British arrival in 1842 that more Chinese Muslims came to Hong Kong from the mainland cities such as Guangzhou (廣州) and Zhaoqing (肇慶) of Guangdong province.[22]

---

18 Weiss, 417, 433.

19 Caroline Pluss, "Hong Kong's Muslim Organization: Creating and Expressing Collective Identities," *China Perspectives* 29 (2000): 21.

20 Weiss, 419.

21 Tang and Tien 1995; Tang 1996.

22 Liu Suying, 1998.

Among the Muslims in Hong Kong, the Chinese Muslims have received the least amount of public attention . Since the British occupation of Hong Kong, the Chinese Muslim community had always been overshadowed by their Indian fellow believers. Considered to be part of the Chinese migrant population, Chinese Muslims have never been treated as a separate "nationality" category *hui* as they would be on the mainland. Akhond Yeung, the secretary in charge of the Chinese Muslim Association, stated that Chinese Muslims arrived before the British. And during the colonial years, these early Chinese had maintained a very low profile in the community as they were usually settlers who did not speak English and were mostly confined to low-income jobs. Both socially and economically, they lagged behind the Indian Muslims and for the most part belonged to the lower class residing alongside the tramway area in Wan Chai.[23] Nevertheless, Tang and Tien also found the names of wealthy Hong Kong Chinese Muslim merchants who were remembered on the memorial stones of at least two mosques in Guangzhou for their contributions to their respective renovations in 1909 and 1921. Tien noted in another study that the rapid rise of economic and political influence of Chinese Muslims in the recent decade has not been matched with due recognition by the non-Chinese Islamic community in Hong Kong. Over the years, the Chinese Muslim Association (established in 1905) has "quietly" played the role of addressing their needs and has facilitated social and religious activities for the Chinese Muslim community. With the handover in 1997, the Chinese Muslim Association has become an increasingly important liaison between the Chinese Muslims in Hong Kong and the Muslim organizations on the mainland. Leaders of the Chinese Muslims have gradually

23 Interview on 20/9/2010.

emerged as prominent religious leaders, representing Muslims in Hong Kong in national events held in Hong Kong and the mainland.

III CHINESE MUSLIM WOMEN AND THEIR FAMILIES IN HONG KONG

In this section, I focus on the study of Chinese Muslim families and women. In terms of cultural negotiation, the dual identities of Chinese and Muslim and how they affect the women's home making and understanding of gender roles in the home are of particular interest. Although studies about Muslim women were numerous even before the popularization of the "clash of civilizations" polemic by the United States, most of the studies, focused on women of the Islamic countries and very rarely addressed Islamic women living in non-Islamic states and cultures.[24] A study of the experiences of the Chinese Muslim women living and making multicultural families in Hong Kong provides a valuable contribution for our understanding of religion, culture and gender.

During summer 2010, I met five Chinese women through the contacts provided by the Manager of the Hong Kong Islamic Union, Basmah Lok. Four of the interviews took place at the restaurant and the offices of the Masjid Ammar and Osman Ramju Sadick Centre at Wan Chai, and one interview was conducted at the office of the interviewee's company at Causeway Bay. The youngest of the five women was 35 years old and the oldest 73 years old

24 Wadud 2006; Lughod 1998. There are some recent studies that focus on the examination of cross-cultural experiences of Muslim women who emigrated from Islamic countries to the West. Cf. Aune, Sharma, and Vincett 2007; Karim 2009.

at the time of the interviews. Four of the women work full time, although one works in an honorary capacity, and only one woman has exclusively been a housewife. All of the women have some post-secondary education, and their occupations include school vice-principal, manager, center-in-charge, and self-employed company owner. All five women have been married, with one woman re-married, one woman widowed, and one woman considering a divorce. Three of these women had children and two did not. All of their families appear to do well economically and should be considered middle to upper middle class. The most impressive finding of all is that while the women all defend Islam as a gender egalitarian religion, they also exercise rather broad and flexible interpretations of their faith in their various contexts.

1. Coping with the Modern Society

The dominant view of Islam suggests that there is not a separate entity of state or church as such in Islam. Rather, the Islamic ideal state of government, the Caliphate, encompasses all domains including everything in the juristic, political and economic spheres. It is therefore not only that the state and religious community are one but also that the state and religious authority are embodied in the same person, the Caliph. This emphasis on the integration of the state and religion has, however, led many to conclude that Islam remains in the pre-modern era and that Muslims following the religious precepts without flexibility belong to the archaic world. In the face of the dominant perception of modern as equivalent to secular, one of the greatest challenges for Muslims living as minorities in modern society is to practice the religious instructions including, the most common of which include *salah* (praying five times a day), eating *halal* food, and the application of the veil for women who are faithful. These religious practices easily place the faithful followers at the centre of public gaze and as objects of suspicion in schools, workplaces, or when sharing meals with family and friends who are not Muslim.

Yasmin, who is about 40 years old, is the most educated among the interviewees. She is married with two children and works as a vice-principal of a high school. When she came back from her studies in Malaysia, she found Hong Kong to not be conducive to practicing Islamic teachings because of its weak religious atmosphere.[25] The unfriendly attitude of the general public makes it particularly difficult to raise Muslim children. "When others [at school] see my children as Muslims, they would say something nasty and treated them unfairly. When performing their religious rituals, they would attract unwanted attention and feel rather uncomfortable." For going to service, visiting the mosques, and eating *halal* food, "[the children] would ask why we are different from others." Although Hong Kong is not like France where children are forbidden to wear veils in schools, Yasmin feels it is still quite impossible to ask her daughters to wear veils. According to Mohamed Alli Din, the Chairman of the United Muslim Association of Hong Kong (UMAH) and an outspoken figure in the Islamic community in Hong Kong,[26] South Asian Muslim students often

25 Interview on 17/7/2010.

26 He is known to be liberal in his interpretation of Islam and has often been dismissed by other Muslims. His campaign for the rights of ethnic minorities including ethnic minority prisoners and Filipino migrant workers earns him great respect from the community. Cf. Ho, 67.

feel discriminated against and isolated in the local schools.[27] But as UMAH organized for the building of a new mosque integrated with an English language secondary school and an elderly home in Yuen Long, the local residents strongly protested, citing the fear of the noise from *salah*, possible traffic congestion, worsened community security and the possible adverse effects on the real estate value.[28] In the opinion of Din, the Hong Kong community is not ready to accommodate multiculturality.[29]

The issues of *halal* and veiling also bother the 73 year old Man Kei as she began to take her faith more seriously over the past few years. Man Kei has always been a full time housewife and was widowed after her husband's untimely death at the age of fifty. With her only daughter studying abroad, she is living by herself near Wan Chai. Probably owing to her long time Muslim family lineage and the private space she has as a housewife, she finds practicing Islamic instructions "neither difficult nor easy" in Hong Kong. In her daily life, she goes to service regularly, practices *salah* and ritual cleanliness, and buys meat from Muslim butchers only. The more challenging moments for her remain in the public realm where she has to dine with friends. She does not feel comfortable eating outside her home where she could not be sure of how the food is prepared. She would therefore join them only when socially necessary. For other occasions, "I would mostly excuse myself." As for veiling, she still finds it a pressure. "[It] feels a little simmered [with the veil on]," and she feels "often become the talking

27 The shift of many government subsidized schools from using the teaching medium of English to Chinese resulted in a high dropout rate for South Asian children. The ethnic students in the mainstream schools will always lag behind, feel discriminated against and isolated. Cf. Ho, 70.

28 Ho, 73.

29 Ho, 74.

point in the neighborhood."

As much as the religious instructions place the faithful as the spectacles for their largely non-Muslim neighbors, they serve as a distinct identity marker for the faithful. Reflecting on the challenge of her faith in practice, Zameena, the 51 year old self-employed company owner, admitted that she encounters difficulties in her day to day living. "For example, socially when relating to an adult man who is not a relative, I basically cannot stay with him in a room. ...There are a lot of things I cannot eat; [and I] need to be mindful of all the immoral ideas when watching a film as well." But she also finds her seriousness toward food preparation a sign of her deeper involvement in her faith. "I would clean up my own utensils [when eating out] and ask my family to prepare only seafood when I go back for dinner with them." Referring to the issue of veiling, "it had been some struggle to veil, such a difference from what I had been before. There has naturally been some gaze of disbelief [from people around]." So much so that the colleague who had been supportive of her interracial romance would say in dismay: "It is okay to believe [in Islam] but do you really need to wrap yourself up like this?" And yet she was quite proud of the fact that she was one of the first who immediately put on the veil after conversion, since "a lot more people would take some time to adapting to it." Still, challenges appeared from every corner: people would ask her, "why believing in the religion of the 'ah cha' (阿叉)[30]?" or "aren't you hot [wearing the veil]?" However, she continues to wear the veil and believes this is what a faithful Muslim woman should do.

In all three cases, Yasmin, Man Kei and Zameena, all from different age groups, have been freely adapting the Islamic teachings they know to negotiate

30 Making fun of the common sound "jah" in many Indian names, local Chinese transliterated it into Cantonese "Ah Cha" as a nickname for South Asians in Hong Kong.

with the public space in which they live. The broad environment of emerging confrontation between Islamic teachings and modernity has in many ways shaped their sense of religious responsibility. All three believe that practicing Islamic instructions in their daily life is essential to the demonstration of their seriousness in faith. Yasmin explicitly drew reference to the case of France and lamented the barbarity of the so-called civilization today. Even though people in general do not understand or appreciate Islam and tend to give the Muslims an unwelcome gaze when they see them, *salah*, *halal* and veiling are what they believe constitutes their religious identity. Nevertheless, also due to the relatively relaxed religious atmosphere in Hong Kong, all three are adopting the religious practices at their pace. Man Kei began to wear the veil about five years ago but accepts that members in her family do not have to wear the veil. For Zameena, who used to wear the most fashionable clothes on the market before conversion, would now translate her fashion sense into exploring many different styles and patterns of the veil. "I would spend a lot of time in wearing it in order to look good." As for Yasmin, she believes that Islam has to adapt itself to various contexts and understands that all Muslims must live under the laws of their respective societies. In the secular environment of Hong Kong she would not force the religious instructions on her daughters. "Young girls often love to look pretty. But I believe, they would gradually learn the meaning of [veiling] and put it on themselves one day." Utilizing Chinese pragmatism, Yasmin, Man

Kei and Zameena feel attached to their Islamic identity, and yet each woman exercises a degree of flexibility to accommodate Hong Kong modernity in their individual contexts.

2. Coping with Intermarriages

Aside from the heated issue of veiling, much debate on the relation of Islam to modernity is focused on the rights and place of women in the family. One of the primary issues of feminist contention is that women should not be restricted to the roles of housekeeping and childbearing and thereby be confined exclusively to the domain of home. Many studies of the situation of women in Muslim countries show that their predicament has not been much improved. Despite some modernist Muslim interpretations that attempt to reinstate gender equality into Islamic tradition, there is a wide-spread and strong belief among Muslim men and women that the conservative version of the status of women in Islam is the only authentically Islamic way of life.[31] The most controversial section of the *Qur'an* is Sura 4:34 which has often been interpreted to grant men the "pre-eminence" over women, or that men are " overseers" of women. In the case of an "insubordinate" (*nashiz*) wife, the husband is further granted the authority to admonish her, then desert her in bed and finally beat her up. A *TIME* report on "The Women of Islam" in 2001 quoted professor of religious

31 Ekaterina Yahyaoui Krivenko, *Women, Islam and International Law: Within the Context of the Convention on the Elimination of All Forms of Discrimination against Women* (Leiden: Martinus Nijhoff Publishers, 2009), 212. For example, in Egypt women can have only one spouse, while men are permitted four. In Iran the legal age for marriage is nine for girls, fourteen for boys. The law has occasionally been exploited by pedophiles, who marry poor young girls from the provinces, then use and abandon them.

studies at the University of Louisville Riffat Hassan's critique: "The way Islam has been practiced in most Muslim societies for centuries has left millions of Muslim women with battered bodies, minds and souls."[32]

This depiction is definitely not representative of the billions of Muslim women in the world. In a country where Islam is a minority religion, much negotiation has to be made to contextualize its precepts. In fact, it is commonly acknowledged in Asia that Islam is not limited to one interpretation but a diverse stream of understandings. In her *Qur'an and Woman*, Amina Wadud argues

> ...there is continuity and permanence in the Qur'anic text itself as exemplified even through various readings by their points of convergence. ...However, the assertion that there is only one interpretation of the Qur'an limits the extent of the text. The Qur'an must be flexible enough to accommodate innumerable cultural situations because of its claims to be universally beneficial to those who believe.[33]

And this is exactly what the Chinese Muslim women in Hong Kong do in coping with their marriages. Except for the family values shared largely by the local Chinese community regarding filial piety toward seniors, parental duties, and sibling and spousal respect and care, none of the conservative *Qur'an* interpretation is evident in the accounts of the five women. This does

---

32 Lisa Beyer, "The Women of Islam," *TIME*: *World* (Sunday, Nov. 25, 2001) at http://www.time.com/time/world/article/0,8599,185647,00.html#ixzz1uvSuT4i7, retrieved on 15/5/2012.

33 Amina Wadud, *Qur'an and Woman*: *Rereading the Sacred Text from a Woman's Perspective* (New York: Oxford University Press, 1999), 6.

not mean that the Islamic faith does not play a role in their conduction of families. On the contrary, faith is described as one of the most important factors contributing to successful marriages. And in four of our five cases, faith plays the most essential role in their intermarriages with South Asian men. While three of them converted to Islam because of their husbands, one revived her early Islamic identity because of her marriage. Although all of these Chinese women are serious believers who try to follow Islamic instruction as closely as they can, none accept plainly the will of men as the final authority in the family. Rather, their devotion to the Islamic faith often constitutes a higher authority that leads to a certain evaluation and criticism of the unfaithful acts of men in general and their husbands in particular.

According to Weiss, since marriage became permitted between Indian-Pakistani Muslim disciplinary forces and local Chinese women during Japanese occupation, the number of these marriages rose steadily. While Indian-Pakistani women would still for the most part be arranged to marry back "home," their Indian-Pakistani men seem to have more choice given that the women they married would necessarily convert into Islam. For "local boys," given their living and working in Hong Kong within the Chinese community and their Cantonese language abilities, courtship and marriages with Chinese women happen as a matter of fact. Basmah, the Manager of the Islamic Union, recalls that because of the dominance of South Asians in the Muslim community in Hong Kong, interracial marriages such as those of Yasmin, Zameena, Aleeza and Rania are quite common in the community. Unfortunately, in her observation, many difficulties have emerged from these intermarriages and not many marriages resulted in happy endings.

As a matter of fact, both Yasmin and Zameena found their intermarriage situations to be unbearable. Yasmin sought divorce with her South Asian[34] husband after three years of marriage and remarried with a Chinese Muslim several years back; Zameena has not made up her mind but is contemplating the possibility of divorce. Yasmin is our highest educated interviewee and is considered as one of the most learned in Islam because of her specialized study in Islam at the University of Malaya when she was young. She was first married to a "local boy" who was her colleague at the same company when they met. In the case of Zameena, her husband is an Indian carpet trader she met in Kashmir, who knew nothing about Hong Kong before his first arrival. Despite the different backgrounds of the two South Asian spouses, neither Yasmin nor Zameena is satisfied with the values they and their husbands shared in their respective marriages. And while Yasmin found the main problem to lie in their cultural discrepancy, Zameena believes her problem is also faith related. That is, her husband does not take Islamic teachings seriously enough to make their marriage work.

Yasmin blames the failure of her intermarriage on the difference in culture. Although she and her South Asian husband knew one another quite well before they married, she discovered only after marriage that "his way of thought is vastly different from that of Chinese tradition." There have been many disagreements about their views and ideas toward cultural matters, and she concluded that "the thoughts of South Asians and Chinese are essentially incongruent." Such differences permeated the two families in their responses

34 Given her stress on the problems of Pakistani men in her conversation, there is solid rationale to believe that her former husband is from Pakistan.

to Yasmin's initiation of divorce. For Yasmin, divorce is not particularly controversial in contemporary Hong Kong and she believes that her family also found her decision to be acceptable; but her former husband's family thought only Chinese women would ask for divorce. They believe that Pakistani women would be more faithful and would stay in a lifelong marriage no matter the circumstances. Confident in her knowledge of Islam, Yasmin believes that much more than that of Pakistani tradition, "Islamic family is in fact very close to the ideas of the Chinese tradition, [pertaining to] values such as filial piety." In contrast to what she perceives to be the submissiveness of Pakistani women, she argues that although Islam "encourages women to taking care of the family while men work outside, ...yet as a family, if men can take the time to look after the children, women can work outside as well."[35] Although she did not go into elaborate explanation on the cause of her divorce , her modernist separation of Islamic teachings from the South Asian custom she knows seems to not only justify her move from one marriage to another, but also affirms her role as a vice-principal of her school and a religious leader in the Muslim community.

Zameena is a strong defender of Islamic teachings about women. "Everyone says that Islam oppressed women; it is actually the [Indian] cultural custom." Her main complaints about her husband evolve around his laxity in following his faith. While she is living to the best of her ability in accordance with the instructions of Islam, she thinks her husband fails in many aspects of being a "true" Muslim. Her initial encounter with her husband was all about romance: a handsome carpet trader on the beach of Kashmir and the life-changing conversion and devotion to Islam for her after their marriage. Unfortunately,

35 Interview on 17/7/2010.

their real intercultural encounter began only after marriage during which they found much more divergence than commonality. "When he first came to Hong Kong, I had to work along with taking care of him, and he made a lot of complaints. I have done what I could, go marketing and returning home to cook [after work]. I quarreled with my boss then who thought that I had turned into another person!" And "I thought he [too] would change! He found everything in Hong Kong abominable at his first arrival. I thought he would gradually change." He simply finds Hong Kong to be unlivable. But for Zameena, there is not only the difference of culture. Moving to Kashmir is unthinkable for her not only because of the complete cultural and physical isolation she experienced when staying there, but also because she did not find Kashmir to be "the ideal Islamic environment for [her] faith." In her view, the people there, including her husband and his family, are deeply rooted in their local tradition and custom which are contradictory to the Islamic principles she knows. Even when her husband was in Hong Kong, his mindlessness toward physical and ritual cleanliness was to her a sign of his disrespect to Allah. Reflecting on their twelve tumultuous years together, she believes that "an Islam family, ...if one is to get marry, there must be faith, only then could it be happy. [One] really needs to follow religious instruction and understand Islam." In fact, Zameena feels quite strongly about her own faith and finds it difficult to get along with many Indian-Pakistanis because of their laxity in lifestyles and religious practices.

The intermarriages of Aleeza and Rania and their respective husbands seem to be two of the few successful cases. Depending on the income of their husbands, both Aleeza and Rania spent a lot of time in the work and activities of the Islamic Union in the capacity of semi-volunteers. Both spoke very firmly about the role religious devotion plays in their running of families. And probably because of their positive experiences with their marriages, they seem to adopt relatively "traditional" views of a woman's place in the family. Aleeza believes that a man should be the one who shoulders responsibility and be the breadwinner and model for the family. However, when comparing her mother to her Indian mother-in-law, she finds her mother too strong and her mother-in-law too submissive. Negotiating between the roles modeled by these two women, Aleeza prefers the Chinese way of trying the moderate approach, or hitting the middle way (中庸之道). In reality, not only does she work in her independent job outside the home, she is also a general manager of her organization and has to make many decisions throughout the day. Her humble admission of men as masters of their families likely reflects her wish to balance the interests of work and family as a working woman. In the case of Rania, her desire to be recognized by her devotion and faith is fully demonstrated in her approach to running the family. In line with her faith, she decides to work as a volunteer helping to promote Islam and a housewife overseeing the development of her children. In her ideal family scenario she would prefer her husband to read the *Qur'an* together with her and to not watch television after work; she wishes that her children would take part in the regular services in the mosque instead of spending time in the shopping malls; she takes pride in her son's acceptance of Islam and her daughter's voluntary veiling and expects her to marry a Muslim; and she would treat everyone as a member of her ever extending family and share with them her love. For her, because of her faith, material reward is not important, only love is.[36]

Ironically, both Aleeza and Rania are pessimistic about genuinely faithful interracial relationships. They both knew friends who had had terrible marriages

36 Interview on 31/8/2010.

with South Asian men and ended up in divorce. With shared disappointment, both Yasmin and Zameena hold low opinions about South Asian men in general. Aleeza mentioned offhand that women friends of Indian-Pakistani background would prefer to marry their daughters off to families back in India and Pakistan because they do not think the Indian-Pakistani men in Hong Kong are good enough. More directly, Rania comments that she finds many problems with the Pakistani men in Hong Kong. "Relationship between Pakistani couples is usually not good. Those who are faithful would all detest Pakistani [men], only one [of them] behaves badly the whole religion suffers." Apparently there are Pakistani men in the community who have, in the eyes of the Chinese, tainted the name of Islam by their misdeeds. Referring to many failed intermarriages, Aleeza returns to the question of faith first brought up by Zameena: "When an Indian-Pakistani got married with a Chinese woman, the woman may not know much about his religion, and it is not easy to keep up with one's faith in the extravagant world of Hong Kong, there will be bigger conflicts, because there is in fact no common ground of faith." Overall, in the observations of Aleeza, Rania, and, to a large extent, Zameena, intermarriage does not work when first, the couple does not share a strong foundation in Islam; and second, when the South Asian spouse is not serious enough about his faith to practice Islam in his everyday life. In short, their conclusions weigh the degree of "true" commitment to faith over cultural differences as a factor in intermarriage. But how did that happen? Is devotion to the Islamic faith a sufficient condition in making intermarriage work? Or has Islamic faith, in contrast to its popular negative understanding, empowered the Chinese Muslim women to face their marital crises with the interpretative tools of a higher power?

3. Coping with Divorce

The general impression has been that wives in Islamic societies face great difficulty in suing for divorce, and yet husbands can be released from their vows virtually on demand by saying "I divorce you." In some cases, fear of poverty keeps many Muslim women locked in bad marriages, as does the prospect of losing their children. However, as seen from the cases above, divorce is common in the mixed marriages in the Muslim community in Hong Kong because of cultural and religious difficulties. And in the case of Yasmin, the frequent lecturer for Islamic courses, not only did she divorce, but she also remarried and found her decision religiously sound. Among all five interviewees, although there are variant degrees of qualification, divorce is generally acknowledged to be permissible by *Qur'an* 4: 21. The clause includes some detailed instructions such as a cooling period of three months so that the woman is clear of any pregnancy, and/so(?) that she will get all her *mahr* (dowry) and keep the custody of her children if divorce is initiated by the man. And divorce can be initiated independently by women as well. Within the faith, divorce is not encouraged because the Muslim marriage is intended to last. It is only the last resort for spouses who fail to live in kindness with one another. Taking divorce as a lawful option for the irreconcilable differences of married couples allows the parties concerned to make peace afterward. According to Amina Wadud, the Qur'anic wisdom here aims at harmonious reconciliation: "…it is no sin for the two of them if they make terms of peace between themselves, peace is better." (4: 128)[37]

Yasmin is most definite about the *Qur'an*'s permission of divorce and remarriage. "Islam…has given us plenty of rights; some of them are not permitted in other religions. Let's say divorce for instance, there is restriction to men's initiation only in other religions, women are not allowed to initiate it, but in my case I was the one who initiated it." She is well aware of the *Qur'an*'s discouragement of divorce as a general principle, but she is also sure of its permission when necessary. "When something develops to an extent where its disadvantages have outweighed its advantages, it is permissible. The pretext is that we have thought through it, not making any decision in haste. We had thought through it, whether it is appropriate to continue or not."[38] The couple also sought the opinion of a third party and did soul searching through prayers. In short, the process was not taken lightly. Indeed, parting amicably is a way of making peace between the two parties. Despite her remarriage, Yasmin and her former husband remain friends and would occasionally meet and dine at the restaurant of the Islamic Union with their daughters. In the process of contemplation for divorce, Zameena is sure that this is not what Allah likes to see. "But when you run into marital problem, Muslim brothers and sisters would advise you to be bearing, until there is no other way may one initiate divorce."[39] With the *Qur'an*'s affirmation of divorce as the last resort, Zameena does not need to be forced into choosing between divorce and her faith. Rather, faith has been the reason legitimizing her choice to divorce.

37 Wadud, *Qur'an and Woman*, 80.

38 Interview on 17/7/2010.

39 Interview on 14/8/2010.

Having observed many failed marriages, Aleeza contends that the only situation which calls for Muslim women's consideration of divorce is when they discover that their husbands no longer follow the Islamic way. As mentioned above, the weight of faith is a determinant in the women's assessments of their marital crises. Indeed, Yasmin has been very serious about her faith and has become a learned teacher through her completion of the Islamic programme at the University of Malaya. Throughout the interview, she seemed to feel basically guiltless as a divorcee and showed no remorse in her decision, either in terms of her religious belief or her social position in the community. She stands firm as she defends this as the right of a Muslim woman guaranteed by the *Qur'an*. Reasoning in a more sophisticated way, Zameena prefaced her thoughts on divorce with her pride over her recent spiritual ascendance. "Honestly, my husband is not a good follower. As I learn more about my religion, the more distance is felt in my relationship with him." From clashes of cultural values, personal behavior and styles of living for intermarried couples, the difficulties are "transformed" into a sophisticated justification of women's rights in the initiation of divorce by way of faith. As expressed by both Yasmin and Zameena above, a faith assessment is exercised on both parties of the couple concerned and a divorce is sanctified if it consists of three factors: first, that the man is not a "true" follower of Islam; second, that the woman has reached a level of piety much more advanced than that of her husband; and third, as scripturally instructed, it is a last resort to achieving reconciliation and making peace with one another. In sum, Islam turns out to be much more modernist than many people would think. In comparison to evangelical Christians in Hong Kong who still see divorce as something violating the divine will, Islam is much more open to siding with the welfare of women who face marital difficulties, and as such, Islam is more ready to address the issues of changing marital relationships in today's society. Most interestingly, the religion that the world believes to be most oppressive to women in the family turns out to be a more liberating tool for the Hong Kong-Chinese Muslim women in need.

IV CONCLUSION

In an early volume on *Today's Woman in World Religions* edited by Arvind Sharma in 1994, Jane I. Smith argues that despite the diverse cultures and situations in reality, there is a certain universality espoused by Islam regarding the basic understanding of the traditional roles for women. And whether one likes it or not, the question of women is caught at the centre of the tensions between the resort to Islamic fundamentalism, traditionalism, or revivalism and Muslims' struggle to reconcile their heritage with the ongoing legacy of Western imperialism and the challenges of the modern world. As a result, the question of Muslim women is the key to the discussion and debate about the meaning of being a Muslim in all modern societies.[40] However, these arguments and debates take place without more careful examinations on the ground. If one also takes into consideration the gap between official teachings and the diversity of interpretations and practices on the ground. In brief, the experiences of the five women in this study introduce a necessarily complex picture of any religious

40 Jane I. Smith, "Women in Islam," in *Today's Woman in World Religions*, ed. Arvind Sharma (New York: State University of New York Press, 1994), 303.

community which is often situated at the centre of historical, political and social crossroads, weaving together many threads of cultures in a social tapestry for some deep and profound understanding. In this picture, women play a key role in the interweaving process and contribute to complicate the understanding of religion and culture with their quiet presence as well as active agency in negotiation.

Of the five women interviewed, the only case with a "straightforward" Chinese family genealogy is that of Man Kei. Her experience has not been elaborated on because of the attention given to intermarriage above. Man Kei's family is actually more typical of the emigrated Chinese Muslims who have carried strong dual traditions of both Chinese *and* Muslim cultures. It is a characteristic of a "traditional" Chinese family that members of the full extended family network stay closely in touch. They were especially helpful when Man Kei's daughter, son, and husband had consecutively suffered from chronic and terminal diseases, from which she eventually lost her infant boy and her middle-aged husband. And yet it is at the same time characteristic of a faithful Islamic family that religion plays the key to Man Kei's continuous striving despite her loss. In her recall, religion makes sense out of her otherwise unbearable life and provides her with a sense of purpose to live on. "Thanks to Allah who teaches me to see through [the meaning of life]." And "if I do well now, I shall be accountable to Allah when we meet later."[41] However, given the implicit and explicit multicultural facets of the Muslim community in Hong Kong, is it really meaningful to talk about Chinese or Muslim families as such in the case of Man Kei and beyond?

41 Interview on 31/8/2010.

One does not have to go to the abundant literature reviewing the diversities in belief and practices in Chinese and Muslim families to dispute the point. Neither is it useful to engage in the question of whether the Chinese tradition or the Islamic tradition is more oppressive to women. Rita Gross once argued that since every male dominated society includes female members, it is important to understand how women, who rather than remain powerless, react to such male dominance as it is warranted by the official tradition . The question for us would rather examine ways that women have exercised their "informal" power, as distinct to official authority, to make their lives meaningful and livable for their loved ones as well as for themselves.[42] Indeed, there is no Chinese or Muslim family in their "pure" sense, or women in complete subordination or full freedom in either system as generally believed. What we see in the cases of Yasmin, Zameena, Aleeza, Man Kei, and Rania is the blending of their religious devotion in terms of *salah*, eating *halal* food, and veiling with modern urban values including work-family balance, flexible parenting, women's right to divorce, and more egalitarian gender roles, and all done in the broad context of Chinese familial practices such as filial piety, caring for sibling relationships and a strong sense of male responsibility.

In the everyday realities of the women interviewed for this study, rather than a doubling effect generated from the meeting of patriarchies, there is some new space created out of their convergence because no single tradition has the final say as a consequence. When Yasmin and Zameena lifted up Islamic teachings for the defense of their decision or intention to divorce, religion has offered them alternative references for negotiating with their husbands for an exit from

42 Rita M. Gross, *Feminism & Religion: An Introduction* (Boston: Beacon Press, 1996), 68-69.

their marital crises. And when they feel trapped in their intermarriages, they utilize the difference between Chinese and South Asian traditions and customs to make their cases. In short, I find that the mixture of cultures in the hybrid history and society of Hong Kong has actually offered additional venues for women's negotiation with their expected familial roles and responsibilities and has opened up for them much more room for negotiation in cases of marital crises than in the case of Christianity in Hong Kong.

Bibliography

Beyer, Lisa. 2001. "The Women of Islam." *TIME: World*, November 25. http://www.time.com/time/world/article/0,8599,185647,00.html#ixzz1uvSuT4i7.

Gross, Rita. 1996. *Feminism & Religion: An Introduction*. Boston: Beacon Press.

Ho, Wai-Yip. 2001. "Historical Analysis of Islamic Community Development in Hong Kong:Struggle for Recognition in the Post-colonial Era." *Journal of Muslim Affair* 21(1): 63-77.

Hong Kong Yearbook 2010.

Karim, Jamillah Ashira. 2009. *American Muslim Women: Negotiating Race, Class, and Gender within the Ummah*. New York: New York University Press.

Kristin, Aune, Sonya Sharma, and Giselle Vincent, eds. 2007. *Women and Religion in the West: Challenging Secularization*. Hamphire: Ashgate.

Krivenko, Ekaterina Yahyaoui. 2009. *Women, Islam and International Law: Within the Context of the Convention on the Elimination of All Forms of Discrimination against Women*. Leiden: Martinus Nijhoff Publishers.

Lughod, Lina, ed. 1998. *Remaking Women: Feminism and Modernity in the Middle East*. Princeton: Princeton University Press.

Pluss, Caroline. 2000. "Hong Kong's Muslim Organization: Creating and Expressing Collective Identities." *China Perspectives* 29 (May-June):19-23.

Smith, Jane I. 1994. "Women in Islam." In *Today's Woman in World Religions*, ed. Arvind Sharma, 303-325. New York: State University of New York Press.

Sharma, Arvind, ed. 1994. *Today's Woman in World Religions*. New York: State University of New York Press.

Vaid, K. N. 1972. *The Overseas Indian Community in Hong Kong*. Hong Kong: Centre for Asian Studies, University of Hong Kong.

Wadud, Amina. 1999. *Qur'an and Woman: Rereading the Sacred Text from a Woman's*

Perspective. New York: Oxford University Press.

Wadud, Amina. 2006. *Inside the Gender Jihad: Women's Reform in Islam*. Oxford: Oneworld.

Weiss, Anita M. 1991. "South Asian Muslims in Hong Kong: Creation of a "Local Boy" Identity." *Modern Asian Studies* 25(3):417-453.

杜瑞樂(Thoraval, Joel)著、張寧譯。1991。〈葬禮與祈禱之安排：香港回教信托基金總會歷史概貌〉。收《廣東民族研究論叢》，廣東省民族研究學會、廣東省民族研究所編(第五輯)；221-248。廣州：廣東人民出版社。

湯開建(Tong Kaijian)。1996。〈兩次戰爭時期香港穆斯林的發展和變化(續上期)〉。《東南亞研究》，1:57-60。

湯開建、田映霞(Tong Kaijian and Tien Yingxia). 1995.〈香港伊斯蘭教的起源與發展〉。《東南亞研究》，6:48-51。

劉淑英(Liu Shuying)。1998。〈興學育人，桃李輩出：記香港中華回教博愛社辦學歷程〉。《回民研究》，29, 1: 84-85。

Being Minority and Being Female: Gender and Social Capital among the Nepalese in Postcolonial Hong Kong

TAM Siumi Maria

I BACKGROUND

Historically, the first generation of Nepalese women traveled to British Hong Kong as wives of the Gurkha soldiers in the British Army. They lived in the colony for a period of two to five years as dependents of the soldiers, and were physically secluded, as they were restricted to the barracks. As a colored minority in a predominantly Chinese society, they were misunderstood at best, and socially and culturally discriminated against at worst.

The second generation of Nepalese women consisted of the daughters of these transnational marriages, who experienced a reverse migration back to the mountain kingdom as their mothers' sojourns ended. They were raised in a split household, away from their fathers, but nonetheless brought up among his kin and thus socialized in a highly patriarchal family structure centered on the needs of the male members. In the 1990s these daughters of former Gurkha soldiers returned to Hong Kong, not as individual migrants, but as wives of yet another generation of Nepalese men. Daughters of these transnational marriages constituted the third generation of migrant women. As granddaughters of ex-Gurkhas they sought to settle permanently in their birthplace, and demanded the right to be educated and the right to work. While they considered Hong Kong their second home, and indeed many considered themselves *Hongkongese* (in Cantonese: *heunggongyahn*, people of Hong Kong), they were faced with the daunting prospect of unemployment, domestic abuse, and ethnic discrimination, which their mothers and grandmothers had experienced.

Among the three generations of women migrants, dissimilarities emerge in the motivations and circumstances surrounding their migration decisions. Yet there is an obvious common denominator among them, which is the female submission to arranged marriage, parental authority, and familial duty. In different stages of their lives, gender roles as wife and mother have been central to decisions related to women's livelihoods and futures. This study is based on in-depth interviews of Nepalese residents in Hong Kong between 2006 and 2008. In addition, focus group discussions and participation observation of Nepalese family, religious and community life were carried out. The data collected shows that the women migrants were important building blocks of a transnational network, as well as agents in the maintenance of family and cultural integrity, as they accessed and utilized social capital. In the process, however, the women often found themselves neglected and victimized, becoming a voiceless and invisible subaltern group in metropolitan Hong Kong. In the discussion below, all informants are given pseudonyms. In some instances, personal data are altered to protect individuals' privacy.

II BEING MINORITY IN HONG KONG

Being an ethnic minority is a very complex experience because minority status is multi-layered and multi-determined. According to government figures, there are approximately 15,000 people of Nepalese origin in Hong Kong, making up 0.2% of the total population.[1] Undoubtedly, the Nepalese are the smallest ethnic group in terms of population size. However, they have a unique place in the history of Hong Kong, as they had served in the British Army stationed in Hong Kong between 1948 and 1997. Their famed combat skills and service in Hong Kong have earned them a respect that other South Asians groups do not enjoy.[2] However, since 1997, when China regained sovereignty over Hong Kong, their relationship to the people of Hong Kong also changed. Those Nepalese who chose to stay in Hong Kong could no longer stay separated in their own community as they previously did in the army camps. After the British Army left Hong Kong, Nepalese men's employment opportunities have been limited to occupations that are extensions of their military background. A large majority of them are employed as security guards, construction workers, and nightclub bouncers. The few who are able to break

1 See the periodic reports by the Hong Kong Government, compiled by the Hong Kong Census and Statistics Department: *Population Census Thematic Report –Ethnic Minorities*, Hong Kong Special Administrative Region Government, Hong Kong, 2001; and Bi-Census, Hong Kong Special Administrative Region Government, Hong Kong, 2005.

2 L Caplan, *Warrior Gentleman*: "*Gurkhas*" *in the Western Imagination*, Berghahn Books, Providence, 1995.

out of this job stereotypification are the entrepreneurs, who have started their own small businesses in neighborhoods where South Asians congregate. They typically open grocery stores that sell ingredients and spices for ethnic South Asian dishes, or general supplies stores that sell various items imported from Nepal, including Nepalese folk and pop music CDs and movie VCDs. Most of these small businesses cater toward fellow Nepalese needs, but also trade in other South Asian items to serve Indian and Pakistani customers. Some have started small café style or street corner stalls that sell snacks like momo and masala tea, and the more affluent ones open restaurants that sell both Nepalese and Indian dishes to widen their clientele. An educated few have gone into education, opening a number of kindergartens as well as a primary school that ethnic minority children attend. The Nepalese also have their own temples. Although many of them are Buddhist, they follow the Tibetan tradition and carry out a totally different set of rituals based on a different set of holy scripts. Their temples in Hong Kong are run by the religiously knowledgeable in the community and are nestled in apartment buildings, and priests are regularly invited from Nepal to perform specialized and seasonal rituals. These factors indicate that being an ethnic minority in Hong Kong means leading a lifestyle that is both physically isolated and socially marginalized .

This segregated existence is complicated by one's gender especially as it interfaces with the transnational migration process and the traditional marriage institution. Among the Nepalese women in Hong Kong, while their mobility was not forced in the sense that they were trafficked, it was conspicuously carried out as part of an arranged marriage package. Thus for the women involved, these arranged migration-marriages carried a much higher sense of uncertainty and anxiety. Experiences of individual women interviewees cited below will show how arranged marriage and migration across national borders have combined to produce a ghetto effect for the female Nepalese migrants in their families and in society. As the women tried every day to recreate the Nepalese ideal mother-wife in a Chinese society, they were disenfranchised due to a lack of social capital, especially in three areas: education, employment, and health service. For Nepalese men, this structural lack has led to further problems such as drug addiction and criminal offenses. For women, however, this has further reinforced their gender inferiority and relegation to the domestic sphere.

The knowledge void in these ethnically specific problems could be attributed partly to the "sinicization" of anthropological research in Hong Kong, which has led to a false consciousness that Hong Kong is an ethnically homogenous society, and that ethnic relations and attendant problems do not exist. Since the 1970s, academic interest was focused squarely on sub-ethnicity among the Chinese. Fred Blake and Nicole Constable studied the Hakkas, Hsieh Jiann studied the Huizhou community, and Gregory Gulden studied the Fujianese, to name just a few. An exception is Barbara Sue White who studied the Indians in Hong Kong in the 1980s, but since then little scholarship has emerged. It was the historians (such as Carl Smith) who took interest in the British-Chinese ethnic relationships, but most of the work focused on the expatriates of the early 20th century.[3] By the late 1980s, the focus was on foreign domestic workers and the problems they encountered.[4] It was not until the last five years that ethnic

3 See for example the following works of scholars on ethnicity in Hong Kong society : C F Blake, *Ethnic Groups and Social Change in a Chinese Market Town*, University of Hawaii Press, Honolulu, 1981; N Constable, *Christian Souls and Chinese Spirits: A Hakka Community in Hong Kong*, University of California Press, Berkeley, 1994; C Smith, *A Sense of History: Studies in the Social and Urban History of Hong Kong*, Hong Kong Educational Publishing Co, Hong Kong, 1995; and B S White, *Turbans and Traders: Hong Kong's Indian Communities*, Oxford University Press, Hong Kong and New York, 1994.

4 Examples of this body of work on foreign domestic workers are: N Constable, *Maid to Order in*

minorities of South Asian origin have begun to attract social attention, albeit negatively—they were stereotyped as welfare abusers and a potential threat to the population mix as their numbers increased at the rate of 10,000 (14%) per year.[5]

The construction of a racial harmony discourse in Hong Kong was conveniently carried out by stressing the fact that 95% of the Hong Kong population is of Chinese origin. As the remaining 5%, the ethnic minorities are characteristically listed as consisting of British, Canadians, Japanese, Koreans and persons of South Asian origin, and so on. But a hierarchy exists among the minorities, in both consciousness and practice, and is largely based on class and the Chinese population's experience of British colonialism. Unfortunately, in everyday life this hierarchy manifests as a 19th century misunderstanding of race – one that is ranked according to the shade of skin color. For a long time, "foreigners" in Hong Kong's mainstream Chinese society meant only white people, and the existence of other ethnic groups was simply ignored.

Hong Kong: Stories of Filipina Workers. Cornell University Press, Ithaca, 1997; and, C French, *Filipina Domestic Workers in Hongkong: A Preliminary Survey*. Centre for Hong Kong Studies, Institute of Social Studies, the Chinese University of Hong Kong, Hong Kong, 1986.

5 For responses from social welfare providers, see: Hong Kong Polytechnic University Department of Applied Social Sciences, and Hong Kong Christian Service Project SASA, *A Research Report on the Social Situations of Ethnic Minority Women in Hong Kong*, Hong Kong, 2007. There were also a couple of postgraduate theses written on the subject. One is by S Lotter, *The Nepalese Community in Hong Kong after July 1997*. MA Thesis, Social Anthropology, School of Oriental and African Studies, the University of London, London, 1997. Another one is by K P Yung, *We Have No Choice! Social Exclusion and Citizenship of the Nepalese Community in Hong Kong*, MPhil Thesis, Sociology, the Chinese University of Hong Kong, Hong Kong, 2002.

III THE GENDEREDNESS OF BEING NEPALESE IN HONG KONG

From the beginning of the arrival of the Gurkha regiment before 1997, to the emergence of a business community today, the Nepalese migration to Hong Kong has been a highly gendered phenomenon. In the colonial period, the men served in the army, and the women joined them temporarily as their wives. In the post-colonial period, things have not changed much. While many of the daughters of the ex-Gurkhas were born in Hong Kong and hold permanent residency, they have migrated to Hong Kong not as individuals, but like their mothers as wives of a new generation of male immigrants.

In the following sections I will present data from the individual interviews of women informants. The interviewees were invited to individual interviews through snowball and stratified sampling. Two thirds of the interviewees were born in Hong Kong when their fathers were serving in the British Army stationed in Hong Kong, and the remaining interviewees were born in other British Commonwealth countries, where their fathers were stationed. All of the women settled in Hong Kong in the 1990s and so have lived in Hong Kong for over 10 years. In terms of education, all have received secondary education or hold a bachelor's degree. Regardless of their qualifications, they were able to find only low-income, low-status, and temporary jobs such as construction work, janitorial work, and work as kindergarten teachers. The only exception is a doctor who was trained in a non-commonwealth country, but who was not able to assert her qualifications in Hong Kong. Despite her working experience and professional knowledge, under the current laws she cannot practice independently and must work under the supervision of a local doctor.

In terms of marital status, all but one of the interviewees were married. The exception was the doctor mentioned above, who was engaged, her fiancé also living in Hong Kong. Without any exception, these marriages were arranged, though they varied in the degree of parental intervention and previous knowledge of the husband. In many of these cases, the women knew about the marriage only three days before. A typical recount was that they came home from school one day, and were told that they would be marrying a certain man. They would be shown a photograph of the future husband, and were asked to get ready to move to Hong Kong after the wedding. Arranged marriages often resulted in the interruption of the women's education. For example, one 27-year-old interviewee, Laxmi, was studying in her bachelor's program in Kathmandu when she was informed of her marriage, and had to stop her studies immediately. Similarly, Sushila was working on her master's program on Asian language and culture, but was recalled from overseas to return to Nepal in order to get married.

Among the informants, 32-year-old Lena presented an interesting case. Lena was married at the age of 17. After the wedding her husband returned to Hong Kong, but she was allowed to finish her postgraduate studies before joining her husband in Hong Kong. She stayed with her parents in Pokhara, Nepal's second largest city, and refused to move to her husband's village to live with her parents-in-law. This in effect led to a delayed transferred marriage that freed her from housewifery. However, although Lena was able to finish her studies, her dream of becoming an accountant in Japan did not materialise, as she had to transfer to her husband's home in Hong Kong soon after she completed her studies. But as she did not read or write Chinese, she was not able to find a job in accountancy, her field of training. Her arranged marriage also did not work out. Her husband was much older and they found no common interests between them, even after their child was born. When I interviewed Lena in her home, sitting on the floor

Nepalese style, she was full of grievances. Recalling her experience as a new migrant, she said,

> It [was] very hard for me to find a job or even make new friends. Even now my husband is very quiet, not talking much, and I have to do everything on my own... I got lost 3 times in Tsimshatsui.

Getting lost in Tsimshatsui, one of the busiest districts in Hong Kong, highlights Lena's experience and identity as a migrant lost in another culture. Her helplessness and anxiety was aggravated by the fact that her husband worked 12 hours a day at various construction sites, and often the couple did not see or talk to each other for days. As a wife without the protection of the all-important husband, she lamented that her marriage at age 17 to a man 12 years her senior, based simply on a photograph, was the most regrettable thing in her life. She said she could have enjoyed her life more if she had married later. When I asked her about future plans, she took me by surprise by saying, "I don't know...maybe I'll find another husband."

Lena did not choose to divorce, as she knew very well that a divorced woman runs the risk of being ostracized in the Nepalese migrant community. She would be looked down upon by her own relatives, and would bring shame to her family in Nepal. When I brought up the topic of marriage and divorce in my interviews, regardless of age all interviewees held the view that being married is the marker of a good woman, and one must work hard to live up to that image.

Another informant, Kumari provides a telling contrast. She was born in Hong Kong and as such had the right of abode. However, she also came to Hong Kong as the wife of a man whom she did not know before their wedding. Her mother's relative was the matchmaker, and she admitted that she was scared that she had to take part in a migration-marriage. But her friends convinced her, who she thought "gave her bad ideas that single women [particularly as migrants] would be insecure," and that fellow Nepalese would "gossip" if she lived alone.[6] Kumari recalled that on the day of arrival in Hong Kong she and her husband were picked up at the airport by a relative who let them stay in their apartment for a short period of time. But they could not offer much help, so she and her husband had to start looking for jobs. Very soon she was working at a McDonald's restaurant nearby. She also volunteered at an NGO so that she could acquire more work experience and expand her social network. She then proceeded to find herself a job as waiter at the American restaurant Ruby Tuesday, which paid much better. After a few months, she was working in the housekeeping department of a hotel as a room attendant, which again meant a raise in salary.

But Kumari's marriage was a traumatic experience, as her husband was violent and abusive. At the time of interview she had separated from him, and had started taking a facial massage course at a community center. Her eyes sparkled when she talked about how she would open her own beauty parlor, and how she would help other Nepalese women in training courses that she in turn will offer, so that her Nepalese sisters could stand on their own feet, just like herself. In the meantime, she was helping her ex-husband pay his debts from failed business ventures and gambling, and to raise their son on her own.

---

6 Scholars have pointed out how patriarchal relations have served to restrict women in Nepalese culture and society. See for example: I Majupuria, *Nepalese Women*, Tecpress Books, Bangkok, 1996; B Rana, and N Singh (eds), *Mother Sister Daughter: Nepal's Press on Women*. Vol. 2, Sancharika Samuha, Kathmandu, 2005; A Rana-Deuba, *A National Study on Changing Roles of Nepali Women due to Ongoing Conflict and its Impact*. Samanata Institute for Social and Gender Equality, Kathmandu, 2005; and L N Sangraula, *Foreign Employment for Women: Challenges and Opportunities*, Sancharika Samuha and UNIFEM, Kathmandu, 2003.

Yet she had always found time to do volunteer work in an elderly home or by helping illiterate Nepalese read letters. When I asked if there was anything the government should do for the Nepalese people, she was surprised that this question was even asked. After a few seconds she said the government should expedite the assignment of public housing for single mothers like herself, and provide free Chinese language classes and low-cost childcare.

Obviously Kumari was a very resourceful individual who was able to make use of, and constantly accumulate, various forms of capital, despite an unhappy marriage. She empowered herself by first building up and then constantly expanding her social networks through work and voluntary service, and freed herself from the social and cultural effacement that was so characteristic of Nepalese women in Hong Kong. She had rebuilt a selfhood independent of her husband. Yet despite this extraordinary sense of autonomy, she had retained a strong sense of familial responsibility, and believed that fulfilling wifely duties was "just natural" for women – even after their divorce, she continued to help pay her ex-husband's debts.

IV INSTITUTIONAL PROBLEMS: FAMILISM AND OCCUPATION

This concept of familism and women's roles as daughter, wife and mother is persistent among all informants in the study. Mamita, a thirty-year old school teacher, represented these roles as the fate of all women. She had tried hard to be a dutiful wife and protective mother, but her family life was not what she had imagined before coming to Hong Kong. One of her problems was the living conditions. Her family of three lived in a tiny apartment on the 5th floor of an old village house in the New Territories. The family chose to live there because the rent was affordable, and because almost everyone living in the building was Nepalese. As the building had no elevator, she had to climb the stairs several times a day, bringing heavy groceries home, and taking her child to and from kindergarten in town. Her only child was a victim of malpractice at a local hospital, and Mamita had trouble securing for her child the same education as local Chinese children. She could not understand the government notices mailed to her, and had few friends except the Nepalese women in neighboring apartments, who occupied similarly isolated situations. She said she had to tackle all of these problems on her own, as her husband was away at work most of the day, and the lack of communication between the couple led to the disintegration of their marriage.

However, Mamita justified the failure of her family life as the personality mismatch between herself and her husband, and was unable to see that it could be due to structural factors such as their arranged marriage, parental authority over her mobility, or the Hong Kong government's lack of sensibility towards the conditions of ethnic minorities. Other than hoping that the government would relax its housing policy so that her family could apply for public housing sooner, she did not feel that her negative experience as a migrant wife and mother should be dealt with on a government or social-cultural level. Such personalization of difficulties was common among the interviewees. As a result, it led to a misplacement of problem ownership, which further contributed to the maintenance and reproduction of asymmetric relations; firstly, between mainstream Chinese society and its ethnic minorities, and secondly, between women and men in household power relations.

Employment is another important area in which Nepalese women suffered from gender and ethnic segregation. For Nepalese men, employment opportunities were often defined by ethnic stereotypes. Regardless of their education level and employment background, they were limited to occupations that were related to their supposed physical prowess and an imagined military background, and as such a large majority of them became security guards and construction workers.[7] For the women, employment opportunities are even scarcer. Eight of my informants alternated between fulltime housewifery and unemployment. Those who were employed found work mostly in low-paying and insecure positions, especially those that were an extension of their domestic duties. Among the 23 interviewees, one was a janitor, four were kindergarten or primary school teachers, and one was a minder in an after-school childcare centre. The other available (and acceptable) jobs were those that were considered feminine. Two informants were working as, or training to be, beauticians, and another one was a junior stylist in a hair salon. The entrepreneurial few started their own small businesses. They opened tiny shops in rather worn-out shopping centres in older parts of town, specializing in clothes alteration, facial massage, and hairdressing. They would also sell clothing and costume jewelry from Nepal, as well as cosmetics and undergarments from mainland China. Without exception, these private enterprises catered to fellow Nepalese, and Indians and Pakistanis, as well as the occasional Chinese customers looking for ethnic exoticism.

While these jobs, or owning small enterprises did empower the women migrants and provide them with financial autonomy, nonetheless the nature of the occupations, being defined as feminine and therefore appropriate for good, proper family women, ironically further reinforced the glass walls of gender

7 S Frost, Building Hong Kong: Nepalese Labor in the Construction Sector, *Journal of Contemporary Asia* Vol 34-3, 2004, pp.364-376.

job segregation, and help to perpetuate patriarchal values in accordance with traditional Nepalese culture. Instead of insisting on fair treatment in mainstream institutions such as formal education and professional training which would help them develop skills that would allow them to climb the social ladder, they created ethnic niches to which many retreated. This not only limited their own personal career development but also produced intergenerational subordination for their daughters, leaving systemic discrimination in the form of ethnic segregation and gender segregation unchallenged, and reinforcing the concept that suffering is destiny. It would be unfair to blame the victims, as equitable access to social capital is not only the responsibility of the individual, but also of the society at large. We will now turn to discuss the role of the government in the next section.

V GOVERNMENT ROLE

The introduction of the Race Discrimination Ordinance in 2008 served to remind members of Hong Kong society that ethnic inequality is alive and well, and that it needs to be regulated through legislation.[8] But the lack of open-mindedness and willingness to see ethnic diversity as a social and cultural asset will in the long run dampen any efforts in this direction. Rather, ethnic difference was seen as a burden on social welfare services. A good example is

8 For legal consultation documents, see Hong Kong Home Affairs Bureau, *Joining Hands for Social Harmony with Respect, Affection, Care and Equality: An Introduction to the Race Discrimination Bill*, Hong Kong Special Administrative Region Government, Hong Kong, 2006; and Hong Kong Home Affairs Bureau, *Legislative Council Brief – Race Discrimination Bill*, Hong Kong Special Administrative Region Government, Hong Kong, 2006.

the notorious education reform, which includes the policy to "integrate" all ethnic minority children into the mainstream educational system. This policy was simplistically interpreted as placing minority children in regular classes with local Chinese-speaking students, and taught by local teachers in Chinese as a medium of instruction. The policy elides the specific needs of ethnic minority school children—one blatant problem is the lack of development in the basic needs of school children—and holds no provisions for enhancement programs in Chinese as a second language. Disadvantaged in language and lacking tools to communicate and to learn, minority children underperformed in the schooling system, which translated into underachievement in secondary school and a barrier to university education. Researchers in education studies (such as Coleman and Hoffer 1987) show that social capital and education are highly correlated. While there are no ethnic-specific statistics showing how Nepalese girls are disadvantaged in Hong Kong's schooling system, studies on the education system in Nepal may shed some light on the social complexity of the issue. According to a UNGEI report, while girls' enrollment rates in primary school level is high, there is a lack of quality learning opportunities for girls, which reflects "how communities still give priority to boys when it comes to quality education" (Nora Fyles, senior advisor on education of the Canadian International Development Agency, quoted in Corporal 2012). In Corporal's view, Nepal is a society where "boys are still much preferred over girls who are often considered burdens to the family, the latter bear the brunt of inadequate educational opportunities. Boys are expected to get higher education and get good jobs" (Corporal 2012).

A constant strategy that the Hong Kong government employs is to outsource ethnic minority services to non-government organizations. Often fixed-term contracts are meted out, but it is uncertain how efficacious the programs are in eliminating unequal access to social resources for ethnic minority groups. More comprehensive services for the Nepalese are provided for as part of South Asian service programs by various Catholic and Christian charity organizations. These organizations have begun providing employment training and language classes to Hongkongese of Nepalese origin. In Nepal, volunteers such as Christie Lam and her friends, who had started a school in the hills in Dhading, are providing education to village children in the vicinity.[9]

VI CONCLUSION

As the data presented above shows, the patriarchal ideology and family system that originated from Nepal is an important factor in keeping migrant Nepalese women ghettoized. Coupled with gender and ethnic inequality in mainstream Chinese society, being both female and an ethnic minority in Hong Kong makes it doubly difficult for Nepalese women to realize individual potential and exercise their citizens' rights. A policy aiming to improve the situation of minority groups must take into consideration gender-specific factors that intervene into the factors challenging individuals' lives. Past research has shown that sustainable development is best practiced through providing women with social capital, as they are directly engaged in the maintenance of the family and socializing children. Providing women with instruments of change will help break cycles of poverty and underdevelopment. To achieve this

9 See D C Cheung's journal report, 'School in the Sky: Hong Kong Girl Bringing Warmth to Nepal Mountain Region', in the Christmas special edition of *Ming Pao Weekly*, 24 December 2005, pp. 36-50.

goal, it is imperative that women are able to participate as partners of change, rather than as recipients of "help." More importantly, they should be treated, and treat themselves, as individuals with their own rights in public and private spaces, and not only as part of the family system in which they fulfill duties as daughters, wives and mothers.

Bibliography

Blake, C. F. 1981. *Ethnic Groups and Social Change in a Chinese Market Town*. Honolulu: University of Hawaii Press.

Caplan, L. 1995. *Warrior Gentleman: "Gurkhas" in the Western Imagination*. Providence: Berghahn Books.

Cheung, D. C. 2005. "School in the Sky: Hong Kong Girl Bringing Warmth to Nepal Mountain Region." *Ming Pao Weekly*, December 24, 36-50.

Coleman, J. S., and T. Hoffer. 1987. *Public and Private Schools: The Impact of Communities*. New York: Basic Books.

Constable, N. 1994. *Christian Souls and Chinese Spirits: A Hakka Community in Hong Kong*. Berkeley: University of California Press.

______. 1997. *Maid to Order in Hong Kong: Stories of Filipina Workers*. Ithaca: Cornell University Press.

Corporal, L. L. 2008. "NEPAL: Gender Inequality in Education Has Deep Roots." http://www.ipsnews.net/2008/06/nepal-gender-inequality-in-education-has-deep-roots/.

French, C. 1986. *Filipina Domestic Workers in Hongkong: A Preliminary Survey*. Hong Kong: Centre for Hong Kong Studies, Institute of Social Studies, the Chinese University of Hong Kong, Hong Kong.

Frost, S. 2004. "Building Hong Kong: Nepalese Labor in the Construction Sector." *Journal of Contemporary Asia* 34(3):364-376.

Hong Kong Census and Statistics Department. 2001. *Population Census Thematic Report –Ethnic Minorities*. Hong Kong Special Administrative Region Government, Hong Kong.

______. 2005. *Bi-Census*. Hong Kong Special Administrative Region Government, Hong Kong.

Hong Kong Home Affairs Bureau. 2006. *Joining Hands for Social Harmony with Respect, Affection, Care and Equality: An Introduction to the Race Discrimination Bill.* Hong Kong: Hong Kong Special Administrative Region Government.

______. 2006. *Legislative Council Brief–Race Discrimination Bill.* Hong Kong: Hong Kong Special Administrative Region Government.

Hong Kong Polytechnic University Department of Applied Social Sciences, and Hong Kong Christian Service Project SASA. 2007. *A Research Report on the Social Situations of Ethnic Minority Women in Hong Kong.* Hong Kong: Hong Kong Polytechnic University.

Lotter, S. 1997. "The Nepalese Community in Hong Kong after July 1997." MA Thesis, University of London.

Majupuria, I. 1996. *Nepalese Women.* Bangkok: Tecpress Books.

Rana, B., and N. Singh, eds. 2005. *Mother Sister Daughter: Nepal's Press on Women.* Vol. 2. Kathmandu: Sancharika Samuha.

Rana-Deuba, A. 2005. *A National Study on Changing Roles of Nepali Women due to Ongoing Conflict and its Impact.* Kathmandu: Samanata Institute for Social and Gender Equality.

Sangraula, L. N. 2003. *Foreign Employment for Women: Challenges and Opportunities.* Kathmandu: Sancharika Samuha and UNIFEM.

Smith, C. 1995. *A Sense of History: Studies in the Social and Urban History of Hong Kong.* Hong Kong: Hong Kong Educational Publishing Co.

White, B. S. 1994. *Turbans and Traders: Hong Kong's Indian Communities.* Hong Kong and New York: Oxford University Press.

Yung, K. P. 2002. "We Have No Choice! Social Exclusion and Citizenship of the Nepalese Community in Hong Kong." MPhil Thesis, Chinese University of Hong Kong.

Intergenerational Exchange Patterns Between Elderly Korean Women and Their Adult Children

LEE Shin-Young

I INTRODUCTION

1. Problem Statement

South Korea reached aging society in 2000, and is expected to enter aged society by 2018 and super-aged society by 2026. According to data from the National Statistical Office, 38.3% of elderly respondents believe their families are responsible for supporting them, while 37.8% believe it is the joint responsibility of their families, the government and their communities, and 18.4% believe it is their own responsibility to support themselves. The data show that the percentage of those who believe that families should take care of the elderly dropped, while the percentage of those who believe it is the joint responsibility of their families, government and community, or their own responsibility increased from four years ago. However, 61% of the respondents replied that they were not prepared for life after retirement, which is at least 20% more than the 39% who said that they were prepared. For the reasons for not being prepared, 54.4% said they could not afford it while 39.5% said they planned to rely on their children. When asked about how they would make a living after retirement, 51.9% of the respondents said they themselves or their spouses would earn money, 37.6% said they would depend on relatives or their children for living expenses, and 10.4% said they would rely on support from the government and social organizations. This data suggests that children are regarded as one of the most important resources for provisions of care for the elderly parents who have not been able to prepare for life after retirement. It holds particularly true when government-provided welfare services for the elderly are underdeveloped.

The unofficial network of an elderly person includes their family members such as their children and spouses, relatives by blood, and friends and neighbors. Previous studies on the elderly report that social support from unofficial networks is important because such support affects the quality of life and mental health of the elderly. A survey on elderly women living alone in farming and fishing villages found that with more frequent phone calls from their children, more neighbors and more frequent visits with their neighbors, came higher quality of life (Kim, Kang and Kim 2008). Other studies have reported similar findings: for elderly women living alone, their quality of life was affected by the level of closeness with their family and neighbors, and exchange of social support (Kim, An and Kang 2008). An investigation on the correlation of social support and elderly depression showed that the aged tended to have lower levels of depression when they were better aware of their family support and engaged in more frequent contacts with their friends (Rho and Mo 2007). The factors affecting the mental health of senior citizens living alone included not only their economic status and level of health, but also how often they came in contact with their children and whether and how much they received help from people around them (Han and Lee 2009). Another study reported that the intergenerational exchange of social support between elderly parents and adult children was closely related to the elders' level of satisfaction and psychological sense of well-being (Han and Han 2004; Lee 2003). Studies also found that elders' quality of life was higher when they maintained frequent contact and close relationships with their family rather than their relatives , friends or neighbors (Choi and Lee 2003).

Early studies on social support focused on the quantity and types of social support elderly parents received from their children. However, recent studies have paid attention to the intergenerational exchange of social support as elderly parents have, for instance, provided support for their adult children in the form of baby-sitting their grandchildren and doing others rather than only being recipients of support. Therefore, there are a number of ongoing studies on the intergenerational exchange of social support or mutual support in the relationships between elderly parents and adult children (Cheong 2007; Han and Han 2004; Lee 2003; Lim 2009; Yoon 2003). While some findings indicate that the elders who provided social support enjoyed a higher quality of life than those receiving support (Kim, An and Kang 2008; Lowenstein et al. 2007), there is a report that the elderly had a higher level of satisfaction with their lives when they had a balance in their exchange of support with their children (Kim and Kim 2000).

Studies on the exchange of social support are mostly conducted on the elderly population as a whole, and only a few of the surveys focus exclusively on elderly women. The female elderly population is 1.6 times bigger in number than the male elderly population and has a longer average life expectancy, but faces poorer health and economic conditions. In addition, elderly women appeared to have higher rates of dissatisfactory relationships with their children than their male counterparts (Statistics Korea 2011). Therefore, studies on social support for elderly women who live in relatively poorer conditions are significant in that they do not view the elderly population as a homogeneous group and, thus, provide basic data for the development of tailor-made services for the aged population who face a variety of needs.

In the meantime, the types of elderly households are undergoing rapid change. The comparison of results from the Survey on Service Needs of Older Persons in Korea in 2004 and 2008 reveals that while the percentage of single elderly households and elderly couple households respectively increased, the percentage of the households where elderly parents lived with their children decreased. More specifically, the rate of the single elderly households rose by 6.1% from 20.6% in 2004 to 26.7% in 2008, and the elderly couple households rose by 5.3% from 34.4% to 39.7%, while the rate of the aged living with their adult children dropped by 10% from 38.6% to 28.6% during the same period (Cheong et al. 2005; Ministry of Health and Welfare 2009). Both the rate of one-elderly-person households and one-elderly-couple households are expected to continue rising as a report by the National Statistical Office (Statistics Korea 2010) showed that 6 out of 10 people aged 65 or over replied that they did not want to live together with their children in the future. As this signals changes in the makeup of elderly households, we need to look at the social support provided for each type of household.

2. Subject for Inquiry

This study explores the intergenerational exchange of social support between elderly mothers and their adult children. Both structural and functional aspects as well as the extent and types of social support to and from both directions are studied. The households are categorized into two types: one-elderly-person household and one-elderly-couple household.

This study focuses particularly on the following questions.

First, what are the structural characteristics of the intergenerational exchange of support shown among elderly women, namely, the number of offspring, frequency of contact with and visits to and from their children and the geographical distance between the elderly women and their children's places of residence? Is there any difference in the characteristics between the two types of households?

Second, which types of social support are exchanged to what extent in each area of intergenerational exchange, and is there any difference between the two types of households? Third, what are the factors that affect the types of intergenerational social support that elderly women both provide and receive?

II THEORETICAL BACKGROUND

1. Characteristics of Aged Women

When elderly women were compared with their male counterparts in terms of demographic, economic, physical, social, and emotional characteristics, both genders showed a distinct difference in each of the areas. First, when compared in census demographics, while the number of men aged 65 and over was 2.19 million, women in that age bracket numbered 1.6 times more at 3.167 million. As of 2009, the average expected remaining years of life for elderly men was 17 years, while it was 21.5 years for elderly women, which projects an increase of 2.9 years for men and 3.5 years for women from 10 years ago (Statistics Korea 2011).

Second, data on their economic status revealed that the economic activity rates for men and women aged 65 and over as of 2010 were 40.6% and 21.7% respectively. The rate of future job seekers among the male elderly was as high as 72% while it was only 46.8% among the female elderly. In the same age bracket, the rate of female recipients of the Basic Livelihood Security service was 9.0%, 1.9 times more than the rate of male recipients at 4.9% (Statistics Korea 2011).

Third, the main cause of death of elderly men was cancer, followed by cerebrovascular disease, heart disease, chronic lower respiratory disease and diabetes, while cancer, cerebrovascular disease, heart disease, diabetes and pneumonia in that order were the major killers of women aged 65 and older (Statistics Korea 2011). In 2008, when asked how they perceived their physical condition, 28.4% of men and 13.6% of women aged 65 and over responded that they were in good condition, while 33.2% of men and 30.7% of women responded that they were in mediocre condition and 38.3% of the male respondents and 58.5% of the female respondents perceived their physical condition as being poor. These numbers indicate that more elderly women perceive their health to be poor than do elderly men (Statistics Korea 2010).

Fourth, the data demonstrates that elderly men and women spent about 7 hours and 6 hours respectively on engaging in leisure activities, and that elderly women spent more hours on religious and networking activities than elderly men did (Statistics Korea 2011).

Fifth, elderly women living on their own scored 2.87 on a scale of 5 with 5 indicating the best quality of life in the quality of life survey (Kim, An and Kang 2008), and the average quality of life score of elderly women living alone in rural areas was a bit higher at 2.94 (Kim, Kang and Kim 2008). The female elderly were more susceptible to depression than their male counterparts (Kim 2009). Similar findings were produced in a survey which used the Zung Self-Rating Depression Scale: elderly women living alone showed a higher level of depression than elderly men living alone (Seo and Kim 2003). On the other hand, some studies find that male seniors were more depressed than female seniors. A survey on people aged 65 and older who lived alone in the suburban areas of Tokyo showed that 40.7% of men and 30.5% of women complained of depression (Sun et al. 2007). A study on the level of depression among frail senior citizens living alone in cities in Korea also found that male seniors showed higher levels of depression than did female seniors (Kim and Seo 2010).

As for the level of satisfaction with the relationship with their children, elderly women were found to be less satisfied at 7.3% than their male counterparts at 5.5% (Statistics Korea 2011). The number of male divorcees aged 65 and over was 4,346, making up 3.7% of the total male divorcees of all ages, while aged female divorcees numbered at 1,734, accounting for 1.5% of the total female divorcees. This is an increase of 2.6% and 1.1% respectively from 10 years ago. The number of remarriages among people aged 65 and over was also on the rise with 2,099 men and 702 women in that age bracket remarrying in 2010, which is respectively 2.2 times and 3.5 times more than the number of remarriages in 2000 (Statistics Korea 2011).

As studies show, elderly women are poorer, in a worse state of health, and with lower levels of psychological well-being than elderly men. As the number of elderly women is expected to grow with the increase in average life expectancy, elderly women will remain a focal point for senior welfare policies.

2. Intergenerational Social Support Exchanged by Elderly People

Social support can be measured both quantitatively and qualitatively. The qualitative measurement focuses on satisfaction in relationships while the quantitative measurement evaluates the structural and functional aspects of social support. The structural aspect includes the frequency of contact or visit, geographical proximity, and the size of a support network. The functional aspect mainly focuses on the various types of support from a support-provider (Cantor and Little 1985; recited in Choi and Lee 2003)

Scholars define the sub-categories of social support in diverse ways. Seo and Kim (2010) include forms of support such as economic, emotional and physical (accompaniment to hospitals) support. Some studies include physical support such as accompanying elders to hospitals in the instrumental support category. For example, Bae Jin Hee (2004) divided social support into instrumental, informational and emotional support. Instrumental support includes taking care of house chores such as meal preparation and cleaning, nursing, accompanying elders to hospitals, or providing or lending living expenses or pocket money. Informational support involves helping elders to understand documents or laws. Emotional support is measured by whether there is someone who actually cares for or pays attention to elderly people, and whether he or she is reliable and can be trusted. Lim Hyo Yeon (2009) also included caring for or nursing ill people, helping with house chores and providing help when one is away from home in the category of instrumental support, while defining emotional support as giving counsel to elderly people when they are worried or concerned about something.

Lee Hyong Sil (2003) categorized social support into financial, instrumental and emotional support, and included in the category of instrumental support not only assisting in house chores or grocery shopping, but also providing counseling. Some studies conducted overseas did not include physical support in any of the categories above (Lowenstein, et al. 2007; Wang and Li 2008). As indicated above, the sub-categorization of social support varies depending on the researchers. My own research divides social support into categories of emotional, instrumental and physical support.

Intergenerational support takes many forms, such as unidirectional support either from adult children to their aging parents or from aging parents to their adult children, or mutually exchanged support. A study conducted by Choi Jeong Hye (2009) is among many that consider one-sided support extended by adult children to their aging parents; in her study, she compared patterns of filial piety activities of adult children in Korea and in the United States. Choi found that financial caregiving was the most prevalent form of caregiving among Korean adult children, followed by emotional and service caregiving. By comparison, adult children in the United States were found to be most actively engaged in emotional caregiving activities, followed by service and financial caregiving. A study on single elderly females in need of public assistance found that, among all types of support provided by adult children, financial, emotional and physical support accounted for 76.6%, 85.9% and 47.6% respectively (Seo and Kim 2010).

More recent studies focus on both the provision and reception sides of social support exchanged between aging parents and their adult children, rather than just on one-sided support giving. Studies in other countries found that elderly people received more emotional and instrumental supports than they provided (Lowenstein et al. 2007; Wang and Li 2008). Cheong Byeong Eun (2007) studied the reciprocity of intergenerational support and found that elderly parents received most from their adult children physical support, followed by emotional and financial support. Emotional support was most frequently exchanged, and tended to flow from parents to their children, while financial support was the least frequently exchanged, and tended to flow from adult children to their aging parents.

Other nationwide surveys on elderly people also examine both the receiving and giving aspects of intergenerational support. A 2004 study on financial, physical, instrumental and emotional support provided or received by elderly parents found that the support provision rate was in the 50% range for the categories of listening to problems, cleaning, laundry, and meal preparation, followed by financial support at 21.7%, nursing at 11.2% and baby-sitting grandchildren at 18.2%. The reception rate of such support as financial assistance, cleaning, laundry, meal preparation or listening to problems was over 70%, followed by nursing at 25.1% (Cheong et al. 2005).

Some studies moved beyond only looking into the degree of reception or provision of social support, and tried to identify various types of elderly people in terms of intergenerational social support. Kim and Kim (2000) found that the receiving (those who only receive support from children), mutual, giving and no-exchange types accounted for 25.2%, 65.2%, 1.6% and 8.9% of all elderly people respectively. Han and Han (2004) categorized intergenerational support into mutual, receiving, giving and no-exchange types. When it came to measuring financial support, the giving type in which only adult children provide support to their elderly parents predominated, while emotional support mainly consisted of the mutual type where parents and their adult children exchange support both ways. For instrumental support, the no-exchange type in which no support goes back and forth between the two parties was the most prevalent type. Lim Hyo Yeon (2009) conducted a survey on 1,020 elderly people living alone in the city of Osaka, Japan and found that the mutual type and the low-exchange type dominated emotional and instrumental support respectively.

Factors determining the type of social support include gender, age, health, and financial capability. Single elderly women were found to be receiving more instrumental and emotional support from their adult children than their male counterparts (Suh and Kim 2003). Lee Hyong Sil (2003) found that elderly men were providing more financial support than elderly women, and that elderly women tended to receive such support more than their male counterparts. Progression in age rarely affected the social support provided by adult children, but diminished the amount of social support provided by aged parents. The health status of aging parents does affect the reciprocity of social support. Healthy elderly people were found to provide support more than to receive it (Cheong 2007; Liten 2004). Other previous studies also showed that aging but financially able parents could indeed provide financial support to their children more than depend on their children for money. Aged parents (aged 55-75) with high incomes were very likely to provide financial support to their adult children (Grundy 2005). Cheong Byeong Eun (2007) also found that financial capability is a significant variable in the exchange of financial support.

III METHOD OF INQUIRY

1. Research Data and Subjects

This research is based on the "2008 National Data on the Elderly," a recent survey mandated by the Welfare of the Aged Act, on the health and welfare of elderly people across the nation. The survey was conducted as of June 30, 2008 on people aged 60 or older living in average housing in 16 cities or provinces in Korea. 15,146 elderly people in 12,567 households were selected for the survey. Among them, 8,961 women were again selected for this study . A total of 5,626 elderly females were selected for analysis; this sample includes single-elderly-woman and elderly-couple households, both living separately from their adult children.

2. Methods of Inquiry

The study analyzed socio-demographic characteristics including age, location of residence, education level, religion, monthly income, instrumental activities of daily living, and subjective health status.

The study measured the number of non-cohabitant children, frequency of contact, frequency of visits, and the distance between residences in order to evaluate the structural components of the social support networks of elderly women. The study categorizes social support into emotional, instrumental and physical support. Each category then was measured for degree of support by asking subjects a total of four questions with one question per each category. The degree of emotional support was measured by asking how often they listen to each other when they are worried. To understand the degree of instrumental support, we asked how much support such as cleaning, meal preparation and laundry is exchanged. As for physical support, subjects were asked how often they exchanged such support as nursing, caring or hospital accompaniment. The degree of each support was then scored from 1 for rt, we asked how much support

3. Methods of Analysis

Frequency- and percentage-based descriptive statistics have been used to identify the general characteristics of the elderly women surveyed, the number of their non-cohabitant children, the frequency of contact or visit, and the degree and types of social support. Chi-square test was also carried out to understand the difference in social support by household type, and logistic regression analysis was used to identify factors determining the type of social support.

IV STUDY RESULTS

1. General Characteristics of the Surveyed Elderly Women

The socio-demographic characteristics of the elderly women surveyed are shown in <Table 1>. Out of the total 5,626 elderly women, 2,738 were living alone (48.7%) and 2,888 were living with their husbands (51.3%). Those aged 60-69 accounted for 46%, those aged 70-79 accounted for 43%, and those aged 80 or older accounted for 11% in this category. Those in their 60s or 70s took up 89% of the total. 61.1% of the elderly women in their 60s were living with their husbands, which is twice as large as the figure of single-elderly-female households at 30%. A majority of those aged 80 or older, however, were living alone.

Table 1. General Characteristics of the Surveyed Elderly Women (Unit: %)

Variable	Category	Total (N=5626)	Single-Elderly-Woman Household (N=2738)	Elderly-Couple Household (N=2888)	χ^2
Age	60-69	2587(46.0)	822(30.0)	1765(61.1)	652.107***
	70-79	2420(43.0)	1412(51.6)	1008(34.9)	
	80 or older	619(11.0)	504(18.4)	115(4.0)	
Location of Residence	Rural	2562(45.5)	1385(50.6)	1177(40.8)	54.755***
	Urban	3064(54.5)	1353(49.4)	1711(59.2)	
Education Level	No Education	2391(42.5)	1601(58.5)	790(27.4)	587.548***
	Elem. Graduation	2330(41.4)	889(32.5)	1441(49.9)	
	Middle or High School Graduation	810(14.4)	225(8.2)	585(20.3)	
	Community College or Beyond	95(1.7)	23(0.8)	72(2.5)	
Religion	Buddhist	2267(40.3)	1116(40.8)	1151(39.9)	1.749
	Protestant	1191(21.2)	583(21.3)	608(21.1)	
	Catholic	420(7.5)	201(7.3)	219(7.6)	
	No Religion	1673(29.7)	800(29.2)	1673(29.7)	
	Others	75(1.4)	38(1.4)	75(1.4)	
Monthly Income	less than 500,000	4241(75.9)	1930(71.1)	2311(80.5)	75.500***
	500,000-1m.	1005(18.0)	600(22.1)	405(14.1)	
	1m.-2m.	277(5.0)	160(5.9)	117(4.1)	
	2m. or more	67(1.2)	30(1.1)	37(1.3)	
Instrumental Activities of Daily Living	Completely Dependent	22(0.4)	7(0.3)	15(0.5)	3.338
	Partially Dependent	78(1.4)	42(1.5)	36(1.2)	
	Completely Independent	5526(98.2)	2689(98.2)	2837(98.2)	
Subjective Health Status	Very Bad	777(13.8)	454(16.6)	323(11.2)	80.868***
	Bad	3045(54.2)	1547(56.5)	1498(51.9)	
	Average	823(14.6)	351(12.8)	472(16.4)	
	Good	924(16.4)	367(13.4)	557(19.3)	
	Very Good	52(0.9)	18(0.7)	34(1.2)	

***:p<.001

54.5% of the elderly women surveyed were living in cities while 45.5% were residing in farming villages. As for household type, there were about 10% more single-elderly-woman households than elderly-couple households in farming villages. But cities had more elderly-couple households (59.2%) than single-elderly-woman households (49.4%). When it came to education level, 42.5%

of the women never went to school and 41.4% graduated from elementary school only, which means that roughly 84% of the surveyed elderly women had an elementary school-level or lower education background . A mere 1.7% had community-college level or higher education. Among those who never went to school, 58.5% were living alone, twice as many as the percentage of those living with their husband at 27.4%. As for religion, Buddhists, Protestants and Catholics accounted for 40.3%, 21.2% and 7.5% of the total respectively. 29.7% or approximately 1/3 of the women surveyed had no religious affiliation. The study found no difference in terms of religion between the single-elderly-woman households and elderly-couple households.

For data on monthly income, 75.9% of the elderly women were paid less than 500,000 KRW while 18% were receiving 500,000 ~ 1,000,000 KRW. 94% of them were receiving less than 1,000,000 KRW per month on average, which means their income level is low overall. Among those paid less than 500,000 KRW per month, there were about 10% more elderly-couple households (80.5%) than single-elderly-woman households (71.1%).

98.2% of the surveyed were fully able to carry out instrumental activities of daily living on their own, and there was no difference in this area between the single-elderly-woman and elderly-couple households. A test on subjective health status found that 13.8% of the surveyed women thought their health conditions are very bad, 54.2% not good, 14.6% average and 16.4% said that they were healthy. In other words, 68% of elderly women believed that their health was not in good shape. More women who lived alone (73.1%) responded that their health was in bad shape compared to women living with husband (63.1%).

2. Structure of Social Support

To understand the structural aspect of social support, we looked into the size of social support networks, frequency of contact or visits, and the distance between residences. First, we investigated the number of non-cohabitant children to measure the size of social support networks, and the results are as shown in <Table 2>. Among all surveyed elderly women, those with 3 or 4 non-cohabitant children accounted for 45% of the total, followed by those with 5 or 6 at 29.4% and those with 1 or 2 at 19%. 22.9% of the single-elderly-woman households had 1 or 2 non-cohabitant children, which is higher than 15.2% of the elderly-couple households. Those with 3 or 4 non-cohabitant children made up 38% of the single-elderly-woman households and 52% of the elderly-couple households. The difference in the number of non-cohabitant children between the single-elderly-woman households and the elderly-couple households was within the p<.001 range, which means the difference is statistically meaningful.

Table 2. Number of Non-Cohabitant Children (Unit: Number (%))

	Total	Single-Elderly-Woman Household	Elderly-Couple Household	χ^2
1-2	901(19.0)	482(22.9)	419(15.2)	
3-4	2624(45.0)	1110(38.0)	1514(52.0)	
5-6	1716(29.4)	898(30.7)	818(28.1)	294.740***
7 or more	385(6.6)	248(8.4)	137(4.7)	
Total	5626(100.0)	2738(100.0)	2888(100.0)	

***:p<.001

The question of how often elderly females and their non-cohabitant children contact each other has been answered by looking into the frequency of two different types of contact: contact by phone or letter, and contact by visiting. First, the frequency of contact by phone or letter is shown in <Table 3>. 24.1% of the surveyed said they stayed in contact with each other every day while 28.7% said about two or three times a week. Contact once a week accounted for 26.2% of the total. Overall, 79% of elderly women said that they talked to their children at least once a week.

Table 3. Frequency of Intergenerational Contact (Unit: Number (%))

Category	Total	Single-Elderly-Woman Household	Elderly-Couple Household	χ^2
Almost None	28(0.5)	22(0.8)	6(0.2)	
Once or Twice a Year	54(1.0)	31(1.1)	23(0.8)	
Once or Twice a Quarter	143(2.5)	100(3.7)	43(1.5)	
Once or Twice a Month	921(16.4)	525(19.2)	396(13.7)	88.208***
Once or Twice a Week	1476(26.2)	692(25.3)	784(27.1)	
Two or Three Times a Week	1615(28.7)	725(26.5)	890(30.8)	
Almost Everyday	1357(24.1)	619(22.6)	738(25.6)	
No Answer	32(0.6)	24(0.9)	8(0.3)	

***:p<.001

When it came to household type, 22.6% of the single-elderly-woman households and 25.6% of the elderly-couple households were found to stay in contact with their children almost every day, and 26.5% and 30.8% of the same groups above talked to their children two or three times a week. Contact once a week accounted for 25.3% and 27.1% of the respective groups. 83.5% of the elderly-couple households talked to their children at least once a week, which is higher than 74.4% of the single-elderly-woman households.

The frequency of visits is shown in <Table 4>. 29.4% of elderly women responded that they and their non-cohabitant children visited each other once or twice a month. 10.9% responded that they met each other almost every day, while 20.8% responded that they visited once a week.

Table 4. Frequency of Intergenerational Visit (Unit: Number (%))

Frequency	Total	Single-Elderly-Woman Household	Elderly-Couple Household	χ^2
Almost None	43(0.8)	34(1.2)	9(0.3)	91.001***
Once or Twice a Year	437(7.8)	270(9.9)	167(5.8)	
Once or Twice a Quarter	940(16.7)	516(18.8)	424(14.7)	
Once or Twice a Month	1653(29.4)	784(28.6)	869(30.1)	
Once or Twice a Week	1170(20.8)	530(19.4)	640(22.2)	
Two or Three Times a Week	731(13.0)	315(11.5)	416(14.4)	
Almost Everyday	611(10.9)	261(9.5)	350(12.1)	
No Answer	41(0.7)	28(1.0)	13(0.5)	

***:p<.001

In terms of household type and visiting, those who responded almost every day took up 9.5% and 12.1% of the single-elderly-woman households and the elderly-couple households respectively. Those who responded that they visit two or three times a week accounted for 11.5% and 14.4%, and once a week made up 19.4% and 22.2% of the same respective groups above. 48.7% of the elderly-couple households were found to be visiting or were visited by their children at least once a week, which is slightly higher than 40.4% of the single-elderly-woman households. Once or twice a year accounted for 9.9% of the single-elderly-woman households, higher than 5.8% of the elderly-couple households. Overall frequency of contact or visit was found to be higher among the elderly-couple households than the single-elderly-woman households.

Table 5. Distance between Residences of Elderly Women and Non-Cohabitant Children

(Unit: Number (%))

	Total	Single-Elderly-Woman Household	Elderly-Couple Household	χ^2
Within 30 Min. on Foot	455(8.1)	204(7.5)	251(8.7)	
10 to 30 Min. on Foot	484(8.6)	214(7.8)	270(9.3)	
Within 30 Min. by Car	1375(24.4)	627(22.9)	748(25.9)	
30 Min. to One Hour by Car	1151(20.5)	586(21.4)	565(19.6)	
One to Two Hours by Car	884(15.7)	441(16.1)	443(15.3)	30.100***
Two to Three Hours by Car	538(9.6)	276(10.1)	262(9.1)	
Three or More Hours by Car	626(11.1)	316(11.5)	310(10.7)	
Live Overseas	14(0.2)	8(0.3)	6(0.2)	
No Answer	99(1.8)	66(2.4)	33(1.1)	

***:p<.001

<Table 5> shows the distance between the residences of the elderly women and their non-cohabitant children who had been identified as visiting each other most frequently. In the case of single-elderly-woman households, 30 minutes or less by foot accounted for 15.3%, within one hour by car 44.3%, one to two hours by car 16.1% and two or more hours by car 21.6%. For elderly-couple households, within 30 minutes by foot accounted for 18.0%, within one hour by car 45.5%, one to two hours by car 15.3%, and two or more hours by car 19.8%. Roughly 45% of the elderly people surveyed were living within a one-hour driving distance from their non-cohabitant children.

3. Extent and Types of Intergenerational Social Support

This study researched the giving and receiving patterns of the intergenerational social support between elderly women and their non-cohabitant offspring in terms of emotional, instrumental and physical support. <Table 6> shows the results. For the extent of emotional support provided by elderly people, 7.7% of the one-elderly-woman households and 5.2% of the elderly-couple households surveyed said that they never listened to their children about their problems, while 22.6% and 17.0% of the same groups above said that they did not pay much attention. However, 58.5% of the single-elderly-woman households and 62.9% of the elderly-couple households said that they listened to their children their children about their problems, while 22.6% and 17.0% of the same grouresponded that they listened to their children's problems very often. Overall, a majority of the respondents were found to provide emotional support, but single-elderly-woman households were found to provide less emotional support (69.5%) than elderly-couple households did (77.6%) (p<.001).

Regarding how often elderly people get emotional support from their children, 6.2% of the single-elderly-woman households and 4.7% of the elderly-couple households said that they did not receive any emotional support from their children while 15.7% and 14.9% of the same respective groups responded that they did not get much emotional support. However, 64.2% and 65.5% of the same groups above said that they are emotionally supported by their children while 13.8% and 14.7% of them were found to receive very much emotional support. Overall, a majority of the people surveyed said that they received emotional support, but the difference between the single-elderly-woman households and the elderly-couple households was not great enough to be statistically significant.

As for the extent of instrumental support provided by elderly parents, 35.2% of the one-elderly-parent households and 27.4% of the elderly-couple households said that they never provided their children with instrumental support such as cleaning, meal preparation and laundry, while 42.6% and 39.7%

of the same groups responded that they did not provide much of such support. 19.2% of the one-elderly-parent households and 28.2% of the elderly-couple households were found to help their children to some point with cleaning, meal preparation and laundry, while those helping their children very much were low in number with 2.9% and 4.6% of the abovementioned groups respectively. Overall, those elderly parents who provided instrumental support were not as many as those who did not, but one-elderly-parent households (22.1%) were found to provide instrumental support less than elderly-couple households (32.8%) did (p<.001).

Table 6. Degree of Social Support Exchanged Between Generations (Unit: %)

	Extent of Support	Provide Support: One-Elderly-Parent Household	Provide Support: Elderly-Couple Household	χ^2	Receive Support: One-Elderly-Parent Household	Receive Support: Elderly-Couple Household	χ^2
Emotional Support	Never	7.7	5.2	56.226***	6.2	4.7	8.103
	Not Much	22.6	17.0		15.7	14.9	
	Average	58.5	62.9		64.2	65.5	
	Very Much	11.0	14.7		13.8	14.7	
Instrumental Support	Never	35.2	27.4	88.528***	23.1	21.6	12.603*
	Not Much	42.6	39.7		30.4	33.6	
	Average	19.2	28.2		39.0	39.0	
	Very Much	2.9	4.6		7.5	5.7	
Physical Support	Never	36.0	30.7	30.570***	20.5	21.0	9.683*
	Not Much	44.5	44.4		24.7	27.4	
	Average	16.6	20.8		42.7	41.6	
	Very Much	2.8	3.9		12.0	10.0	

*: p<.05, ***:p<.001

A close look into how often elderly parents receive instrumental support from their adult children revealed that 23.1% of the one-elderly-parent and 21.6% of the elderly-couple households did not receive any instrumental support such as cleaning, meal preparation and laundry, while 30.4% and 33.6% of the same groups said that they did not receive very much instrumental support. 39% of both groups responded that they received instrumental support, but those receiving a great amount of instrumental support were found to be greater in number within one-elderly-parent households (7.5%) than in elderly-couple households (5.7%). In general, there were more elderly people receiving instrumental support than those who did not, but a larger percentage of the one-elderly-parent households (46.5%) were found to be receiving more instrumental support than elderly-couple households (44.7%) ($p<.05$).

As for the extent of physical support extended by elderly parents, 36.0% of the single-elderly-parent households and 30.7% of the elderly-couple households surveyed told that they never provided such physical support as nursing, caring and accompanying to hospital while 44.5% and 44.4% of the same respective groups said that they did not provide such support much. 16.6% of the single-elderly-parent households and 20.8% of the elderly-couple households responded that they gave physical support to their children to some extent, and 2.8% and 3.9% of the same groups said that they provided a great amount of physical. On the whole there were less elderly people providing physical support than those who did not, and single-elderly-parent households (19.4%) were found to provide more physical support than elderly-couple households (24.7%) ($p<.001$).

As for the extent of physical support received by elderly people, 20.5% of the single-elderly-parent households and 21.0% of the elderly-couple households said that they never received from their children physical support such as nursing, caring and hospital accompaniment, while 24.7% and 27.4% of the same respective groups said that they did not receive much of such support. 42.7% of the single-elderly-parent households and 41.6% of the elderly-couple households responded that they received physical support from their children to some extent, and 12% and 10% of the same groups said that they were receiving a great amount of such support. Overall, there were more people receiving physical support than those who did not, and more of the single-parent-households (54.7%) were found to be receiving physical support than the elderly-couple households (51.6%) were ($p<.05$).

Next, we looked into the types of intergenerational social support, and the results are summed up in <Table 7>. Social support has been categorized into giving, receiving, mutual and no-exchange types. For example, if an elderly female only provides emotional support to her children by listening to their problems, she falls under the type of giving emotional support. On the other hand, if an elderly female confides her problems to her children and not the other way around, she is the receiving type. If the support is provided by both parties, they are categorized as the mutual type, and if there is no exchange of such support, then the relationship falls into the no-exchange type.

In the area of emotional support, the mutual type has been found the most in all types of households, followed by the no-exchange type, the receiving type and the emotional type at the end. The receiving type accounted for 10.8% of the one-elderly-parent households, which is roughly twice as large as the rate of the elderly-couple households at 5.2% ($p<.001$). 75.1% of the elderly-couple households fell under the mutual type, which is about 8% larger than 67.3% of the one-elderly-parent households ($p<.001$). The no-exchange type was discovered slightly more among the one-elderly-parent households (19.6%) than in the elderly-couple households (17.1%) ($p<.01$). In summary, when worried, more of those in the one-elderly-parent households looked to their children for emotional support than those in the elderly-couple households did, and a relatively low number of one-elderly-parent households were found to be the mutual type.

Table 7. Types of Intergenerational Social Support (Unit: %)

Category	Type	One-Elderly-Parent Households	Elderly-Couple Households	χ^2
Emotional Support	giving	2.3	2.5	.424
	receiving	10.8	5.2	60.034***
	mutual	67.3	75.1	41.914***
	no-exchange	19.6	17.1	6.016**
Instrumental Support	giving	5.2	8.8	28.482***
	receiving	29.5	20.8	56.853***
	mutual	17.0	24.0	42.359***
	no-exchange	48.3	46.4	2.160
Physical Support	giving	1.6	1.9	.696
	receiving	37.0	28.8	43.167***
	mutual	17.8	22.8	22.271***
	no-exchange	43.6	46.4	4.653*

*: p<.05, **: p<.01, ***:p<.001

The no-exchange type has dominated all types of households in terms of instrumental support. The giving type accounted for 5.2% of the one-elderly-parent households, which is slightly lower than 8.8% of the elderly-couple households surveyed (p<.001). On the other hand, there were roughly 10% more receiving type of people found among the one-elderly-parent households (29.5%) than in the elderly-couple households (20.8%) (p<.001). The mutual type made up 24.0% of the elderly-couple households, which is about 7% greater than 17.0% of the one-elderly-parent households ($p<.001$). Overall, more of the one-elderly-parent households were found to receive such instrumental support as cleaning, meal preparation and laundry than the elderly-couple households, and a relatively low number of those in the one-elderly-parent households exchanged such support in a mutual fashion.

In terms of physical support, there were roughly 10% more receiving type of people found in the one-elderly-parent households (37.0%) than in the elderly-couple households surveyed (28.8%) ($p<.001$). The mutual type accounted for 22.8% of the elderly-couple households and 17.8% of the one-elderly-parent households ($p<.001$). 43.6% of the one-elderly-parent households were found to be the no-exchange type and 46.4% of the elderly-couple households were identified in the no-exchange category ($p<.05$). More of those in the one-elderly-parent households were receiving physical support from their children than those in the elderly-couple households, which indicates that the former might not have as good health conditions as the latter.

4. Factors Affecting Different Types of Social Support

Types of social support are a dichotomous variable in which certain types are assigned the value of 1 while the others get 0. Therefore, the dichotomous logistic regression analysis has been conducted to identify factors affecting various types of intergenerational social support. Only the demographic, socio-economic and medical conditions of elderly women were taken as independent variables for this study.

<Table 8> shows the results of the dichotomous logistic regression analysis conducted on the factors impacting emotional support. The chi-square (df=7) value has resulted in the range of $p<.001$ except for the giving type, therefore

the research model is statistically appropriate. As for the receiving type, such variables as household type, age, instrumental activities of daily living and subjective health status were found to be statistically significant. Household type and age were the statistically significant ones for the mutual type while education, monthly income, instrumental activities of daily living and subjective health status proved to be statistically significant for the mutual and no-exchange types.

Table 8. Factors Affecting Emotional Support

Variable	Giving		Receiving		Mutual		No-Exchange	
	B	EXP	B	EXP	B	EXP	B	EXP
Household Type[1)]	.111	1.118	-.534***	.586	.222***	1.249	-.073	.929
Age	-.137	.872	.304***	1.355	-.112*	.894	.017	1.017
Location of Residence[2)]	.058	1.060	-.035	.965	.016	1.016	-.018	.982
Education Years	-.151	.860	-.164	.849	.156***	1.168	-.116*	.890
Monthly income	-.158	.854	-.048	.953	.182***	1.200	-.202**	.817
Instrumental activities of Daily Living	.005	1.005	.045**	1.046	-.058***	.943	.044***	1.045
Subjective Health Status	-.050	.951	-.222***	.801	.210***	1.234	-.182***	.833
Constant	-3.147***	.043	-1.900	.150	.421	1.523	-1.011***	.364
-2LL Chi-square(df=7)	1267.273 4.285		2939.734 135.379***		6473.668 214.139***		5233.088 90.030*	

1) Single-Elderly-Parent HS=0, Elderly-Couple HS=1 2) Farming Village=0, City=1
*: p<.05, **: p<.01, ***:p<.001

The one-elderly-parent households had a higher probability than the elderly-couple households to receive emotional support, while the elderly-couple households were more likely to be identified as the mutual type than the one-elderly-parent households. Progression in age increased possibilities for becoming the receiving type (p<.001), but decreased the likelihood of falling under the mutual type (p<.05). Those with higher education and higher monthly incomes were more likely to be the mutual type (p<.001). Those with lower instrumental activities of daily living had a higher probability of becoming the receiving type (p<.01) or the no-exchange type (p<.001) while becoming less likely to be the mutual type (p<.001). When the subjective health status improves, people are more likely to become the mutual type (p<.001) while lowering the possibility of being identified as the receiving or the no-exchange type (p<.001).

Table 9. Factors Affecting Instrumental Support

Variable	Giving		Receiving		Mutual		No-Exchange	
	B	EXP	B	EXP	B	EXP	B	EXP
Household Type[1)]	.160	1.174	-.181**	.834	.304***	1.355	-.104	.901
Age	-.523***	.592	.347***	1.414	-.190***	.827	-.031***	.970
Location of Residence[2)]	-.081	.922	-.169**	.845	-.184**	.832	.252	1.287
Education Years	.266***	1.305	-.133**	.876	.014	1.014	-.011	.989
Monthly Income	-.100	.904	.037	1.037	.052	1.053	-.028	.972
Instrumental Activities of Daily Living	-.189***	.827	.071***	1.074	-.055**	.947	-.031**	.970
Subjective Health Status	.132*	1.141	-.189***	.828	.222***	1.249	-.076*	.927
Constant	-.691	.501	-1.519***	.219	-1.463***	.231	.545**	1.725
-2LL	2712.631		5993.439		5525.514		7682.604	
Chi square(df=7)	135.538***		277.823***		136.196***		37.170***	

1) Single-Elderly-Parent HS=0, Elderly-Couple HS=1 2) Farming Village=0, City=1

*: p<.05, **: p<.01, ***:p<.001

<Table 9> summarizes the results of the dichotomous logistic analysis on the factors affecting instrumental support. The value of chi-square(df=7) resulted in the range of p<.001 in all types of instrumental support, which indicates that the research model is statistically appropriate. Statistically significant variables for the giving type included age, years of education, instrumental activities of daily living and subjective health status while household type, age, location of residence, years of education, instrumental activities of daily living and subjective health status turned out to be significant for the receiving type. Household type and location of residence were used as significant variables for the mutual type, and age, instrumental activities of daily living, and subjective health status proved to be statistically significant for the mutual and no-exchange types.

In terms of household type, the single-elderly-parent households were more likely to be the receiving type than the elderly-couple households while the latter were more likely to be the mutual type than the former. Progression in age increased the probability of one being the receiving type (p<.001) while decreasing the likelihood of becoming the giving, mutual or no-exchange types (p<.001). Elderly people in farming villages showed a higher probability of being categorized under the receiving or the mutual type than their counterparts in cities (p<.01). Those with higher education were more likely to be the giving type (p<.001), and less likely to become the receiving type (p<.01). Low instrumental activities of daily living increased the odds of one being the receiving type (p<.001), while decreasing the probability of becoming the giving, mutual or no-exchange type (p<.001). High subjective health status led to greater chances of one becoming the giving type (p<.05) or the mutual type (p<.001), and lower chances of becoming the receiving type (p<.001) or the no-exchange type (p<.05).

<Table 10> summarizes the results of the dichotomous logistic analysis on

factors affecting physical support. In all types, the value of chi-square(df=7) turned out to be in the range of p<.05 or p<.001, which indicates the research model is statistically appropriate. Variables like household type, age, location of residence, years of education, instrumental activities of daily living and subjective health status proved to be statistically significant for the receiving type. As for the mutual type, such variables as age, location of residence, instrumental activities of daily living and subjective health status turned out to be statistically significant. The no-exchange type included age and monthly income as significant variables.

Table 10. Factors Affecting Physical Support

Variable	Giving		Receiving		Mutual		No-Exchange	
	B	EXP	B	EXP	B	EXP	B	EXP
Household Type[1)]	-.118	.889	-.138*	.871	.126	1.134	.048	1.050
Age	-.243	.784	.279***	1.322	-.164**	.849	-.134**	.875
Location of Residence[2)]	.405	1.499	-.175**	.839	.224**	1.251	-.017	.983
Education Years	.184	1.203	-.092*	.913	.076	1.079	.002	1.002
Monthly Income	-.058	.943	.084	1.088	.056	1.057	-.106*	.899
Instrumental Activities of Daily Living	-.039	.962	.043***	1.044	-.053**	.949	-.020	.981
Subjective Health Status	.087	1.091	-.169***	.844	.198***	1.219	-.006	.994
Constant	-3.743***	.024	-.920***	.398	-1.554***	.211	.326	1.386
-2LL Chi-square(df=7)	988.121 14.467*		6874.506 190.338***		5498.310 127.972***		7658.424 25.179***	

1) Single-Elderly-Parent HS=0, Elderly-Couple HS=1 2) Farming Village=0, City=1

*: p<.05, **: p<.01, ***: p<.001

In terms of household type, the single-elderly-parent households showed higher probability to fall under the receiving type than the elderly-couple households ($p<.05$). Those who are older had higher chances of becoming the receiving type ($p<.001$) while showing lower chances of being considered as the mutual or the no-exchange type ($p<.01$). Elderly people in cities were more likely to become the mutual type than those in farming villages ($p<.01$) while the latter were more likely to become the receiving type than the former ($p<.01$). Those with fewer years of education showed higher chances of becoming the receiving type ($p<.001$). Those with lower monthly incomes were more likely to become the no-exchange type. Low instrumental activities of daily living increased the odds for the receiving type ($p<.001$) while lowering chances of becoming the mutual type ($p<.01$). High subjective health status led to higher chances of becoming the mutual type ($p<.001$) and those who viewed themselves as not healthy were more likely to become the receiving type ($p<.001$).

V CONCLUSION

1. Summary of Research Results and Limitations

This study is based on the "he study is based on Results," the latest study that had taken its samples from representative groups of elderly people across the nation, and looked into whether elderly women exchanged support with their non-cohabitant children in emotional, instrumental and physical areas, and what types of support were exchanged.

Emotional social support was found to be exchanged most frequently between elderly females and their non-cohabitant children. When it came to emotional support, the amount of support turned out to be high both ways. An analysis has also been made on the characteristics of different types of support such as emotional, instrumental and physical support. The most prevalent was the mutual type in the emotional support. And the no-exchange type dominated instrumental and physical support, followed by the receiving type. This indicates that elderly women rarely provided instrumental and physical support to their children while receiving such support most of the time.

The results above suggest that, among all elderly people, a high percentage of elderly women only receive social support rather than provide or exchange it. The rate of such exclusive reception by elderly women increases disproportionately with age. This suggests that progression in age of elderly women is highly likely to exacerbate their economic, physical and emotional difficulties. But it also indicates that if their medical or economic conditions permit, elderly females could still exchange support with their children rather than only receive support. Therefore, when drafting welfare policies for senior citizens, policymakers need to pay keen attention to gender difference and differentiate the extent or the type of assistance accordingly. This study is meaningful in that it has categorized different types of intergenerational social support involving elderly females and identified factors affecting them. However, it has stopped short of considering elderly females' relationships with their children and other interactions when analyzing the different types of social support exchanged between elderly women and their adult children. It also did not look into possibly different situations facing elderly men. Future studies will need to bring such variables into focus as well. In addition, social relationship networks of elderly females with other people such as relatives, friends and neighbors deserve a close look in the types of social support exchanged.

2. Korea's Welfare Policies for Elderly Women

In this last chapter, we will discuss the welfare policies for elderly women currently in place in South Korea.

Age makes a clear difference in the medical conditions of elderly people. A high percentage of elderly people consider themselves to be not healthy. Accordingly, the medical insurance compensations paid to senior citizens aged 65 or higher accounts for 31.6% of the total cost (Statistics Korea 2011). Medical checkups and health education are being provided currently as part of the governmenter accouns to prevent senior citizens from falling ill and for early detection of diseases. In addition, considering the increasing odds of dementia with age, the government enacted the Dementia Control Act in 2011.

Traditionally, the care-givers for elderly people have been their adult children or daughters-in-law. The norms of filial responsibility for aging parents, however, have changed and an increasing number of women are now joining the workforce. All this has made taking care of elderly parents a greater burden than ever, which sometimes served as the cause for domestic conflicts. Such family troubles in some cases could turn into the abuse of elderly people. About 2,500-3,000 cases of elder abuse are reported annually at 20 senior citizen protection agencies across the nation. Considering the lack of awareness of elder abuse and the social tendency of feeling uneasy about reporting to authorities, we believe that the number of elder abuse cases is even greater than official estimates. The maltreatment of senior citizens mostly takes place in the home environment. Having recognized the difficulty of getting an insider abuse of elderly people. About 2,500-3,000 cases of elder abuse are reported annually at 20 senioresolve family problems by family members or within the community rather than directly stepping in for resolution. An increasing number of elder abuse cases, however, prompted the government in 2004 to amend the senior citizen welfare act and began providing the government-sponsored counseling services on elder abuse, which had previously been provided by local volunteers. The primary purpose of such change was to take preventative and protective measures for elderly citizens by way of professional and systematic management. The related law mandates the installation of an elder abuse hotline, the establishment of professional protection agencies for elderly citizens, the mandated requirement of reporting elder abuse cases and other related procedures.

As part of the government cases and ent of professional protection agencies for elderly citizens, theizens by way of professional and systematicg the government-sponsored oblems by family members or within the community rathficiaries of the Long-term Care Insurance System for the Elderly include elderly people with geriatric diseases, and they can benefit from the system after being tested for severity classification. Beneficiaries receive household assistance (home care, home bathing, home nursing, day-and-night care, short-term care and care equipment rental) and facility assistance (a sanatorium for the elderly and cohabitation housing for the elderly). As of 2010, 315,994 people qualified for the Long-term Care Insurance System for the Elderly and there were 3,751 long-term care centers (Ministry of Health and Welfare 2011).

Elderly females face financial difficulties. As of 2010, elderly women accounted for about 9% of the beneficiaries of the Basic Livelihood Security System. The government enacted the Basic Old-Age Pension Scheme in April 2007 and enforced it in January 2008 in order to tighten the public safety net for income security and stable livelihood for the elderly. The Basic Old-Age Pension Scheme provides compensation to 70% of the senior citizens aged 65 or older with limited income and wealth.

As this study shows, one-person-only households are more likely to become the receiving type than elderly-couple households, and this is why greater attention needs to be directed toward elderly people living on their own. Elderly people living alone confront worse physical, financial and psychological circumstances than average elderly people. Especially given that elderly females on average live longer than their male counterparts, the focus can understandably be narrowed on the issue of elderly females living alone. The government is also expanding services for elderly people living alone by starting the Basic Elder Care Services for example . This program targets people aged 65 or older without nursing needs. Applicants are evaluated for income, health, residence and social networks, among other criteria, and the beneficiaries are selected in order of their needs for the services which are provided free of charge. The services consist of regular safety checks through home visits, or phone calls for four hours a month, as well as preventative services such as livelihood training and other related services.

According to the Korea National Statistical Office (Statistics Korea 2011), the rate of "twilight" divorce and remarriage is on the rise. Although 80.9% of the senior citizens still respond that it is better to stay in marriage, a growing number of people are beginning to think that divorce could be an option. This indicates that elderly couples also face marital problems and that they now value the pursuit of individual happiness more than persevering in unhappy marriages for the sake of their children. So, the rate of "twilight" divorce could continue to rise. A sensible division of roles and smooth communication are crucial for maintaining a happy marital life in old age. To that end, there is a clear need to train professional counselors for senior couples so that they can identify problems and rebuild good relationships.

When facing reduced public assistance for the elderly by the government, elders may rely on family to play an important role by compensating for such lack of support. However, due to an increasing senior population, rising life expectancies, low fertility rates, and more women joining workforce, the care of elderly citizens cannot remain exclusively the responsibility of their families, and it is increasingly urgent for the government to actively intervene with resolutions. The government needs to create welfare policies that are not just focused on troubled senior citizens, but on the entire senior population so that elders are not separated or isolated from their family members or from the community. The welfare policies should also help change public perceptions about elderly people so that senior citizens are no longer viewed as passive and dependent, but as active and productive members of the family or society as a whole.

Bibliography

Bae, Jin-Hee. 2004. "Social Support and Life Satisfaction of the Rural Elderly: Focusing on the Function of Support by Their Children and Neighbors." *Social Welfare Policy* 20: 197-216.

Cantor, M., and V. Little. 1985. "Aging and Social Care." In *Handbook of Aging and Social Science* (2nd), eds. R.H. Binstock and E. Shanas, 745-782. New York: Van Nostrand Reinhold.

Cheong, Byeong-Eun. 2007. "The Reciprocity of Intergenerational Support Exchange and its Characteristics." *Journal of the Korean Gerontological Society* 27(2):503-518.

Cheong, Kyung-Hee et al. 2005. *2004 National Data in the Elderly*. Seoul: Korea Institute for Health and Social Affairs

Choi, Jeong-Hye. 2009. "Comparison of Adult Children's Quality of Relationship and Care Provision for Elderly Parents in the U.S. and Korea." *Journal of the Korean Gerontological Society* 29(2):611-627.

Choi, Yong-Min and Lee Sang-Joo. 2003. "Relationship between the Quality of Life and the Social Support Network for Single Home-Owned Old People." *Journal of Welfare for the Aged* 22:193-217.

Grundy, E. 2005. "Reciprocity in Relationships: Socio-Economic and Health Influences on Intergenerational Exchanges between Third Age Parents and Their Adult Children in Great Britain." *The British Journal of Sociology* 56(2):233-255.

Han, Hye-Kyung and Lee Yu-Ri. 2009. "A Study on Factors Impacting on the Mental Health Level of the Elderly People Living Alone." *Journal of the Korean Gerontological Society* 29(3):805-822.

Han, Min-A and Han Gyoung-Hae. 2004. "Patterns of Intergenerational Support Exchange and the Psychological Well-Being of Adult Children in Korea." *Journal of Korea Association of Family Relations* 9(1):135-152.

Kim, Dheong-Seok and Kim Ik-Ki. 2000. "Patterns of Intergenerational Support Exchange and the Life Satisfaction of the Elderly Parents in Korea." *Journal of the Korean Gerontological Society* 20(2):155-168.

Kim, Hee-Nyon and Seo Hong-Lan. 2010. "The Effects of Self-Efficacy on the Depression of Lonely Frail Elders." *Journal of Welfare for the Aged* 48:59-82.

Kim, Soo-Hyun, Kang Hyun-Jung, and Kim Yun-Jeong. 2008. "The Effects of a Social Network for Female Elders Living Alone in Rural and Fishing Villages on Their Quality of Life." *Korean Journal of Family Welfare* 13(3):51-71.

Kim, Young-Joo. 2009. "Mediating Effects of Social Supports on the Decrease of Depression of the Rural Elderly." *Journal of Welfare for the Aged* 46:77-104.

Kim, Yun-Jeong, An Jeong-Shin, and Kang In. 2008. "An Ecological Approach to Quality of Life of Single Household Old Women." *Journal of Korea Association of Family Relations* 13(2):23-42.

Lee, Hyong-Sil. 2003. "Intergenerational Social Support Exchanges and Life Satisfaction Among the Rural Elderly: Sex and Age Group Differences." *Journal of Korean Home Economics Association* 41(4):57-69.

Lim, Hyo-Yeon. 2009. "Exploring Relationships between Life Satisfaction and Patterns of Support Exchange of the Elderly Living Alone and Their Children in Metropolitan City in Japan." *Journal of the Korean Home Economics Association* 47(5):59-66.

Liten, H. 2004. "Intergenerational Exchanges Patterns and Their Correlates in an Aging Israeli Cohort." *Research on Aging* 26(2):202-223.

Lowenstein, A., R. Katz, and N. Gur-Yaish. 2007. "Reciprocity in Parent-Child Exchange and Life Satisfaction among the Elderly: A Cross-National Perspective." *Journal of Social Issues* 63(4):865-883.

Ministry of Health and Welfare. 2009. *2008 National Data in the Elderly*. Seoul: Ministry of Health and Welfare.

______. 2011. *Ministry of Health and Welfare Year Book 2011*. Seoul: Ministry of Health and Welfare.

Rho, Byeong-IL and Mo Seon-Hee. 2007. "The Effects of Levels and Dimensions of Social Support on Geriatric Depression." *Journal of the Korean Gerontological Society* 27(1):53-69.

Seo, Hong-Lan and Kim Hee-Nyon. 2010. "Factors Affecting Psychological Well-Being of Frail Elderly Women Living Alone." *Mental Health and Social Work* 35:176-202.

Statistics Korea. 2010. "Statistics of the eldery." http://www. mw.go.kr

______. 2011. "Statistics of the eldery." http://www. mw.go.kr

Suh, Kyung-Hyun and Kim Young-Sook. 2003. " Investigation of Social Support and Mental Health among the Elderly People Living Alone." *Journal of Welfare for the Aged* 21:7-26.

Sun, W., M. Watanabe, Y. Tanimoto et al. 2007. "Factors Associated with Good Self-Rated Health of Non-Disabled Elderly Living Alone in Japanese: A Cross-Sectional Study." *BMC Public Health* 7:297-305.

Wang, P. and S. Li. 2008. "The Effects of Intergenerational Support on the Changes in Cognitive Functioning of the Rural Elderly in China." *Asia-Pacific Population Journal* 23(3):75-88.

Yeh, S. and S. Lo. 2004. "Living alone, Social Support, and Feeling Lonely among the Elderly." *Social Behavior and Personality* 32(2):129-138.

Yoon, Hyun-Sook. 2003. "The Impact of Intergenerational Support Exchange to the Psychological Well-Being of Older Parents." *Journal of the Korean Gerontological Society* 23(3):15-28.